The Complete Traveller's

Gairloch & Torridon

Angela Nicholson

Thistle*Press*

Quality guides to Scotland

Cover photograph:
An Teallach from Inverianve Waterfalls Walk (Walk No. 20)

Published by
Thistle*Press*
Insch, Aberdeenshire,
AB52 6JR, Scotland.

ISBN 0 9520950 0 9

British Library Cataloguing-in-Publication Data.
A catalogue record for this book is available from the British Library

Printed in Scotland by
Nevisprint, Fort William.

CONTENTS

Part I
General Information

Part II
Travel Guide

Part III
Heritage and Environment

LIST OF MAPS

Part I

General Information

INTRODUCTION

When Queen Victoria visited Gairloch and Torridon in September 1877 she was greatly impressed by the wild and magnificent scenery of this remote corner of Scotland. In her diary she wrote of the "...grand, wild, savage-looking, but most picturesque Glen of Torridon..." and of the "...grand and romantic..." Loch Maree. Today these same qualities continue to draw many thousands of visitors from all over the world to this spectacular area each year.

The Gairloch/Torridon region is not only a paradise for the hill-walker and birdwatcher. Within a relatively small geographical radius are to be found safe sandy beaches, picturesque waterfalls, a spectacular 9-hole golf course, remote hill lochs teeming with brown trout and boats galore to take you exploring around the many sheltered bays of this rugged coastline.

Where else can you have tea at a lighthouse, scramble amongst some of the oldest rocks in the world, see sub-tropical plants flourish at the same latitude as Siberia and laze on a deserted beach watched only by inquisitive seals?

"The Complete Traveller's Guide To Gairloch and Torridon" will tell you where to go, what to do and what to see, together with something of the history and legends of this fascinating area. Practical aspects such as where to eat and where to buy petrol on a Sunday are covered. Handy village maps are also included. Whether you are touring by car, backpacking or renting a holiday cottage, this little book contains something for everyone. *"The Complete Traveller's Guide To Gairloch and Torridon"* is packed full of useful information that no visitor should be without.

TRAVELLING AROUND

MAPS

For hillwalkers, fishermen and others requiring detailed map coverage of the countryside, the Ordnance Survey 1:50,000 Landranger series is excellent value. Two maps cover most of the area detailed in this guide - Sheet 19: Gairloch & Ullapool area and Sheet 25: Glen Carron and surrounding area. In addition, two maps covering peripheral areas may be of interest - Sheet 20: Beinn Dearg & surrounding area and Sheet 24: Raasay & Loch Torridon.

HOW TO GET THERE

By Car

Most visitors to Gairloch and Torridon arrive by car. From Inverness, follow the A9 northwards for about 7 miles and then turn on to the A835. From here there are two choices available to the motorist. To explore the southern part of the region via Achnasheen and Kinlochewe, turn left on to the A832 shortly after Garve. Alternatively, continue to follow the A835 northwards until you reach Braemore Junction and then turn left on to the A832 to enter the region from the north via Aultbea and Poolewe. On the west coast, those travelling from Kyle of Lochalsh can follow the A890 north to Achnasheen.

By Rail

Despite its remoteness, the area is relatively well served by rail. The little village of Achnasheen lies on the famous Inverness to Kyle of Lochalsh line and trains call there several times a day (twice on Sundays). If you like scenic railway journeys, this is definitely not one to be missed. From *Inverness*, the train first crosses the River Ness and then the Caledonian Canal before travelling westwards along the shore of the Beauly Firth. There are lovely views across the Firth to the fertile farming region of the Black Isle and the towering mass of Ben Wyvis. After crossing the River Beauly, the train turns north to the old cattle town of *Muir of Ord*, the first stop. Continuing northwards, the line crosses the River Connon before stopping at *Dingwall*. Here, the track divides into two: the northern branch continues to Wick and Thurso, while the western branch turns inland, hugging the shore of Loch Garve before arriving at the little settlement of *Garve*. The line now climbs to Corriemoillie Summit and then descends to the north shore of Loch Luichart, arriving shortly at *Lochluichart Station*. From here, the track swings between Loch a' Chuilinn and Loch Achanalt. The next stop is *Achanalt*, from where the line winds along Strath Bran, through stunning mountainous country to *Achnasheen*. The track now turns south-westwards down Glen Carron, passing several lochs and the towering mountains of Coulin and Achnashellach before arriving at *Achnashellach Station.* The line continues alongside the River Carron to *Strathcarron.* To the right there are spectacular views across Loch Carron to the little village of the same name. The line hugs the lochside, arriving shortly at *Attadale* and then continues around the shore to *Stromeferry.* To the right, Loch Carron begins to open up, giving a panoramic view of the mountains on the Applecross Peninsula. The track continues along the coast to *Duncraig* and the picturesque village of *Plockton* and then turns inland across the crofting land of Drumbuie to *Duirinish.* The final stretch runs south along the coast with magnificent views of Skye, before terminating at *Kyle of Lochalsh.* Most trains include a trolley service of cold snacks and hot and cold drinks and the special Hebridean Heritage and Atlantic Heritage trains which run during the summer have dining car service. The Hebridean Heritage train carries a special Observation Car with on-board commentary for which an extra charge is payable. Cyclists should check with Scotrail in advance of travel as carriage space for cycles is very limited on board this service and prior reservations are required (a £3.00 reservation fee is charged). A new service recently introduced on the Inverness-Kyle line is the "Young Explorer Train" - a train comprised entirely of the traditional coaching-stock which has much more room for cycles, backpacks and climbing gear etc (cycle reservations are still required, however). Young Explorer Trains run between May and September inclusive. For up to date information on timetables and fares telephone Inverness (0463) 238 924.

By Bus

The WESTERBUS service makes regular runs between Inverness and Gairloch. Westerbus is operated by Gairloch Garage. For confirmation of timetables and fares telephone (0445) 2255. There are two routes to choose from: Gairloch-Dundonnell-Inverness and Aultbea-Achnasheen-Inverness.

Gairloch-Dundonnell-Inverness: Runs every Monday, Wednesday and Saturday, but not on 25/26 December or 1/2 January. The timetable is as follows:

Gairloch Post Office	0750
Gairloch Strath Post Office	0800
Poolewe Post Office	0815
Aultbea	0830
Laide	0840
Badcaul	0900
Dundonnell	0908
Braemore	0930
Garve	0955
Contin	1005
Strathpeffer	1010
Dingwall County Building	1020
Inverness (Farraline Park)	1045

Inverness (Farraline Park)	1705
Dingwall County Building	1735
Strathpeffer	1745
Contin	1750
Garve	1800
Braemore	1830
Dundonnell	1850
Badcaul	1855
Laide	1915
Aultbea	1920
Poolewe Post Office	1940
Gairloch Strath Post Office	1955
Gairloch Post Office	2000

Aultbea-Achnasheen-Inverness: Runs every Tuesday, Thursday and Friday, but not on 25/26 December or 1/2 January. The timetable is as follows:

Aultbea	0800
Poolewe Post Office	0815
Gairloch Strath Post Office	0830
Gairloch Charleston (road end)	0835
Kerrysdale	0840
Loch Maree	0855
Kinlochewe	0910
Achnasheen	0930
Garve	0955
Contin	1005
Strathpeffer	1010
Dingwall County Building	1020
Inverness (Farraline Park)	1045

Inverness (Farraline Park)	1705
Dingwall County Building	1735
Strathpeffer	1745
Contin	1750
Garve	1800
Achnasheen	1825
Kinlochewe	1845
Loch Maree	1900
Kerrysdale	1910
Gairloch Charleston (road end)	1915
Gairloch Strath Post Office	1925
Poolewe Post Office	1940
Aultbea	1955

GETTING AROUND

Although most people holidaying in the Gairloch/Torridon region have their own car, there are two convenient ways for the independent traveller to get around the area.

By Postbus

In addition to delivering the mail, the postbus carries passengers and can pick you up or drop you off at several points on the postal round. The Gairloch-Torridon area is served by two postbuses: the Achnasheen postbus (very convenient for those arriving by train) and the Torridon postbus. Fares are usually around £1-£3 per single journey. Timetables are as follows:

Achnasheen Postbus: Runs Monday-Saturday. Departs from the village post office. To confirm postbus times and fares, please contact Achnasheen Post Office. Tel. (044 588) 241.

Laide		0905
Aultbea		0915
Poolewe		0930
Gairloch		1010
Loch Maree Hotel		1035
Kinlochewe		1055
Achnasheen	arrives	1125
	departs	1215
Kinlochewe		1235
Loch Maree Hotel		1255
Gairloch		1325
Poolewe		1410
Aultbea		1430
Laide		1445

Torridon Postbus: Runs Monday-Saturday. Departs from the village post office except Y.H. - departs from Youth Hostel. To confirm postbus times and fares, please contact Alligin Post Office. Tel. (0445) 791 233.

Torridon Y.H.		0905
Torridon		0907
Diabaig		0925
Alligin		0945
Torridon		1000
Torridon Y.H.		1010
Annat		1015
Kinlochewe	arrives	1045
	departs	1340
Annat		1430
Torridon Y.H.		1445
Torridon		1455
Alligin		1610
Diabaig		1630
Torridon		1658
Torridon Y.H.		1700

The Torridon postbus arriving at Kinlochewe at 1045 connects with the 1055 postbus to Achnasheen. At Achnasheen there are train connections for Inverness and the Kyle of Lochalsh (see By Rail above).

By Bus

On school days, the excellent WESTERBUS service makes runs to many of the villages in the Gairloch area. There are four routes to choose from: Gairloch to Red Point, to Melvaig, to Kinlochewe and to Mellon Charles. Please note that routes and times are subject to alterations in accordance with the needs of Gairloch High School and for weather conditions. The Westerbus service is operated by Gairloch Garage. For confirmation of timetables and fares telephone (0445) 2255.

Gairloch-Red Point: Timetable is as follows:

Gairloch High School		1535
Gairloch Garage	0740	1536
Kerrysdale	0745	1545
Shieldaig	0747	1550
Badachro	0750	1555
Port Henderson	0752	1600
South Erradale	0755	1610
Red Point	0800	1620

Red Point	0800	1620
South Erradale	0810	1625
Port Henderson	0820	1628
Badachro	0825	1630
Shieldaig	0830	1633
Kerrysdale	0835	1638
Gairloch Garage	0843	1640
Gairloch High School	0845	

Gairloch-Melvaig: Timetable is as follows:

Gairloch High School	0730	1535
Strath Post Office	0732	1537
Big Sand		1550
North Erradale		1600
Melvaig	0800	1620

Melvaig	0800	1620
North Erradale	0820	
Big Sand	0830	
Strath Post Office	0843	1648
Gairloch High School	0845	1650

Gairloch-Kinlochewe: Timetable is as follows:

Gairloch High School		1535
Gairloch Garage	0730	1537
Loch Maree Hotel	0750	1600
Kinlochewe	0805	1615

Kinlochewe	0805	1615
Loch Maree Hotel	0820	1630
Gairloch Garage	0843	1645
Gairloch High School	0845	

Gairloch-Mellon Charles: Timetable is as follows:

Gairloch Garage	0730	1530
Gairloch High School		1535
Poolewe	0740	1550
Aultbea	0750	1605
Mellon Charles	0800	1620

Mellon Charles	0800	1620
Aultbea	0815	1630
Poolewe	0830	1640
Gairloch High School	0845	1643
Gairloch Garage	0847	1645

For travel around the Gairloch area, see also the Gairloch-Dundonnell-Inverness and Aultbea-Achnasheen-Inveness WESTERBUS routes detailed above.

Local bus services from Torridon to Shieldaig/Strathcarron and from Torridon to Kinlochewe are operated by Mr D. MacLennan of Shieldaig. To confirm times and fares, telephone (052 05) 239. Timetables are as follows:

Torridon-Shieldaig-Strathcarron: From 1st June-30th September buses operate Monday-Saturday. From 1st October-31st May this service operates on Mondays, Wednesdays and Fridays only.

Shieldaig		0945
Torridon P.O.		1000
Shieldaig		1015
Kishorn		1035
Lochcarron		1050
Strathcarron	arrives	1100
	departs	1220
Lochcarron		1230
Kishorn P.O.		1245
Shieldaig		1305
Torridon P.O.	arrives	1320
	departs	1325
Shieldaig		1340

At Strathcarron there are train connections for Inverness and the Kyle of Lochalsh (see By Rail above).

Shieldaig-Torridon-Kinlochewe: This service operates on school days only.

Shieldaig (Hillside)		0730	1530
Torridon Junction		0745	1545
Kinlochewe	arrives	0805	1605
	departs	0807	1615
Torridon Junction		0827	1635
Shieldaig (Hillside)		0842	1650

In addition to the above services, HIGHLAND SCOTTISH OMNIBUSES operate service no.156 from Torridon to Plockton via Shieldaig, Kishorn, Lochcarron, Strathcarron, Attadale, Stromeferry and Achmore. For information on fares and timetables, telephone Inverness (0463) 233 371. For reservations and bookings, telephone (0463) 224 659.

SINGLE TRACK ROADS

Many of the roads in the Gairloch/Torridon area are single track. Please note that it is an *offence* to hinder traffic which is travelling behind you. Pull into the nearest passing place and allow following traffic to overtake. Similarly, use passing places to permit on-coming traffic to pass.

FISHING

The superb fishing to be had in the Gairloch/Torridon region attracts thousands of fishermen to the area each year. Amidst some of Scotland's most spectacular scenery lie innumerable sparkling lochs and rivers positively teeming with brown trout, sea trout and salmon. Two of Europe's most famous trout lochs, Fionn Loch and Loch Maree, are situated in the area, providing some of the most exciting fishing in the country. There is something for everyone, from easily accessible roadside rivers to remote hill lochs entailing several miles' walk over rough moorland. All fishing is strictly controlled and prior permission should always be sought from the owner.

When out fishing, please bear in mind the following points. Always wear a life-jacket when out on a small boat. When walking in the hills, follow the Country Code and check that you will not be interfering with deer stalking. If you are walking to isolated hill lochs, equip yourself sensibly - follow the recommendations for walkers given in the Selected Walks section.

LOCH/RIVER PERMITS AND BOAT HIRE

Please note there is no Sunday fishing.

Aeroplane Loch - Brown trout. £3.00 per rod per day, bank fishing. Boat: £6.00. Permission: Shieldaig Lodge Hotel, Badachro, Gairloch. Tel. (044 583) 250. Hotel guests have priority.

Aultbea Hill Lochs - Brown Trout. 22 hill lochs in the Aultbea area are managed by Aultbea Estates. Permission: Mr Macdonald, Old Smiddy, Laide. Tel. (0445) 731 425. A useful location map is available from the Old Smiddy and boat hire can be arranged.

Badachro River - Salmon and sea-trout spate river fishing, July to October. £9.00 per rod per day. Permission: Shieldaig Lodge Hotel, Badachro, Gairloch. Tel. (044 583) 250. Hotel guests have priority.

Diamond Loch - Brown trout. £3.00 per rod per day, bank fishing. Boat: £6.00. Permission: Shieldaig Lodge Hotel, Badachro, Gairloch. Tel. (044 583) 250. Hotel guests have priority.

Dubh Loch - Permission: Wildcat Stores, Gairloch. Tel. (0445) 2242.

Fairy Lochs - Brown trout. £3.00 per rod per day, bank fishing. Boat: £6.00. Permission: Shieldaig Lodge Hotel, Badachro, Gairloch. Tel. (044 583) 250. Hotel guests have priority.

Fionn Loch - Trout. Permission: Mr K. Gunn, The Radio Shop, Strath, Gairloch. Tel. (0445) 2400. Also, Mr H. Davis, Creag Beag, Charleston, Gairloch. Tel. (0445) 2322.

Gairloch Hill Lochs - Trout. Over 30 lochs in the hills to the east of Gairloch are managed by the Gairloch Angling Association. £1.00 per rod per day. Boat fishing is available. Permission: Mr K. Gunn, The Radio Shop, Strath, Gairloch. Tel. (0445) 2400 or Wildcat Stores, Gairloch. Tel. (0445) 2242.

Loch A'Bhaid-Luachraich - Brown trout. £5.00 per rod. Permission: Inverewe Garden Visitor Centre, Poolewe. Tel. (044 586) 229. Discounts for members of the National Trust For Scotland.

Loch A'Chroisg - Brown trout, pike and perch. Boat fishing. Permission: Glendocherty Craft Shop, Kinlochewe. Tel. (044 584) 220. Permission for bank fishing: Ledgowan Lodge Hotel, Achnasheen. Tel. (044 588) 252.

Loch Bad A Cheamh - Brown trout. Boat, 2 rods, 0900-1800: £12.00. Evenings-1800 onwards: £5.00. Fly fishing only. No bank fishing. Permission: The Anchorage, Pier Road, Gairloch. Tel. (0445) 2402.

Loch Bad Na H-Achlaise - Brown trout. Two boats available. Permission: Shieldaig Lodge Hotel, Badachro, Gairloch. Tel. (044 583) 250. Hotel guests have priority.

Loch Bad Na Scalaig - Permission: Wildcat Stores, Gairloch. Tel. (0445) 2242.

Loch Bharranch - Brown trout and sea trout. Boat fishing. Permission: Glendocherty Craft Shop, Kinlochewe. Tel. (044 584) 220.

Loch Ghiuragarstidh - Brown trout. £5.00 per rod. Permission: Inverewe Garden Visitor Centre, Poolewe. Tel. (044 586) 229. Discounts for members of the National Trust For Scotland.

Loch Kernsary - Brown trout, sea trout and salmon. Boat, 2 rods, 0900-1800: £8.00. Evenings-1800 onwards: £4.00. Fly fishing and spinning. No bank fishing. Permission: The Anchorage, Pier Road, Gairloch. Tel. (0445) 2402.

Loch Maree - Brown trout, sea trout and salmon. Boat, engine and ghillie per day: May and June-£35; July and August-£60; September and October-£45. Permission: The Anchorage, Pier Road, Gairloch. Tel. (0445) 2402.
Spring salmon fishing-April to June; sea trout- June to October; brown trout. 8 boats for hire (2 people per boat) with mandatory ghillies. Fly fishing only from 1 July to end of October. Trolling and spinning are permitted from April to June. Permission: Mr F.M. Buckley, Loch Maree Hotel, Loch Maree. Tel. (044 584) 288. Spring salmon fishing-April to June; sea trout-July to October. £7.00 per rod per day. Boat: £7.00 per day. Permission: Kinlochewe Holiday Chalets, Kinlochewe. Tel. (044 584) 234.

Loch Na Curra - Brown trout. Boat, 2 rods, 0900-1800: £12.00. Evenings-1800 onwards: £5.00. Bank fishing: £2.00 per day. Fly fishing and spinning. Permission: The Anchorage, Pier Road, Gairloch. Tel. (0445) 2402.

Loch Na H-Oidhche - Brown trout. Boat, engine, fuel, 2 rods: £18.00 per day. Bothy, boat, engine, fuel, gas and logs: £15 per day/night per head. Bank fishing: £2.00 per day. Fly fishing only. Permission: The Anchorage, Pier Road, Gairloch. Tel. (0445) 2402. Brown trout. Permission: Mr H. Davis, Creag Beag, Charleston, Gairloch. Tel. (0445) 2322.

Loch Nan Dailthean - Brown trout. £5.00 per rod. Boat hire: £3.50. Permission: Inverewe Garden Visitor Centre, Poolewe. Tel. (044 586) 229. Discounts for members of the National Trust For Scotland.

Loch Squod - Permission: Nirvana Crafts, Poolewe. Tel. (044 586) 335.

Loch Tollaidh - Brown trout. Boat, 2 rods, 0900-1800: £12.00. Evenings-1800 onwards: £5.00. Bank fishing: £2.00 per day. Fly fishing and spinning. Permission: The Anchorage, Pier Road, Gairloch. Tel. (0445) 2402.
Also, Mr K. Gunn, The Radio Shop, Strath, Gairloch. Tel. (0445) 2400. Nirvana Crafts, Poolewe. Tel. (044 586) 335.

Lochan An Iasgaich - Salmon and sea trout, May to October. £12.50 per rod, 0900-1800; boat: £8.00, 0900-1800. Evenings-1800 onwards: £8.00 per rod; boat: £5.00. Permission: Loch Torridon Hotel, Torridon. Tel. (0445) 791 242.

River Kerry - Salmon and sea-trout spate river fishing, May to October. Permission: Creag Mor Hotel, Gairloch. Tel. (0445) 2068.

River Torridon - Salmon and sea trout. 2 beats of 3 rods. £10.00 per rod, 0900-1800. Evenings-1800 onwards: £7.00. Permission: Loch Torridon Hotel, Torridon. Tel. (0445) 791 242.

Spectacles Loch - Brown trout. £3.00 per rod per day, Bank fishing. Boat: £6.00. Permission: Shieldaig Lodge Hotel, Badachro, Gairloch. Tel. (044 583) 250. Hotel guests have priority.

Equipment Hire: Complete fly fishing outfits for hire - rod, reel, line and landing net - £5.00 per day plus £10 deposit. Contact: The Anchorage, Pier Road, Gairloch. Tel. (0445) 2402.

Ghillie Service: Derek Roxborough, S.A.N.A. angling instructor and Secretary of the Gairloch Angling Club, offers guided hill loch fishing for brown trout. Flies tied to order. He also operates a rod repair and hire service. Contact: D.W. Roxborough, The Old Police Station, Gairloch, Ross-shire, IV21 2BP. Tel. (0445) 2057.

SEA ANGLING

The many sea lochs around the Gairloch/Torridon region offer excellent sport for the fisherman. Species which frequent the waters include haddock, whiting, skate, mackerel, flounder, pollock and ling. Several establishments offer skippered sea-angling trips.

M.V. KERRY, a well equipped modern boat, operates daily (except Sundays) from Gairloch Pier. 3-hour sea-angling cruises depart at 0930 Monday-Friday and at 1400 on Saturdays. Bait and fishing rods are supplied. M.V. Kerry is also available for group charters at £100 for a full day (0930-1700) and £70 for a half day (0930-1230). The price includes up to 10 anglers. Bookings: Gairloch Cruises, The Post Office, Pier Road, Gairloch. Tel. (0445) 2175.

THE ANCHORAGE runs daily sea angling trips throughout the summer season and can cater for families and groups. For further details contact: The Anchorage, Pier Road, Gairloch. Tel. (0445) 2402.

LOCH TORRIDON HOTEL can help you arrange angling trips with local fishermen on Outer Loch Torridon. Minimun number 5 people. Contact: Loch Torridon Hotel, Torridon. Tel. (0445) 791 242.

If you wish to hire your own boat, contact WEST HIGHLAND MARINE LTD, Badachro, by Gairloch. Tel. (044 583) 291. Their large hire fleet includes rowing boats (with outboard motors), skiffs, dinghies and yachts. Skippered trips are also offered and sea angling tackle is available for hire.

12 and 14ft boats with full safety equipment are also available for hire from WATERSIDE, The Pier, Poolewe. Tel. (044 586) 420.

ACCOMMODATION

SELF CATERING AND B. & B. DIRECTORY

The Gairloch/Torridon area has a wide selection of excellent self catering and Bed & Breakfast accommodation. Please quote this guide when contacting the following advertisers.

AULTBEA (Guesthouse) Comfortable family guesthouse overlooking Loch Ewe. Home-made meals in a quiet atmosphere, ensuite bedrooms with colour TV, tea/coffee facilities, central heating throughout. Ideal area for a quiet restful holiday, bird watching, walking etc. Inverewe Gardens 9 miles. B & B or D B B. SAE for brochure and details from Mrs A. MacRae, Mellondale Guest House, 47 Mellon Charles, Aultbea, Ross-shire, IV22 2JL. Tel: 0445 731 326. *Display advert*

AULTBEA (Guesthouse - Self-catering Flats - Caravan) Spacious, comfortable, modern guesthouse. STB 1 Crown, Commended. 2 luxury self-catering flats recently converted. STB 4 Crown, Highly Commended. 1 family caravan, comfortable and well-equipped. All with spectacular loch views. Details from Tom and Helen Lister, Oran an Mara, Aultbea, Ross-shire, IV22 2HU. Tel: 0445 731 394.

AULTBEA (Self-catering Houses) Come and see the splendours of the West Coast and stay in comfortable, well-equipped houses. Overlooking Loch Ewe with panoramic views of the Dundonnell or Torridon hills. Ideal for climbing, hill walking or a gentle stroll. Water sports and fishing or just touring and taking in the beautiful scenery. Details from Mrs K. M. Mitchell, Riverside, Poolewe, Ross-shire. Tel: 0445 86 484. *Display advert*

AULTBEA (Self-catering Flat) Self-contained first-floor flat overlooking small loch within easy reach of the sea. Close sandy beaches. Perfectly situated for hill walking etc. Accommodation comprises 2 bedrooms, sleeping 4. Lounge/kitchen, shower room with toilet. Price per week £145 - £210. Advance booking to Mrs R. Wiseman, 39 Mellon Charles, Aultbea, Ross-shire, IV22 2JL. *Display advert*

BADACHRO (B & B) A warm welcome awaits you at "Harbour View". We offer B & B £17, dinner optional £8-50. Accommodation: 2 double, 1 twin, 1 family plus chalet annex. All rooms en-suite. STB 3 Crowns, Commended. Brochure available. Details from Liza and Graham Willey, Harbour View, Badachro, Gairloch, Ross-shire, IV21 2AA. Tel: 0445 83 316.

BADACHRO (Self-catering Cottage) Apronhill House, an original crofter's cottage set alone on a hillside in 1 acre fenced ground. Near all shops and 3 beaches. The area around Gairloch is renowned as one of the most beautiful in Britain, with wild magnificence of mountain, forest, loch and glen, and glorious safe sandy beaches from which swimming can be enjoyed. 70 yard walk to reach Apronhill in splendid isolation. Details from Liz Grigor Duvill, Aros, Badachro, Gairloch, Ross-shire, IV21 2AB. Tel: 0445 83 317.

ORMISCAIG, AULTBEA

Lochview Holidays *Luxury Self-Catering*

Come and see the splendours of the West Coast and stay in comfortable, well-equipped houses. Overlooking Loch Ewe with panoramic views of the Dundonnell or Torridon Hills. Ideal for climbing, hill walking or a gentle stroll, water sports and fishing or just touring and taking in the beautiful scenery.

Bookings and enquiries to:

Mrs K. M. Mitchell, Riverside, Poolewe, Ross-shire. Tel: (044586) 484.

AULTBEA

Self-catering Flat

Self-contained first-floor flat overlooking small loch within easy reach of the sea. Close sandy beaches. Perfectly situated for hill walking etc. Accommodation comprises 2 bedrooms, sleeping 4. Lounge/kitchen, shower room with toilet. Price per week £145 - £210.

Advance booking to Mrs R. Wiseman, 39 Mellon Charles, Aultbea, Ross-shire, IV22 2JL.

MELLONDALE

Guest House

AULTBEA

Comfortable family guesthouse overlooking Loch Ewe. Home-made meals in a quiet atmosphere, ensuite bedrooms with colour TV, tea/coffee facilities, central heating throughout. Ideal area for a quiet restful holiday, bird watching, walking etc. Inverewe Gardens 9 miles. B & B or D B B.

SAE for brochure and details from Mrs A. MacRae, Mellondale Guest House, 47 Mellon Charles, Aultbea, Ross-shire, IV22 2JL. Tel: 0445 731 326.

GAIRLOCH (Guesthouse) AA selected, purpose-built, non-smoking guesthouse; ideally positioned near the sea and village, with uninterrupted views across loch to Torridon mountains. Large enclosed carpark. High standards, with wash basins, tea making facilities, central heating. On cooler evenings, comforting open fire in lounge. Table d'hote dinner and multichoice breakfast. Details from Horisdale House, Strath, Gairloch, Ross-shire, IV21 2DA. Tel: 0445 2151.

GAIRLOCH (Self-catering House) The house is 4 miles from Gairloch village, and half a mile from superb beach overlooking Skye. Very comfortably furnished, fully equipped excluding sheets and towels. Sleeps 6-7 people. TV, washing machine, fridge all provided. Prices from £175-£250. Gas fire with central heating. Electric for cooking etc. Both 50p coin meters. Details from Mrs I.A. Hunter, Myrtle Croft, 20 Big Sand, Gairloch, IV21 2DD. Tel: 0445 2129. *Display advert*

GAIRLOCH, TORRIDON (Self-catering Cottages/Chalets) Mackay's Agency - specialists in holiday property letting, with cottages, farmhouses and chalets throughout Scotland. We have an excellent selection of self-catering properties in the Gairloch, Torridon and Shieldaig area. Enjoy the independence of your own holiday home from £25 per person per week. Full colour brochure available - Tel: (24hrs) 031 226 4364 or write: Dept G/T, Mackay's Agency, 30 Frederick Street, Edinburgh, EH2 2JR. *Display advert*

LAIDE (B & B) Superior Bed & Breakfast accommodation with private facilities catering for an intimate atmosphere. Dinner a speciality with home cooking and baking. Private dining room. One family room, one double room. Rooms fully ensuite c/w television. Fully laid out garden overlooking The Minch. 10 miles NE of Inverewe Gardens, 15 miles NE of Gairloch on A832. For details contact Bill and Mavis Hart, "Cul na Mara", Sand Passage, Laide, Wester Ross, IV12 2ND. Tel: (0445) 731 295.

MELLON UDRIGLE (Self-catering Chalets) Tastefully furnished self-catering chalets with colour TV and bed linen by sandy beach. Spectacular views towards Summer Isles. Ideal setting for sea/loch fishing. Dinghy included. Wonderful coastal and hill-walking. Location Ceol-na-Mara, Mellon Udrigle, nr Laide. Details from Arran Properties Ltd, PO Box 624, St Helier, Jersey, JE4 8YZ. Tel: 0534 27 264.

POOLEWE (Self-catering Cottages) 1 1/4 miles from Inverewe Gardens, two traditional cottages, sleeping 4/6 persons. Situated in a very secluded spot by River Ewe and looking towards Loch Maree. STB 4 Crown, Commended. Try a holiday in this tranquil setting and you will think on it for many years. Details from Mr A. Urquhart, Torwood, 15 Croft, Poolewe, Ross-shire, IV22 2JY. Tel: 0445 86 268.

POOLEWE (Caravans) 2 caravans, each on its own, situated on our croft. Central for touring, 5 mins from village and swimming pool, 15 mins Inverewe Gardens. Fully equipped except linen, mains water supply. Electricity 10p meter, gas supplied for cookers. £100/week, nightly if available. Details from Mrs Margaret Newton, Andmar, 1 Londubh, Poolewe, Ross-shire. Tel: 0445 86 413.

GAIRLOCH
Self-catering House

The house is 4 miles from Gairloch village, and half a mile from superb beach overlooking Skye. Very comfortably furnished, fully equipped excluding sheets and towels. Sleeps 6-7 people. TV, washing machine, fridge all provided. Prices from £175-250. Gas fire with central heating. Electric for cooking etc. Both 50p coin meters.

Mrs I.A. Hunter, Myrtle Croft, 20 Big Sand, Gairloch, IV21 2DD. Tel: 0445 2129.

Specialists in holiday property letting with cottages, farmhouses and chalets throughout Scotland. We have an excellent selection of self-catering properties in the Gairloch, Torridon and Shieldaig area.

Enjoy the independence of you own holiday home from £25 per person per week.

Full colour brochure available:
Tel: (24hrs) 031 226 4364
or write: Dept G/T, Mackay's Agency, 30 Frederick St, Edinburgh, EH2 2JR

SOUTH ERRADALE (Self-catering Flat) Upstairs self-catering flat at address below. Living-room, kitchen, bathroom and 2 bedrooms sleeping 4. Comfortably furnished with electric heating in each room. Quiet seaside location with sandy beach nearby. Magnificent views of Skye and the Torridon mountains. Ideally situated for hill-walking and fishing. Details from Mrs C.M. Thomson, 18 South Erradale, Gairloch, Ross-shire, IV21 2AU. Tel: 0445 83 202.

TORRIDON (B & B - Self-catering Cottage - Caravan) Annat Lodge, Annat, Torridon. B & B in 200 year old cottage overlooking Loch Torridon and mountains. Warm welcome. Wholesome breakfast includes home-made bread and marmalade, free-range eggs, ground coffee etc. Bedrooms have wash-hand basin or en-suite facilities. £14-£16 per person. Near hotel. Also self-catering caravan and cottage, sleep 4. Details from Gill and Graham Wilson, Annat Lodge, Annat, Torridon, by Achnasheen, Ross-shire, IV22 2EU. Tel: 0445 791 200.

TORRIDON (B & B) Dinner, bed and breakfast at Heather Cliff, Alligin, Torridon. Walking, climbing, boating, fishing or just relax in well fed comfort in the heart of magnificent scenery. Bed and breakfast £12-50, dinner £8. Open February to November. Details from Mrs P.J. Rose, Heather Cliff, Alligin, Torridon, by Achnasheen, Wester Ross, IV22 2HB. Tel: 0445 791 256.

CAMP AND CARAVAN SITES

The area is well served by camp and caravan sites, most of which are set amidst spectacular scenery.

Gairloch Holiday Park, Strath, Gairloch, Ross-shire. Booking enquiries to: Mrs J. Forbes, 70 St Andrews Drive, Bridge of Weir, Renfrewshire, PA11 3HY. Tel. (0505) 614 343 or (0445) 2373. This 6 acre grassy site is situated at Strath in the historic fishing and crofting village of Gairloch. From the A832, take the B8021 Melvaig road and after 1/4 mile turn right at the Millcroft Hotel. The site lies just behind the hotel but despite this there are beautiful views across Loch Gairloch to the mountains of Torridon and the Isle of Skye. This is an ideal site for those who wish to explore the village of Gairloch on foot. Several food shops are located within easy walking distance. **Facilities:** 50 pitches for tents and caravans (electric hook-ups are available). Toilet block with hot water and showers. Laundry, including drying and ironing facilities. Camping gas is available. Pets are accepted by arrangement and there are chemical toilet disposal facilities. The site is open from April to October inclusive.

Gruinard Bay Caravan and Camping Park, Laide, by Achnasheen, Ross-shire, IV22 2ND. Tel. (0445) 731 225. This 2 1/2 acre grassy site is set right on the seafront at Laide on the A832. On a clear day, the views across Gruinard Bay to the Summer Isles and the mountains of Coigach and Assynt are breathtaking. The site overlooks a beautiful sandy beach and is adjacent to the picturesque ruins of the ancient Chapel of Sand. There is a small general store within easy walking distance of the site and petrol is also available locally. **Facilities:** 47 pitches for tents and caravans (electric hook-ups are available). Tasteful log windbreaks provide extra shelter and privacy for tents. Toilet block with hot water and showers. Laundry with ironing facilities. Camping gas is available and pets are accepted by arrangement. There are chemical toilet disposal facilities. The site is open from April to October inclusive.

Inverewe Caravan Site, National Trust For Scotland, Poolewe, Ross-shire, IV22 2LF. Tel. (044 586) 249. This 4 acre site is situated by the A832 in the picturesque village of Poolewe, next to the BP filling station. The village offers excellent restaurant and shopping facilities, together with a recently built swimming pool. The world famous Inverewe Garden is only a short walk away. The site is a mixture of grass and tarmac and although situated by the seafront, views are obscured by a brick shed and trees. This site can become very busy at the height of the season. **Facilities:** 50 pitches for tents and caravans. Toilet block with hot water and showers. A key is required for the toilet block - if you arrive after the on-site National Trust shop has closed (around 8pm), you will be unable to gain entry to the block. Laundry with drying facilities. Camping gas is available and pets are accepted by arrangement.

There are chemical toilet disposal facilities. Credit cards are accepted. The site is open from April to September inclusive.

Kinlochewe Caravan Club Site, Kinlochewe, Achnasheen, Ross-shire, IV22 2PA. Tel. (044 584) 239. This 5 acre site is situated in the small village of Kinlochewe, at the junction of the A832 and the A896 - ideally placed for exploring the Beinn Eighe National Nature Reserve, Loch Maree and the mountains of Torridon. The village has a beautiful setting dominated by the quartz-capped peaks of Beinn Eighe which, in sunlight, appear to be snow-covered. The caravan site is a mixture of grassland and tarmac. There is a small Mace supermarket and takeaway food shop within easy walking distance of the site. **Facilities:** 60 caravan pitches (electric hook-ups are available). Toilet block with hot water and showers. Laundry with drying facilities. Camping gas is available and there is a pay phone for residents' use. Pets accepted by arrangement. There are chemical toilet disposal facilities. Credit cards are accepted and the site is open from April to September inclusive.

Sands Holiday Centre, Gairloch, Ross-shire, IV21 2DL. Tel. (0445) 2152. This beautiful 55 acre grassy site is set in a rural location beside the sea, 3 miles out from Gairloch on the B8021 Melvaig road. The site is run by the Cameron family and the land forms part of their sheep farm - children will love watching the sheep shearing which takes place during July. An added advantage to the Sands Holiday Centre is that you must pitch at least 20 feet from your neighbour - an excellent rule which ensures a reasonably quiet holiday. The site is set amidst the rolling sand dunes which form the backdrop to the long expanse of Big Sand Beach - a beautiful sheltered sandy beach, safe for swimming and ideal for watersports. There are panoramic views across the Sound of Raasay to the Isle of Skye. **Facilities:** There is room for 172 caravans (30 pitches have electric hook-ups) and 200 tents in a separate area. There are no individual pitches (apart from the electric hook-ups) so you can set up your tent or caravan wherever you like. Toilet facilities are good, with two large toilet blocks and a smaller one which contains a unit for the disabled. The toilet blocks have hot water and showers. There is a separate covered dishwashing area for the tent section. The metered laundry facilities include 3 washing machines, a spin dryer, 4 tumble dryers and 2 irons with ironing boards. A small supermarket on site sells bread, milk and groceries in addition to camping equipment, Calor and Camping Gas, books and fishing tackle. The shop is open from Monday-Saturday, 0830-1830; Sunday 1000-1200 and 1500-1700. Pets are accepted by arrangement and there are chemical toilet disposal facilities. There is also a children's play area and a pay phone for residents' use. Site charges include fishing on local lochs and rivers. Sailboards, canoes, water skis and rowing boats can be hired on site from Gairloch Watersports, who also provide tuition, if required. The site has its own slipway. The Sands Holiday Centre is open from April to October inclusive.

Camping is also possible at the following sites:

Badcaul: Camping is permitted at Badcaul which is situated about 5 1/4 miles to the north-west of Dundonnell. Enquire where you see the sign by the main A832. **Facilities:** None.

Inveralligin: After descending to the village, you will see a grassy area by the river on your right, just before the road forks at the telephone box. Tents and caravans are permitted to stop here for 20p per night. **Facilities:** None.

Kinlochewe to Torridon Road: There are two small forestry plantations owned by the National Trust For Scotland situated by the main road, about 3/4 mile from Torridon village. Free camping is permitted in the East Plantation which is light and airy and contains mature trees (the other plantation is fenced to prevent damage by animals and should not be entered). **Facilities:** None.

Mellangaun: If you take the B8057 from Poolewe to Cove, you will pass the beautiful sandy beach at Mellangaun. Tents and caravans are permitted to use the firm grassy area at the back of the beach. This is a beautiful site, with views across Loch Ewe to the Isle of Ewe. **Facilities:** None.

Taagan: This is the only area within the Beinn Eighe National Nature Reserve where camping is permitted. The grassy site is situated to the right of the A832, about 1 1/2 miles north-west of Kinlochewe. The site is open from Easter to September only. **Facilities:** Toilet block with cold water and drinking water.

Torridon: There is a small camp site in a grassy field opposite the Torridon Visitor Centre in Torridon village. Although adjacent to the village road, the field is edged with bushes which provide a reasonable amount of privacy. A fee of £2.50 per tent per night is charged. **Facilities:** There is a toilet block close by which has hot water, showers and a kitchen sink.

YOUTH HOSTELS

Carn Dearg Youth Hostel, Gairloch: Grade 2, sleeps 52. Tel. (0445) 2219. The Carn Dearg Youth Hostel is situated on the coast, some 3 miles west of Gairloch. The hostel lies close to the south end of the beautiful beach at Big Sand, with views out to South Rona, the Isle of Skye and, on a clear day, Lewis and Harris. The shops at Strath, 2 1/2 miles from the hostel, include a supermarket, bakery and butcher's shop.

Craig Youth Hostel, Diabaig: Grade 3, sleeps 16. This is one of the most remote Youth Hostels in Britain and is definitely recommended for people who like to get away from it all. There is no road to the hostel - reaching it entails either a two mile walk over rough moor from Diabaig or a five mile walk from Red Point. The hostel is well sign-posted in both directions and the walker is rewarded by panoramic views of Skye, South Rona, Raasay and the Applecross peninsula. Please remember that in such a remote area everything you need for your stay will have to be carried in.

Torridon Youth Hostel: Grade 1, sleeps 80. Depending on how busy the hostel is, family rooms may be available by prior arrangement. Tel. (044 587) 284. The hostel is located in the quiet village of Torridon at the head of Upper Loch Torridon. There are good views across the loch to the remote Applecross peninsula. This is an ideal location for those who wish to explore the Torridon mountains - Beinn Alligin, Beinn Dearg, Liathach and the hills of the Ben-Damph Forest are all close at hand. There is a small supermarket in the village within easy walking distance of the hostel.

INDEPENDENT HOSTELS

There are several independent hostels in the Gairloch/Torridon area, each privately owned and operated with a minimum of rules. No membership is required to use these hostels. Accomodation is in small bunkrooms or dormitories and fully equipped kitchens and hot showers are available. The type of bedding provided varies from place to place, so please check with the individual establishment when booking.

Cnoc Alluin Bunkhouse, Strath, Gairloch. Contact: Douglas Gibson. Tel. (0445) 2085. The Cnoc Alluin Bunkhouse is conveniently situated in the historic village of Gairloch, within easy walking distance of several food shops. Cycles and outdoor equipment can be hired from the bunkhouse, thus making it an excellent centre from which to explore the area. Local transport can be arranged, as can guided hill-walks, loch fishing and sea angling. You can also arrange to be collected from Inverness or Achnasheen.

Kinlochewe Hotel Bunkhouse, Kinlochewe, Wester Ross. Tel. (044 584) 253. This hostel is situated in the small village of Kinlochewe, close to the Beinn Eighe National Nature Reserve and the south end of Loch Maree. It sleeps 18 people and meals are available by arrangement. There is a Mace supermarket and takeaway food shop within easy walking distance. The hostel is open all year.

Sail Mhor Croft Hostel, Camusnagaul, Dundonnell, Garve, Ross-shire. Tel. (085 483) 224. The Sail Mhor Croft Hostel is situated in the country, in the little crofting settlement of Camusnagaul, overlooking Little Loch Broom. The huge mass of An Teallach forms a backdrop to the croft house and indeed the hostel takes its name from one of the peaks of this mountain: Sail Mhor, which in Gaelic means "big heel". The hostel sleeps 16 people (in 8 and 4-bedded rooms) and meals are available by arrangement. The nearest shop is the Dundonnell Stores, 4 miles north-west of the hostel, down the minor road signposted to Durnamuck/Badluarach. The Sail Mhor Croft Hostel is open all year.

Inveralligin Field Centre, Alligin, Loch Torridon, Wester Ross, IV22 2HB. Contact: Dr Jeremy Robertson or Dr Annika Robertson. Tel. (0445) 791 247. Although mainly offering wildlife holidays and courses, bunkhouse accomodation is occasionally available when the Field Centre is not fully booked. The centre sleeps 12 people (in 6-bedded rooms) and meals are available by arrangement. There is also a drying room for wet hill-walking gear. The nearest shop is about 4 miles away in Torridon.

Rua Reidh Lighthouse Exploration Centre, Rua Reidh Lighthouse, Melvaig, Gairloch, IV21 2EA. Contact: Fran Cree or Chris Barrett. Tel. (044 585) 263. The Rua Reidh Lighthouse primarily offers adventure holidays, but bunk-bed accomodation is occasionally available when the centre is not fully booked. Accomodation is in the Old Keeper's House which is set within the walls of the lighthouse compound (the light tower is now automated). The centre sleeps 18 people (in 4 and 6-bedded rooms) and meals, including packed lunches, are available. The nearest shop is in the Sands Holiday Centre, 9 1/2 miles away.

PACKAGE/ACTIVITY HOLIDAYS

Discover, Brownhill House, Annat, Torridon, IV22 2EZ. Contact: Cam MacLeay. Tel. (0445) 791 218. Guided walking holidays in the Torridon area. Packages arranged. Guided walks are available to suit all levels, from easy walks through glens and along stalker's paths to wilderness walking and high top exploration.

Inveralligin Field Centre, Alligin, Loch Torridon, Wester Ross, IV22 2HB. Contact: Dr Jeremy Robertson or Dr Annika Robertson. Tel. (0445) 791 247. Highland wildlife and marine studies. Based in the former schoolhouse in the isolated village of Inveralligin, the centre offers a variety of all-inclusive week long holidays from April to October. Personally guided by Jeremy and Annika Roberston (who both have Ph.D.'s in ecology), the courses will enable you to discover the diverse plant and animal life of the Scottish mountains, moorland, lochs, and sea. Groups are small (a maximum of 12 people) and itineraries are flexible and can be adapted to take account of individual abilities and interests. All courses include hill-walking and boat trips to sites of special interest. Facilities at the centre include a drying room, sampling equipment, binocular microscopes and a comprehensive library. Accomodation is in small dormitories (two 6-bedded rooms), but reasonably priced bed and breakfast accomodation can be arranged locally for those who would prefer this. Self-catering and full-board options are available and vegetarian meals can be arranged. Prices include transport to and from Inverness, if required, and there are special discounts for group and family bookings. A helpful leaflet is available from the centre which contains full information on all the courses on offer throughout the year.

Rua Reidh Lighthouse Exploration Centre, Rua Reidh Lighthouse, Melvaig, Gairloch, IV21 2EA. Contact: Fran Cree or Chris Barrett. Tel. (044 585) 263. Situated at the tip of an isolated moorland peninsula some 12 miles north of Gairloch, the centre offers seven and fourteen day adventure holidays throughout the year. There are a variety of exciting activities to try, including canoeing, rock climbing, abseiling, hill walking, swimming, camping, fishing, lobster potting, orienteering and birdwatching. Learn how to read a map, build your own shelter, light a fire and cook food which you have collected or caught for yourself. All activities are personally supervised and Fran and Chris have between them a total of 22 years experience in the field of adventure holidays thus ensuring a safe stay. There are separate weeks for 13-15 year olds, 16-20 year olds and adults and within each group the programme can be adapted to take account of individual interests and abilities. Accomodation is in the Old Keeper's House set within the walls of the lighthouse compound. 4 and 6-bedded rooms sleep up to 18 people and there is also a double room, a twin room and a family room. The centre contains a cosy sitting room with log fire and an extensive range of reference books are available for consultation. Prices include full board, transport to and from Inverness, all activities and all equipment - rucksacks, sleeping bags, waterproofs, wetsuits, technical and safety equipment. Special discounts or self-catering at a reduced rate may be available for groups of 10 or over. Contact the centre for their illustrated leaflet which contains full information on the activity holidays available at the lighthouse.

There are a number of other operators based outwith the region who operate activity holidays in the Gairloch/Torridon area:

Highland Contours, Delny Post Office, Barbaraville, Invergordon, Ross-shire, IV18 0NA. Contact: June or Maurice Ewing. Tel. (086 284) 2258. Guided walking holidays and off-the-road backpacking expeditions to wilderness areas. Graded programme to suit all abilities. Equipment hire available. Collection from public transport, if required.

Highland Safaris, Cnocmor, Strathpeffer, Ross-shire, IV14 9BT. Tel. (0997) 421 618. Leisurely holidays by mini-coach and boat. Weekly from Easter to September.

Lady Trek, "Foxgloves", Leacanashie, Lochcarron, Ross-shire, IV54 8YD. Contact: Jean Stewart. Tel. (052 02) 238. Leisurely guided walks. Weekly holidays include visits to Torridon together with walks in Applecross, Kintail and the Isle of Skye. Vegetarian meals by arrangement. Ladies only weeks are available.

North-West Frontiers, 19 West Terrace, Ullapool, Ross-shire, IV26 2UU. Tel. (0854) 612 571 or (0854) 85 231. Fax. (0854) 612 025. Guided walking holidays. Weekly from May to October. Small groups and a flexible programme to allow for individual interests.

Puffin Cycle Tours, Miltonburn, Aviemore, Inverness-shire, PH22 1RD. Tel. (0479) 810 214 or (0479) 810 787. Leisurely 3-7 day cycling holidays. Various areas, including Torridon. Small groups (maximum 8 people). Guided or unaccompanied. Operates from May to September.

GENERAL TOURIST SERVICES

TOURIST INFORMATION CENTRE

The only Tourist Information Centre in the area is located in the village of Gairloch. Tel. (0445) 2130. During the summer months, the centre is open Monday-Saturday, 0900-1900 and Sunday, 1000-1800. In winter, open Monday-Friday, 0900-1700. The centre sells a selection of local maps and books and also has general information about other parts of Scotland. Staff can offer free advice and information on the local area and a range of useful leaflets are available. The centre also operates a "Book-A-Bed-Ahead" service, which is a good way of ensuring advance Bed & Breakfast or hotel accomodation in this popular area. Staff can locate establishments with vacancies and make reservations for you. Bookings are normally accepted up to 24 hours in advance. A small fee is charged for national bookings and may also be charged for local bookings. Bureau de Change facilities are available at the centre.

BANK

The Bank of Scotland, Gairloch, Ross-shire, IV21 2BE. Tel. (0445) 2015. Open Monday-Friday, 0915-1230 and 1330-1645. Cash advances are available from Visa, Access, Mastercard and Eurocard credit cards. Bureau de Change facilities are also available (currency and travellers' cheques). The bank has an outside cashline machine which accepts the following cards: Bank of Scotland, Royal Bank of Scotland, Barkleys Bank and Lloyds Bank.

BOAT HIRE/CRUISES

MV KERRY CRUISES, GAIRLOCH (Sea Fishing - Cruises) Daily sea angling trips and cruises from Gairloch Pier during Summer months. Modern boat with full facilities. Angling gear and bait supplied. Book at the Post Office, Pier Road, Gairloch Tel: 0445 2175. Further details from John D. MacKenzie, MV Kerry, Gairloch Cruises, Pier Road, Gairloch, Ross-shire, IV21 2BT. Tel: 0445 2317 (Mon - Sat).

WEST HIGHLAND MARINE LTD, BADACHRO (Boat Hire - Sailing Trips) West Highland Marine operating from Badachro Bay, Gairloch offer a large selection of boats for hire for sea angling or just for pleasure. Full safety equipment provided. Sailing trips on one of our modern yachts can also be arranged. For a brochure or further information contact: West Highland Marine Ltd, Badachro, Gairloch, Ross-shire, IV21 2AA. Tel: 0445 83 291. *Display advert*

MUSEUM

GAIRLOCH HERITAGE MUSEUM, GAIRLOCH (Museum - Restaurant)
This award-winning museum illustrates all aspects of the past life of Gairloch Parish from the Stone Age to the present day. The attached licensed restaurant serves coffee, teas and meals all day. Both open April to end September, daily except Sundays 10am to 5pm. Museum also open October to March by arrangement telephoning 0445 2287. Restaurant open until 9pm in Summer. Located near the Tourist Information Office. *Display advert*

PETROL

Achnasheen: ACHNASHEEN FILLING STATION. Located on the A832. Tel. (044 588) 238. Open Monday-Saturday, 0900-1730. From end March-September, also open Sunday, 0900-1730. Leaded and unleaded petrol, diesel. Credit cards accepted.

Aultbea: BRIDGEND STORES. Tel. (0445) 731 204. Located in the village, down a minor road on the right, just after the bridge over the Allt Beithe. Pumps are located next to the shop. Open Monday-Saturday, 0900-1300 and 1400-1730. Closed Sunday. Petrol and Calor Gas. Credit cards are not accepted.

Dundonnell: DUNDONNELL SERVICE STATION. Located on the A832, opposite the Dundonnell Hotel. To obtain petrol, call in to the hotel bar. Open Sunday-Wednesday, 0900-2000; Thursday-Saturday, 0900-2300. The small shop sells O.S. Maps, photographic film, Camping Gas and Calor Gas. Visa and Access cards are accepted.

Gairloch: GAIRLOCH GARAGE. Tel. (0445) 2255. Located on the A832, close to the Gairloch Hotel. Open Monday-Saturday, 0900-1800. Closed Sunday. Credit cards are accepted for petrol only.

Kinlochewe: KINLOCHEWE SERVICE STATION. Tel. (044 584) 227. Located on the A832, close to the Torridon road junction. Open daily 0900-1800, including Sunday. Leaded and unleaded petrol, diesel and oils. Also sells newspapers, maps, sweets and soft drinks. Accepts credit and charge cards (Access, Visa, Switch, Supercharge, Agency, All Star, Dialcard and Overdrive).

Laide: R. MACLENNAN GENERAL STORES. Tel. (0445) 731 252. Located on the A832, just at the Laide junction. Open Monday-Saturday, 0830-1300 and 1400-1730. Closed Sunday. Access and Visa are accepted for petrol. The small shop sells general groceries and fishing tackle and also incorporates a Post Office.

Poolewe: LOCHEWE SERVICE STATION. Tel. (044 586) 239. Located on the A832, just as you enter Poolewe from Gairloch. Open daily 0900-2000, including Sunday. The small shop has a tea and coffee machine and a cool drinks cabinet and also sells bread, milk and sandwiches. Credit cards are accepted. The garage has excellent mechanics and if you are having engine trouble, this is the place to go for efficient and friendly service.

INVEREWE CARAVAN SITE. Tel. (044 586) 249. Located on the A832, next to the National Trust camp and caravan site. Open Easter-September only. Petrol is sold Monday-Saturday, 0900-1700. Closed Sunday. Credit cards are accepted. A good selection of shrubs, conifers and heathers are usually on sale next to the shop.

LOCHEWE SERVICE STATION, POOLEWE (Petrol - Shop - Fish & Chips) All types of repairs undertaken. Services, MOTs, etc. Open 7 days. Also shop and "Chippy Hut". Lochewe Service Station, Poolewe. Tel: 0445 86 239.

---

24 HOUR VEHICLE RECOVERY SERVICE

Aultbea: A. FORBES & SONS. Tel. (0445) 731 200.

Poolewe: LOCHEWE SERVICE STATION. Tel. (044 586) 239.

SELECTED SHOPS

TAYLORS OF POOLEWE, POOLEWE (General Store & Post Office) For all your daily needs. Fresh bread, pies and pastries baked daily on the premises. Full range of groceries, fresh fruit and vegetables, off-licence, newspapers, gifts, maps, toys, post office. Holiday orders welcome. Open 9am - 6pm Monday to Saturday, 9am - 8pm June, July and August. Poolewe Post Office, Poolewe, Achnasheen, IV22 2JU. Tel: 0445 86 240.

BUY SOMETHING DIFFERENT, DIABAIG (Craft Shop - Teas - Self-catering) Locally made unusual goods for sale at the entrance to the village of Diabaig. Open Wednesday to Friday, 11am to 10pm, June to September. Refreshments. Also, year round self-catering accommodation. Details from David and Gillian Ferguson, 8 Diabaig, Achnasheen, Ross-shire, IV22 2HE. Tel: 0445 81 258. *Display advert*

EWE & ME, GAIRLOCH (Craft Shop) A shop full of beautiful gifts and crafts all chosen with care for you to give with love. We warmly invite you to come and feast your eyes on our selection of the best of Scottish and beyond. Ewe & Me, Strath, Gairloch, Ross-shire. Tel: 0445 2397. *Display ad*

HIGHLAND LINE CRAFT CENTRE, ACHNASHEEN (Craft Shop/Workshop) Visitors can watch gold and silver jewellery, silver spoons etc. being made by Tony M. Holland. A good selection of jewellery from inexpensive earrings to costly original pieces and a wide range of silver spoons in stock. Also a comprehensive range of the best Scottish craftwork, pottery, glass, wood, leather, knitwear etc. Located next to the Railway Station. Open all year (phone in winter months). Highland Line Craft Centre, Achnasheen, Ross-shire, IV22 2EE. Tel: 0445 88 227. *Display advert*

USEFUL TELEPHONE NUMBERS

Doctor: Aultbea - Tel. (0445) 731 221
Gairloch - Tel. (0445) 2229.
Poolewe - Tel. (044 586) 288.

Dentist: Gairloch - Tel. (0445) 2240, Wednesdays.

Police Stations: Aultbea - Tel. (0445) 731 222.
Gairloch - Tel. (0445) 2017.

Taxi Service: Hy Jack P/H Cabs, 10 Glebe Park, Gairloch. Tel. (0445) 2452. Local and long distance hire - train station, airport etc. Also tours and pub service.

Weather Forecast: 6 day weather forecast for the Highland region - Tel. (0898) 654 601.

Gairloch Telephone Number Changes: Gairloch telephone numbers may change while this guide is available. All four figure numbers will become six figure by prefixing with 71. Example: Old number 2xxx, New number 712xxx.

Part II

Travel Guide

ACHNASHEEN TO KINLOCHEWE

As soon as the traveller turns on to the A832 shortly after the little village of Garve he will notice a change in the pace of day-to-day life. Gone is the bustle of the Inverness to Ullapool road, and in its place is a quieter road, where motorists drive at a more leisurely speed to take in the magnificent scenery which now begins to unfold. The gentle rolling farmland of the east gives way to heather moorland and, to the left of the road, the hills of the Strathconnon Forest open up, giving a taste of the grandeur to come.

After Loch Luichart, the broad expanse of Strath Bran comes into view and from here on, the road parallels the course of the River Bran and the track of the scenic Inverness to Kyle railway. This section of road has been much improved in recent years thanks to E.C. funding. Before long, the traveller arrives in the sleepy village of Achnasheen, the true starting point of our guided journey.

ACHNASHEEN

A small loop road on the left, just before the Shell Petrol Station, takes you down to the village proper. The name "Achnasheen" means "Field of Storms", a reference perhaps to the type of weather which often greets the visitor here. Achnasheen remains much the same as it was when Queen Victoria arrived by train on September 12, 1877 en route for Loch Maree. "...there are only a small station and two or three little cottages." she recorded in her diary. The Queen's personal observations were published in 1884 in the form of a book, *"More Leaves From The Journal Of A Life In The Highlands"*, and this did much to publicise the attractions of Loch Maree and Torridon.

The coming of the railway was a great boost to tourism in the area. The Inverness to Kyle line was opened in 1870 and was originally known as the Dingwall and Skye Railway. The popularity of this scenic route continues today, with many visitors choosing to alight at Achnasheen which gives convenient access to the mountains of Torridon. If the visitor chooses to travel further afield by boarding the Post Bus at Achnasheen, he will be following in the footsteps of his Victorian predecessors. At the end of the 19th century, it was possible to procure a seat on the mail-car which collected the post from the morning train. The mail-car ran daily between Achnasheen and Gairloch and was operated by Mr McIver, the landlord of the Achnasheen Hotel. A smaller mail-car also ran daily between Gairloch and Poolewe. It is said that this form of transport was so popular that it was wise to book your seat well in advance. The well-to-do Victorian traveller could choose to hire a horse-drawn carriage from Mr McIver and so conduct his sightseeing in private.

Considering the remoteness of the area and the difficulties presented by the terrain, the 19th century postal service in Gairloch and Torridon was nothing short of amazing. In addition to the daily mail-cars which ran between Achnasheen, Gairloch and Poolewe, runners were hired to deliver the mail on three days each week to outlying villages such as Diabaig and Cove. Even in deepest winter, two deliveries were made by hand each week to the remotest settlements. Before the opening of the railway line, the Gairloch mail-car started out from Dingwall Railway Station on the east coast.

Shopping: ACHNASHEEN POST OFFICE. Tel. (044 588) 241. Early closing Wednesday and Saturday, closed Sunday. In addition to being a post office, the small shop also sells bread, milk, local paintings, newspapers, maps, confectionery, soft drinks, postcards and stationery.

THE HIGHLAND LINE CRAFT CENTRE. Tel. (044 588) 227. Open all year (seven days a week in summer). This is one of the best craft shops in the area, with a good selection of pottery, knitwear, gift toiletries, postcards, tweed skirt lengths and cards. Photographic film is also sold. A unique feature of the Craft Centre is the beautiful gold and silver jewellery made on the premises by Tony M. Holland. Inside the shop, a window looks into the workshop where you can see the jewellery being made. The Celtic crosses on Isle Maree are the inspiration for some of the pieces on sale. If you are looking for an unusual gift, check out the exquisite silver toddy spoons. Tony has been commissioned to craft toddy spoons for members of the Royal Family.

Eating Out: THE ACHNASHEEN HOTEL. Tel. (044 588) 243. Situated next to the railway station, the hotel has a snack bar which serves morning coffee and afternoon tea. Bar and set lunches are available from 1200-1400 and high teas are served from 1700-1830. In the evening you have the choice of a bar supper (1700-2000) or a full dinner (1900-2000). The hotel is open all year and credit cards are accepted. If you are looking for a bargain break, the hotel offers a special package - book for a minimum of 3 night's Dinner, B. & B. and they will include two mini tours of the area absolutely free.

LEDGOWAN LODGE HOTEL. Tel. (044 588) 252. Set in a quiet location a short distance down the A890 Strathcarron road, the hotel serves morning coffee and afternoon tea and a variety of meals throughout the day. Breakfast is available from 0800-0930; bar lunches from 1200-1400; lunches from 1230-1400 and bar suppers from 1800-2100. A full table d'hote dinner is served from 1930-2045. The hotel is open from Easter until October and credit cards are accepted. The Ledgowan Lodge Hotel holds fishing permits for Loch a' Chroisg (see Fishing section).

Toilets: In the railway station, just to the right of the Achnasheen Hotel. There is a separate toilet for the disabled.

Tourist Information Board: Located opposite the Achnasheen Hotel.

Petrol: ACHNASHEEN FILLING STATION. Tel. (044 588) 238. Open 0900-1730, Monday-Saturday. From Easter-October, also open on Sundays, 0900-1730. Petrol, unleaded petrol and diesel. Credit cards are accepted.

The Contin to Poolewe Military Road

The present A832 through Achnasheen follows the line of the old Military Road which was constructed around 1760 by Major William Caulfield. The old road ran from Contin, near Dingwall, to Poolewe, which was then the main port for the Isle of Lewis. The present A832 follows the line of the military road exactly until Slattadale on the shore of Loch Maree is reached. At Slattadale, the military road continued north along the shore of the loch, bypassing the then insignificant settlements around Loch Gairloch. The Contin to Poolewe road was one of the extensive network of military roads which sprang up after the 1715 Jacobite rising. The 1715 rising brought to English attention the fact that the remote north-west Highlands could be easily visited by French, Spanish or Dutch fleets bringing in men or weapons to aid the rebellion. To secure the Highlands, the authorities hit upon the idea of a military road system which would enable soldiers to be moved quickly to any trouble spot. It was hoped that this would provide an effective means of policing the region using only a relatively small force. It appears that the Contin to Poolewe road was maintained for only about 20 years before being allowed to fall into disrepair. By the beginning of the 19th century it was impassable by wheeled vehicles. The standard of maintenance on military roads throughout the Highlands declined rapidly after the death of Major Caulfield in 1767. In 1790 it was announced that military labour would no longer be used to repair the roads and the job was instead contracted out to civilians. This effectively spelt the end of the impressive system and it was not long before most of the military roads fell out of use.

On The Road To Kinlochewe

At Achnasheen, the road becomes single track. Shortly after rejoining the main road, the A890 branches left to Strathcarron and the Kyle of Lochalsh. Continue straight on and, just after the junction, note the striking level terraces on the far side of the river to your left. These are fluvio-glacial terraces, formed around 10,000 years ago at the end of the last Ice Age when the glacier which once occupied this valley began to melt. Rock debris which had been caught up in the ice was deposited here by the rivers and streams of meltwater which flowed out from the melting ice. This resulted in a level plain of boulders and coarse gravel which has since been cut into by the River Bran, producing the terraces which you see today. The entire Gairloch/Torridon region was heavily glaciated during the last Ice Age and there are many such interesting features to be seen in the landscape.

The road now skirts round the north bank of Loch a'Chroisg, one of the many fine trout lochs in the area. To the left rise the hills of Ledgowan Forest while on the right towers Fionn Bheinn. Ahead, the lofty peaks of Beinn Eighe come into view and, just to the left of them, the dark mass of Liathach in Torridon. As you travel further along the loch the hills of Coulin open up to the left. If you wish to enjoy the tranquillity of this splendid place, there is a good parking spot on your left towards the end of the loch, just past the two farm buildings on the right (Badavanich). From here there are good views up and down the loch and, if you have a pair of binoculars, have a closer look at the fantastic frost shattered pinnacles on the Beinn Eighe ridge. As you continue along the road, Beinn Eighe dominates the view ahead. Several of the peaks are capped by quartzite giving the impression, particularly in sunshine, that the mountain is permanently snow-covered.

This grand scene is left behind as the road turns gently to the right and climbs up over the Highland watershed before entering the head of Glen Docherty. The walls of the glen seem to close around you and, in contrast to the open landscape just left behind, the feeling is almost claustrophobic. This steep-sided glen is a classic example of a "U"-shaped glaciated valley. The rocky walls have been scoured bare by the slow-moving action of a glacier. In some areas you can actually see the long scrapes carved by the passing ice. In the bottom of the glen lie ancient river terraces which have been breached by the current stream. Note also the hanging valleys on either side of the glen. The lower reaches of these small valleys have been cut away by the glacier, leaving them "hanging" in mid air. The small burns which gush from them would originally have flowed directly into the main stream, now displaced some 300 metres downwards by the deepening action of the ice.

As the road begins to descend, Loch Maree comes into view for the first time. There is a carpark with an information board on the right of the road from which you can admire one of the most famous sights in Scotland. On a clear day you can see down Glen Docherty and along the full length of Loch Maree - a distance of some 17 1/2 miles. Loch Maree, with its myriad islands, continually vies with Loch Lomond for the title of "most beautiful loch" and from this viewpoint one can see why. The loch is guarded on both sides by towering mountains. On the Letterewe side, these rise steeply from the loch and recede into the distance in varied pastel shades - the impression is that of a beautiful watercolour. The information board in the carpark identifies the various landscape features to be seen from this point.

The Destitution Roads

The road down Glen Docherty is one of the many "Destitution Roads" which were built in the 1850's to provide employment and help relieve the suffering caused by the potato famine of 1846-48. Around 1,000 people were involved in the construction of this road. The Destitution Roads were the idea of the Dowager Lady Mackenzie of Gairloch. The people of the Highlands and Islands, like those of

Ireland, had come to rely upon the potato as their staple food. When the blight began in August 1846, several government steamers were despatched to Gairloch to examine the problem and to determine what might be done to ease the situation. Instead of asking for food supplies to distribute amongst the hungry people, Lady Mackenzie requested that money might be granted to build a road from Slattadale to Rudha n Fhomhair at the upper end of Loch Maree. This area had become largely inaccessible due to the decline of the old Contin to Poolewe Military Road and the Mackenzie family were keen to open up the country around Gairloch. Lady Mackenzie offered to support all those who were unfit to work on the road. The Government eventually agreed and, with a total sum of £10,000, work was begun the following spring. The first turf was cut by Lady Mackenzie's son, Osgood, the founder of Inverewe Garden. A Destitution Committee was then set up and so successful was the construction programme that funds were made available to continue the road to Badachro. Further grants enabled several other roads to be constructed in the area, namely Gairloch to Melvaig, Poolewe to Inverasdale, Poolewe to Aultbea, and Dundonnell to the present Ullapool road at Braemore Junction.

Memorial Cairn: Towards the foot of the glen, a small memorial cairn is prominently situated on a rocky knoll to the right of the road. It commemorates Major Angus J.D. MacDonald of the 1/6th Gurkha Rifles who was killed in the Malayan Campaign on 3 June 1952.

Shopping: THE GLENDOCHERTY CRAFT SHOP. Tel. (044 584) 220. Situated on the left, just after the memorial cairn and over a small bridge. Open Easter to November, Monday-Saturday 1000-1700 and Sunday 1000-1600. Accepts credit cards. This craft shop has a good selection of Scottish books and also sells knitwear, jewellery, shortbread, maps and photographic film. Unusual items include Fair Isle patterned gloves and pill-box hats. The craft shop holds fishing permits for Loch a'Chroisg and Loch Bharranch (see Fishing section).

The road now skirts around an area of forestry before entering the little village of Kinlochewe.

KINLOCHEWE TO TORRIDON

KINLOCHEWE

The village of Kinlochewe has a magnificent setting at the foot of Beinn Eighe. From certain angles, the picturesque white-walled hotel is framed by the sparkling slopes above. The Kinlochewe Hotel was a favourite haunt of Victorian artists and mountaineers and today the village continues to attract climbers and walkers from all over the world.

The name "Kinlochewe" is an anglicisation of the Gaelic "Ceann-loch-iu" which means "Head of Loch Ewe". Thousands of years ago, when the sea level was higher than it is today, the waters of Loch Ewe near Poolewe reached all the way to Kinlochewe. The nearby loch continued to be known as Loch Ewe up until the 17th century and it is from this that the village takes its name. The name of the loch was later changed to Loch Maree, probably to distinguish it from the sea loch at Poolewe into which it now flows via the River Ewe.

As you enter the village, the road crosses the A'Ghairbhe River by means of a small bridge. The original bridge which used to stand here was built c.1843 as part of a famine relief scheme financed by Lady Mackenzie of Gairloch. It had attractive twin stone arches, each with a span of 32 feet, and was known locally as "the Hunger Bridge". The current bridge was built in 1985.

Although quiet today, Kinlochewe was once the scene of many bloody skirmishes between the local Mackenzie clan and Clan Cameron. The Camerons were notorious cattle reivers and they would climb over the hill passes to the village and brazenly attempt to steal the Mackenzie herds. These raids usually provoked fierce fighting.

On 1 August, 1772, Kinlochewe was visited by the English traveller, Thomas Pennant, during his famous tour of the Western Highlands and Islands. Having anchored their boat at Dundonnell on Little Loch Broom, he and his companion, accompanied by some of the local inhabitants, set out over land to see Loch Maree. In his book, *"A Tour In Scotland And Voyage To The Hebrides"*, Pennant describes the accommodation they found in Kinlochewe village. "...the night proved wet and tempestuous; we therefore determined to defer the voyage till next day; and to shelter ourselves in a whisky house, the inn of the place. Mr Mackenzie complimented Mr Lightfoot and me with the bedstead, well covered with a warm litter of heath: we lay in our cloaths, wrapped ourselves in plaids and enjoyed a good repose. Our friends did not lose their sleep; but great was our surprize to see them form their bed of wet hay, or rather grass collected from the fields; they flung a plaid over it, undressed and lay most comfortably, without injury, in what in a little time, must have become an errant hot bed: so blest with hardy constitutions are even the gentlemen of this country!"

In 1888, Kinlochewe received another famous visitor: the poet James Hogg, who was known as The Ettrick Shepherd. In a letter to Sir Walter Scott, Hogg records his journey from Loch Carron to Kinlochewe. The inn at Kinlochewe was not to his liking and he states that it was ill kept and in a poor state of repair. "The windows were broken," he writes, "and the bed was as hard as a stone." There was, however, one saving grace. "They had however plenty of whisky, oatmeal cakes, tea and sugar, with some eggs, and stinking fish, on which I fared sumptuously...".

Shopping: KINLOCHEWE STORES. Tel. (044 584) 252. A Mace supermarket and newsagents selling groceries, fishing tackle and photographic film. Open Monday-Saturday, 0900-2030; closed Sunday. There is also a small Post Office.
OLD VILLAGE HALL ANTIQUES. Tel. (044 584) 277. Situated a short distance down the A896 Torridon road, on the right. A small shop selling a variety of interesting items. Closed Sunday.

Eating Out: THE KINLOCHEWE HOTEL. Tel. (044 584) 253. The hotel serves bar lunches from 1200-1400 and bar suppers from 1800-2000. Morning coffees are also available. In the evening, a table d'hote dinner menu is offered and there is often a tasty carvery. The hotel is open all year and credit cards are accepted.
THE STAG GRILL. A fast food shop which serves a variety of items, including breakfasts, filled rolls and pastries. Takeaway main meals start from around £3.45.

Bike Hire: Mountain bikes are available for hire from the house just to the right of Kinlochewe Holiday Chalets, on the main village road. Apply within or telephone (044 584) 202.

Toilets: In the village carpark, on the right just after the bridge. Usually plenty of hot water. Separate toilet for the disabled.

Petrol: KINLOCHEWE SERVICE STATION. Tel. (044 584) 227. Open daily 0900-1800, including Sunday. Leaded and unleaded petrol, diesel and oils. Also sells newspapers, maps, sweets and soft drinks. Accepts credit and charge cards (Access, Visa, Switch, Supercharge, Agency, All Star, Dialcard and Overdrive).

On The Road To Torridon

From the centre of Kinlochewe, a left turn takes you on to the A896 single-track road to Torridon. The road parallels the course of the A'Ghairbhe River, passing through attractive heather moorland with patches of conifer woodland on either side.

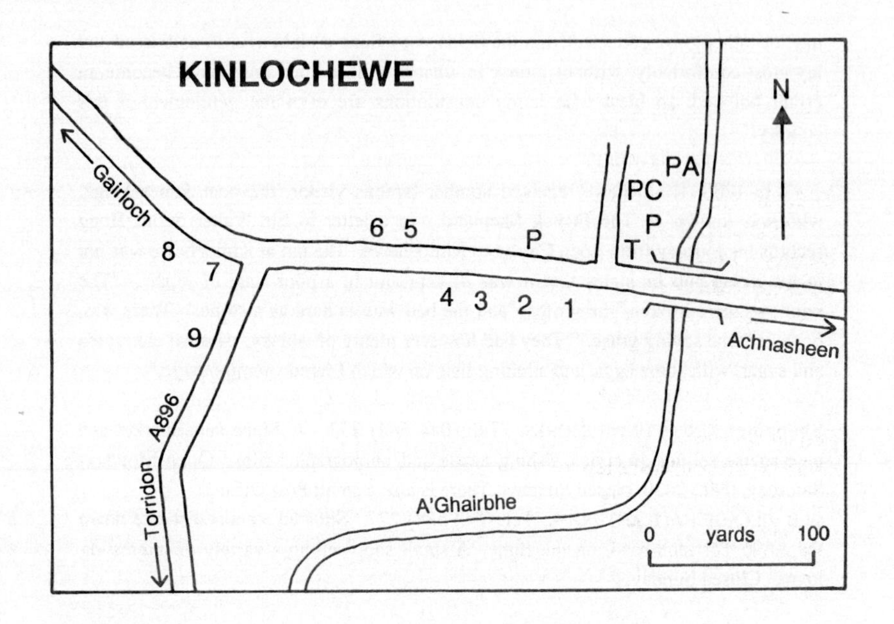

Key
1 - Kinlochewe Hotel
2 - Bunk House
3 - Kinlochewe Holiday Chalets
4 - Bike Hire
5 - The Stag Grill
6 - Kinlochewe Stores/Post Office
7 - Caravan Club Site
8 - Kinlochewe Service Station
9 - Old Village Hall Antiques
P - Parking
PC - Toilet
T - Telephone
PA - Picnic Area

Beinn Eighe towers above the road to the right, while on the left lie the Coulin hills. Before long, Loch Clair is passed on the left, at the inner end of which sits Coulin Lodge. Spectacular views back to Beinn Eighe are to be had from the road to the lodge, particularly in winter when the snow-capped peaks are mirrored in the calm waters of the loch. This is a private road and cars are not permitted, but you can walk in to the far side of the loch. The footpath is part of an 8 1/2 mile public right of way which continues past Coulin Lodge and Loch Coulin and then climbs up over the Coulin Pass before descending to Achnashellach.

When Lord Elphinstone acquired Coulin Lodge in 1881, he added a staircase and interior woodwork which was manufactured from wood cut from the ancient pines on the south side of Loch Coulin. Some of the pines in this area show signs of resin tapping. In the days before sheep-dip, resin was mixed with butter and tobacco juice to produce an effective deterrent against sheep-ticks.

Coulin Lodge occupies an area of land which once contained the shielings of the people of Kinlochewe. Shielings were small buildings which were used in summer when the villagers moved their herds of sheep and cattle on to the peat moors to eat the moss and sedge which grew there. The people lived in the shielings and turned their herds out onto the peat moor, bringing them back twice a day for milking. Today, shieling sites can be recognised as little knolls of green grass which are considerably drier than the surrounding peat moor. The tumbled remains of the shieling buildings can often be seen on such knolls.

The trees which surround Coulin Lodge are a remnant of the great native forests of Scots pine which once covered the lower slopes of Beinn Eighe, Liathach, Beinn Alligin and Beinn Dearg. Looking at the bleak scene today, it is hard to believe that the entire glen was once thickly wooded from Kinlochewe to the sea. Several centuries of clear-felling has resulted in a moorland landscape of scraggy heather. Here and there throughout the peat bog may be found the preserved stumps of ancient trees, exposed after thousands of years of erosion.

Back on the A896, Loch Bharranch and the prominent rocky knoll of Sgurr Dubh are passed on the left. Opposite the loch, a path leads into the Beinn Eighe National Nature Reserve, skirting to the right of a little patch of conifers and then heading straight up the slope for Coire an Laoigh. There is a large quarry cutting on the left of the road, just after the start of the path, where parking is possible. Camping is not permitted within the Reserve. Ahead and to the right, the sheer rocky sides of Liathach now come into view. "Liathach" means "The Grey One" and from this angle the mountain certainly deserves its name.

As the A896 continues, the rugged landscape which unfolds is considered by many to be the finest mountain scenery in Scotland which can be viewed from a main road. The mountains in this area are comprised mainly of Torridonian sandstones and grits which were deposited some 800 million years ago. These sandstone sediments were originally derived from the ancient basement rock of Lewisian gneiss which is around 2,500 million years old - one of the oldest rocks in the world. The Lewisian gneiss once formed a vast continent which lay to the north-west of the present Scottish mainland. Today, this rock still forms most of the Outer Hebrides and can be seen throughout Wester Ross and Sutherland. The gneiss was easily eroded by fast flowing streams and rivers and the resulting debris accumulated at the southern edge of the continent, gradually becoming compressed to form the hard Torridonian sandstone that we see today. Deposition took place in a fairly uniform manner, creating horizontal beds which are only very gently folded. The "steps" which can be clearly seen on the sides of Liathach are the weathered edges of these beds. Torridonian sandstone is the oldest sedimentary rock in the world.

During successive earth movements, the horizontal sandstone beds became tilted and a new horizontal land surface was cut across them. About 600 million years ago, when the entire area was covered by warm, shallow seas, another series of rocks was laid down on top of this new land surface. This series is known as the Cambrian sequence and consists mainly of hard white quartzite. Further earth movements around 420 million years ago tilted the rocks again, moving the underlying sandstone beds back to their original horizontal position and thus setting the overlying quartzite beds at an angle. This complex arrangement is well illustrated as you drive westwards down Glen Torridon. A substantial part of Beinn Eighe is comprised of white quartzite - it reaches road level near Loch Clair - whereas only the summits of Liathach are quartzite.

During the last Ice Age, this whole area was covered by ice-sheets up to 800m thick. The rugged landscape that we see today was carved and shaped by intense glaciation. As the ice moved, it cut deep into the Torridonian sandstone creating valleys with broad, flat bottoms and steep sides. The ice also scoured out bowl-shaped depressions known as corries, many of which are now water-filled. Two magnificent examples are Coire Mhic Fhearchair on Beinn Eighe and Coire na Caime on Liathach. The rock debris which resulted from this process was carried along in the glacier and was deposited where the ice finally melted.

The Valley of a Hundred Hills

As the road continues through the glen, an old ruined cottage is seen to the right and shortly afterwards, a bridge is crossed. To view a unique glacial feature of the area, pull into the carpark on the right, just after the bridge. Look back across the road to Lochan an Iasgair and the long, low white cottage behind it (the Ling Hut). Just above the cottage there are several rounded mounds on the hillside. Once you know what to look for, you will soon see that the entire valley is covered with these mounds. This is the Coire Cheud Cnoc or Valley of a Hundred Hills. The mounds are comprised of sand and gravel which was carried here in the ice of a glacier. As the glacier melted, the sand and gravel was shaped into these distinctive mounds by the action of the meltwater. On the hills above, you can see that the rocks have been completely scraped clean by the ice. There is an information plaque in the carpark which describes the features to be seen in the area.

This carpark is the starting point of two popular walks through National Trust For Scotland land. One walk follows the courses of the Coire Dubh Mor and Coire Mhic Nobuil Rivers on the north side of Liathach and terminates in the vicinity of Torridon House. The other follows the Coire Dubh Mor River to its headwater and then climbs up around the flank of Beinn Eighe to the spectacular Coire Mhic Fhearchair. See Selected Walks for full details.

On The Road To Torridon

Shortly after leaving the carpark and rejoining the A896 to Torridon, there is an excellent view of the many glacial mounds on the hillside to the left. This is a good spot for a photograph. The broad expanse of Glen Torridon now opens up ahead and the road continues alongside the meandering course of the River Torridon. The ice scoured flanks of Liathach rise steeply on the right while on the left lies the smaller hill of Seana Mheallan. This latter looks very pretty after rain when a myriad of sparkling burns tumble down to join the river below. Queen Victoria passed this way in a horse-drawn carriage on Saturday, September 15, 1877, en route for the village of Torridon. The Royal Party were quite amazed at the imposing scale of the landscape as they drove beneath the flanks of mighty Liathach. In her diary the Queen recorded, "Soon after this the grand, wild, savage-looking, but most beautiful and picturesque Glen of Torridon opened upon us, with the dark mural precipices of that most extraordinary mountain Ben Liughach...".

The land to the right of the road is part of the 14,100 acre Torridon Estate which is managed on behalf of the nation by the National Trust for Scotland. This land was formerly owned by the 4th Earl of Lovelace and, upon his death, it was accepted by the Inland Revenue in part payment of estate duty. It was subsequently taken into care by the National Trust for Scotland in May 1967. A few months later, the Trust also acquired the adjoining 2,000 acre property of Alligin Shuas. This land was presented to the Trust by the three sons of Sir Charles and Lady Gordon in memory of their parents who lived in Torridon between 1924 and 1939. The combined properties of Torridon and Alligin Shuas encompass the summit ridge of Beinn Eighe, all seven tops of Liathach, Beinn Alligin and the southern slopes of Beinn Dearg to its skyline.

Just before Glen Cottage is reached, a substantial waterfall plummets down the slopes of Liathach on the right. There is a faint path on the right bank of the stream which makes its way uphill, past the waterfall, to the crags above. This is a popular route for those wishing to climb Spidean a'Choire Leith, the highest peak of Liathach. There is a safe parking spot just past the waterfall, on the left of the road by a bright green rhododendron bush.

The little patch of conifers which surrounds Glen Cottage now comes into view on the right. The picturesque white-washed cottage is a welcome sight after the bleak landscape just traversed. A short distance ahead, the scenery once again becomes austere, with rock slabs and ledges on both sides of the road. When sunlight strikes the polished surface of these rocks, the effect is quite dramatic. Although this area appears to be largely devoid of plant life, the tiered sandstone cliffs above provide an ideal environment for a variety of rare and unusual alpine plants. Here, bands of limestone within the cliffs are being continually eroded by a multitude of small streams, creating patches of fertile soil amidst the poor acidic soils of the Torridonian sandstone. On ledges inaccessible to grazing animals such as sheep and deer, beautiful natural alpine rock gardens are to be found. Species to be seen include Arctic Mouse-ear, Northern Rock Cress, Rose-root, Alpine Club Moss and Starry and Mossy Saxifrage.

To the left of the road, a short distance ahead, lie two small conifer plantations. They stand out as green oases amidst this bare landscape and make an ideal place to stop for a picnic. These trees were planted by the National Trust For Scotland as part of an operation to conserve the plants and wildlife of Torridon. The first plantation contains mature trees and is light and airy, with good grass cover. Camping is permitted in this pleasant wood. The second plantation contains young trees and is fenced to prevent damage by animals. Camping is not allowed in this area.

The road continues along the glen and, as you round a bend, the hills drop away on either side and Upper Loch Torridon comes into view. The village of Torridon is reached by turning right on to the well-signposted minor road at the head of the loch.

Eating Out: LOCH TORRIDON HOTEL. Tel. (0445) 791 242. If you are looking for somewhere to eat, continue along the main A896 instead of turning off to Torridon village. The Loch Torridon Hotel lies on the right, about 1 1/2 miles on from the junction. This attractive Victorian mansion is set within its own grounds, close to the shore of Upper Loch Torridon. The hotel serves morning coffees and afternoon teas and bar snacks are available throughout the day from 1230-2130. Tasty hot and cold buffet lunches are served from 1200-1400 and dinner is available from 1900-2100. The hotel is open from May to October and credit cards are accepted. The Loch Torridon Hotel holds fishing permits for Lochan an Iasgaich and the River Torridon and can also help you arrange sea angling trips in Loch Torridon (see Fishing section).

TORRIDON TO DIABAIG

TORRIDON

The village of Torridon has a picturesque setting at the head of Upper Loch Torridon. The neat cottages lie strung out along the minor road at the foot of Liathach, with beautiful views across the loch to the Applecross Peninsula. The village contains both a Youth Hostel and small camp site, but despite its popularity there is a feeling of tranquillity and isolation.

The name "Torridon" is an anglicisation of the Gaelic "Toirbheartan" which means "A Place of Transference". Local tradition has it that, during the days of the Vikings, boats were lifted from the water at Torridon and carried overland through Glen Torridon to the head of Loch Maree.

The houses which skirt the shoreline at the west end of Torridon village, just before the jetty, form the separate township of Fasag or Fassaig. This is a Clearance township, created in the 19th century when crofting families were cruelly evicted from their ancestral lands in the glens behind the present village to make way for sheep. The only alternative land available to them was close by the water's edge and there they were forced to live as best they could.

The narrow strip of land which projects into the loch just before the village jetty is known as Am-Ploc or Ploc an Doire which is Gaelic for "The Lump" or "The Lump of the Grove". This promontory was once used for open air church services and the stone seats used by the congregation are still visible today. The promontory is known locally as the Church of Ploc.

When Queen Victoria visited Torridon on Saturday, September 15, 1877, she was greatly impressed by the wild isolation of the place. "Hardly anyone ever comes here." she wrote in her diary, "...it was so fine and such a wild uncivilised spot, like the end of the world." The Royal Party drove beyond the village and climbed a hillside to eat lunch and afterwards the Queen and her daughter, Princess Beatrice, spent their time sketching the beautiful view across the loch. The Queen recorded that the village consisted of a small one-storied inn, a school, a merchant's shop and, "...a row of five or six wretched hovels...". Before they left the village, the Royal Party called into the shop and the Queen purchased some comforters, two woollen shawls and a cloak. Of the shopkeeper she wrote, "...the poor man was so nervous he threw almost everything down.".

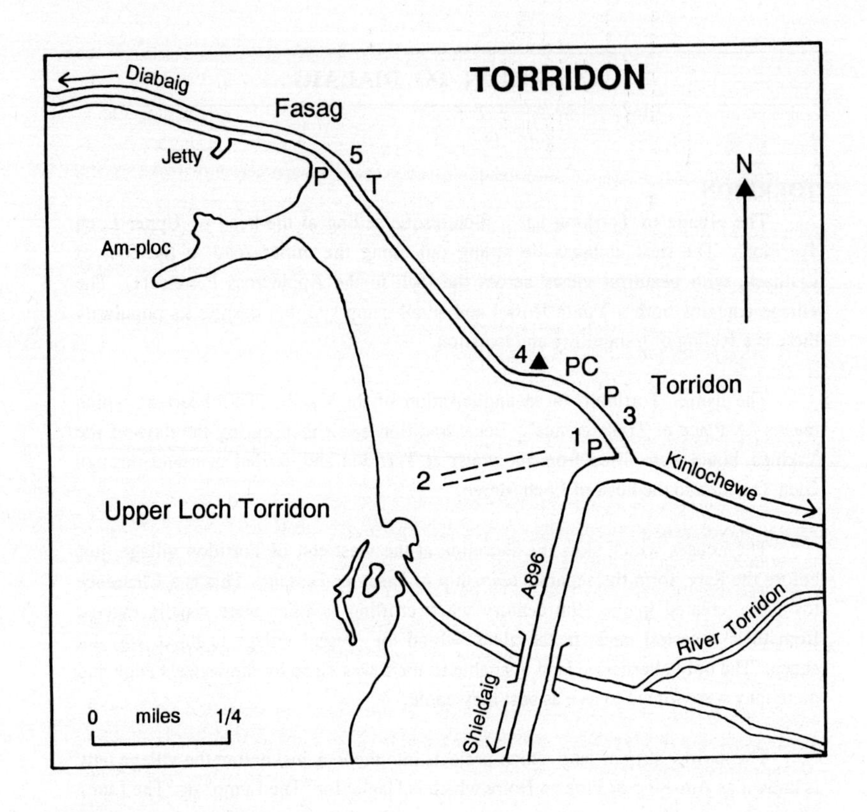

<u>Key</u>

1 - Torridon Countryside Centre
2 - Deer Museum
3 - Camp Site
4 - Torridon Youth Hostel
5 - Torridon General Stores
P - Parking
PC - Toilets
T - Telephone

Throughout the Highlands and Islands there are many interesting stories of the miraculous healing powers of the village wise woman. A visitor to Torridon at the end of the 19th century recorded a remarkable cure which took place in the village. One of the villagers was busily engaged in mending his horse harness when, suddenly, the large needle he was using slipped from his grasp and stuck through the palm of his hand. The village wise woman, who was sitting nearby, came over to the man and plucked the needle from his hand. The injury was so severe that the blood spurted out from the wound and stained the wall opposite. The wise woman took the needle, pointed it at the ground and recited in Gaelic:

"Be your poison within the ground,
May your pain be within the hill.
Wholeness be to the wound,
Rest be to the hurt."

The blood immediately stopped flowing and the wound was completely healed.

Some beliefs concerning magical charms were peculiar to the Torridon region. As you travel through the Highlands, you will often see rowan trees growing close to the houses. These trees were planted deliberately to ward off all forms of evil. The elder tree was believed to have similar powers. In the Torridon region however, bird-cherry was considered to be the most powerful deterrent against evil. When out on the hills, it was common practice to carry a walking stick made of bird-cherry as a charm against becoming lost in the mist. Bird-cherry was also used to tether cows to protect them from spells. Iron was similarly considered to be a powerful charm against evil, but in Torridon it was believed that if an iron implement was used while gathering shell-fish, these creatures would vanish from the beach forever. Legend has it that during Clan feuds people would deliberately plough their enemy's shell-fish beaches at dead of night to deprive them of an important source of food.

Shopping: TORRIDON GENERAL STORES. Open Monday-Saturday, 0900-1300 and 1400-1800; Sunday 0900-1200 and 1430-1700. Small supermarket. Also sells stamps.

Toilets: Situated down the minor road to Torridon village, adjacent to the Youth Hostel. This toilet block contains showers and a kitchen sink and usually has plenty of hot water.

Visitor Centre: TORRIDON COUNTRYSIDE CENTRE. Open from May to September - Monday-Saturday, 1000-1800; Sunday 1400-1800. Admission charges: Adults 80p; Children 40p; Senior Citizens 40p; special rates for groups. The Centre contains a small natural history display and also sells maps, field guides and various National Trust publications. The admission charge includes an audio-visual display on the Highland Year. There is also a Deer Museum (open all year) which contains a collection of jaws and antlers. Adjacent to the Museum is the Deer Park where you can see real deer at close-hand. This is an excellent place to visit if you have children to entertain. The Deer Museum and Park are located about 650 yards from the Countryside Centre, down a well-signposted path. Throughout the summer months, the Countryside Centre operates a series of guided walks which are an excellent way to learn about red deer management at first hand and to see the varied flora and fauna of the Torridon area. You can choose between a low level leisurely hill walk, a walk through deer and eagle country and a strenuous walk on to the high tops. A fee is charged to help defray the cost of providing the Ranger service. For further information and bookings, contact the Ranger, Mr Seamus MacNally, on (0445) 791 221.

On The Road To Inveralligin

On leaving the village, the road skirts around the north shore of Upper Loch Torridon. The beaches here are comprised of attractive red sandstone pebbles and at low tide the unusual orange-brown seaweed is very pretty. Directly across the loch lie the hills of the Ben-Damph Forest. The little settlement of Annat can be made out on the shore opposite and, just to the right of it, at the foot of the woodland, the Loch Torridon Hotel with its distinctive sandstone towers can be seen. This magnificent Victorian mansion was, for many years, the country seat of the Earls of Lovelace. The slopes behind Annat rise in a series of distinct "steps" which are caused by the differential weathering of various hard and soft layers within the sandstone.

Shortly after entering a patch of woodland, the road forks. The left branch is now a private road to Torridon House which lies hidden in the trees at the foot of the Abhainn Coire Mhic Nobuil. Cars are not allowed along this road. However, it is also a public right of way to the village of Inveralligin and you can follow the attractive 1 3/4 mile coastal path on foot. The path joins up with the road at Rechullin, about 1 mile to the east of Inveralligin proper. Unfortunately, parking is not permitted by the fork and you will probably have to travel back towards Torridon to find a place to leave your car.

The right branch of the road winds uphill and gains height quickly, with good views through the trees to the mountains opposite. This section of hillside is clothed in native forest which gives it an altogether kinder feel than the hills in Glen Torridon. As you climb higher, the twin peaks of Beinn Alligin come into view ahead - Tom na Gruagaich on the left and, further back on the right, Sgurr Mhor. Just after you cross a small stone bridge, pull into the large carpark on the left for a view of the waterfall on the Abhainn Coire Mhic Nobuil. The chaffinches in the carpark are so tame they will perch on your wing mirrors to be fed by hand. The best view of the waterfall is to be had from the bridge itself. You can also see the waterfall by walking up the left side of the river for a short distance. A distinct path follows the right bank of the river upstream but the view of the falls is largely obscured from this side. If you take this right hand path, a 15 minute walk will bring you to a left fork which leads to a wooden bridge. From here there is a good view back down the river. Return to the carpark by the same route. This is the termination point of the Coire Dubh Mor walk which is described in the Selected Walks section. You could of course decide to do the walk from this end - there is a National Trust For Scotland information board at the start of the path which gives details of the route.

Another footpath begins at the gate in the left corner of the carpark. Here the branches of the ancient rhododendron bushes have entwined, forming a beautiful tunnel through which the path meanders. There are occasional glimpses of the rocky gorge and cascades on the left. This path continues down past Torridon House and joins the coastal footpath to Inveralligin (see above).

After the carpark, the road continues to climb and emerges suddenly from the trees, giving a clear view across the loch. The scattered white cottages of Inveralligin come into view on the shore below. Jutting into the loch ahead is the rocky peninsula which divides Upper Loch Torridon from Loch Torridon and at its tip lies Eilean a'Chaoil. To the left, directly across the loch, the steep sides of Beinn Damh and Ben Shieldaig begin to open up, revealing the waters of Loch Damh, some 50m above sea level.

INVERALLIGIN

A small road on the left descends steeply to the pretty village of Inveralligin. The village has an idyllic setting, strung out along the shore of the loch with a dramatic view across the water to Beinn Damph. It was here in 1953 that the author Brenda G. Macrow wrote her book "Torridon Highlands", still in print today. The cottage in which she stayed still exists and can be viewed from the outside (it is a private house). To find it, turn right at the phone box just as you enter the village and follow the narrow road over a little bridge. The road ends in a turning circle and parking is not permitted but you will have time to pop out and view the cottage. Follow the footpath along the shore. The cottage lies immediately to the left of "Culdarroch". It is a long, single storey white building with corrugated iron roof. The exterior remains exactly as it was when Brenda Macrow lived there. The little post office to the right of "Culdarroch" also remains unchanged. When Miss Macrow came to Alligin, there was no sealed road to the village. The local bus stopped at the top of the hill and from there, you had to make your way down by means of a rough track which descended steeply by the side of the stream. All provisions, parcels, luggage etc destined for Alligin had to be carried down by hand or brought in by boat.

The footpath continues along the shore to the Inveralligin Field Centre which is based in the former village schoolhouse. The Centre offers residential wildlife holidays and bunkhouse accommodation (see Accommodation section). From the

Centre, the footpath turns inland and crosses the hillside, arriving in the little settlement of Alligin Shuas after about 3/4 of a mile.

At the end of the 19th century, the headland just beyond the Field Centre concealed a Smugglers' Cave which was used for illicit whisky distilling. The "cave" was actually a deep cleft in the rock which was protected and camouflaged by a wall of loose boulders and here the smugglers distilled their whisky right under the noses of the Excisemen who were stationed just across the loch at Shieldaig. The spirit was secretly carried out on foot along the old track or removed by boat under cover of darkness.

Go back across the bridge and turn right at the telephone box to rejoin the main village road. The road now goes round the bay, past several beautiful white-washed cottages. The last one on the left before the jetty is a good example of this classic Scottish style. The neat row of cottages by the jetty must be one of the most photographed scenes in Scotland. There is a parking area on the left, just past the jetty if you wish to take you own picture of this famous view.

The road continues along the shore, terminating in a turning circle by the cottage at Rechullin. This is the starting point of the public footpath which goes back along the coast to the Torridon House turn-off (see above). If you wish to do the walk in this direction there is space to park on the grass verge. Please do not block the turning circle. You will have to retrace your route through Inveralligin to rejoin the main road.

ALLIGIN SHUAS

Shortly after rejoining the main road a small bridge is crossed and then a narrow road descends steeply on the left to the scattered crofting township of Alligin Shuas (Wester Alligin). The township overlooks the sheltered anchorage of Ob a'Bhraighe. When the tide is out the bay is very colourful, with stripes of pink and grey gneiss, black algae, orange-brown seaweed and sandstone pebbles. The road ends in a turning circle but there are several places where it is possible to pull off onto the grass verge. This is the starting point of a 3 1/2 mile footpath which winds its way around the rocky coast to the village of Diabaig. The path is precipitous in places, but the walk is well worth it for the magnificent views to the Applecross Peninsula.

On The Road To Diabaig

The main road from Alligin Shuas onwards contains some very steep sections and is unsuitable for caravans. The road climbs up over a rock strewn moorland, passing the gorge of the Abhainn Alligin with its tumbling waterfall on the right, just before the steep ascent to the Bealach na Gaoithe - the Pass of the Wind. Here the scenery is stark but strangely beautiful: slabs of bare scoured rock as far as the eye can see. The pretty reed-filled lochan at the top of the bealach is a welcome sight. To the left, at the highest point on the road, there is a parking spot with a bench. From here the view over the barren moorland is quite spectacular. The road ahead can be seen winding its way down to the shore of Loch Diabaigas Airde. The blue-grey waters of the loch contrast prettily with the brown moorland and the green grass of the sheep grazings on the shore. Directly ahead, the outer end of Loch Diabaig can be seen. This whole area has been very heavily glaciated and the pink and white gneiss rock slabs to the left of the parking space show the deep scrapes of the passing ice quite clearly.

The road now begins a steep descent to the north shore of Loch Diabaigas Airde. Legend has it that this loch is the haunt of a kelpie or water-horse. Looking back, as the road curves left, you can still see the line of the old path to Diabaig, just below the present road. The farm buildings of Upper Diabaig are passed on the left and after clearing the head of Loch a' Mhullaich the road descends steeply to Diabaig. If you wish to walk down to the village, there is a footpath at the head of the loch which skirts the farm fence and then passes between two crags before descending to the shore.

DIABAIG

The white crofts of Diabaig lie scattered down the steep hillside overlooking Loch Diabaig. The lush green fields and clumps of native forest come as quite a surprise after the bleak landscape of the high moor. A rocky knoll encircles one end of the loch creating a sheltered haven for both fishing boats and the cages of the Diabaig Salmon Farm. This isolated community has an other-worldly feel about it, the silence broken only by the occasional fishing boat returning home with its catch.

About half way down the hill, a right fork leads to Diabaig Post Office which is located in a little hut at the end of the road. The journey along this road affords good views across to the mountains on the Applecross Peninsula. The public footpath to Gairloch via Craig also begins at the end of this road. Craig Youth Hostel is one of the most isolated hostels in Britain, being reached only by a 2 mile walk along the coast from Diabaig or a 5 mile walk from Redpoint near Gairloch. The start of the path is marked by a green sign, just to the right of the Post Office hut. It is well worth walking along the path for the spectacular views alone, even if you are not heading for the Youth Hostel. There is a large passing place on the left, just before the end of the road, where there is room for 4 or 5 cars to pull completely off the road without causing an obstruction. Please do not block the passing place itself. There is also a small quarry cutting on the right of the road where parking is possible.

The main village road continues down to the jetty where there is a large carpark which makes an ideal picnic stop. From here you can gaze across the tranquil waters of the loch to the very tip of the remote Applecross Peninsula or look right, past the little rock of Sgeir Dughall to the open sea. The white crofts of Arinacrinachd on

Applecross can be made out with the naked eye. At low tide, the rocky headland surrounding Loch Diabaig is most colourful, with the same pattern of grey gneiss, black algae and orange-brown seaweed seen elsewhere along the coast. The village jetty is of attractive stone construction with a little store house towards the end. It is often covered with lobster pots, buoys and fishing nets hung out along the wall to dry.

The road continues along the bay for a short distance, and terminates in front of a large white house. To the left of the house there is a blue sign which marks the start of the coastal footpath to Inveralligin (see above).

Once you have visited this isolated spot, it is not difficult to see why it was once the centre of an illicit whisky distilling industry. Distilling was carried out in a seaside cave and at several other locations in the district. At Upper Diabaig an old sheep-fank was converted into a shelter for the smugglers. This illegal activity may have led to the saying, "Is fada Diabaig bho lagh." which means "Diabaig is far from law.".

Shopping: BUY SOMETHING DIFFERENT. Tel. (044 581) 258. Located at the entrance to the village, this little craft shop sells a variety of unusual locally made items. Refreshments are also available. Open June to September, Wednesday-Friday, 1100-2200.

Returning To Torridon

As you begin the steep pull out of Diabaig, consider the difficulties once faced by the local postman in bringing the mail to this isolated spot. Before the road was built earlier this century, the postman had to walk into Inveralligin and back to collect the mail - a total distance of around 10 miles. One postman, who was known as the "Big Post", accomplished this amazing feat every day, except Sunday, for forty years!

On the journey back to Torridon there is another fine viewpoint which is worth stopping at. After passing the viewpoint and the lochan at the top of the Bealach na Gaoithe, the road begins to descend. There is a parking spot and bench on the left of the road, just before the hairpin bend. From here there are panoramic views across the loch to the hills opposite. On the left is Loch Damh, nestling between the hills of Ben Damph and Ben Shieldaig. To the right is the rocky peninsula which separates Upper Loch Torridon from Loch Torridon. You can see over the top of the peninsula to Shieldaig Island which is owned by the National Trust For Scotland. The 32 acres of the island are almost entirely covered by native Scots pine. Behind Shieldaig Island rises Beinn Bhan, the highest of the Applecross mountains.

KINLOCHEWE TO GAIRLOCH

Much of the A832 beyond Kinlochewe has recently been converted to double-track. There are several parking areas along the shore of Loch Maree where you can pull off the road and enjoy the magnificent view across the water to the hills of Letterewe. The beauty of this area greatly impressed Queen Victoria when she passed this way in a horse-drawn carriage on September 12, 1877, en route for the Loch Maree Hotel. She recorded in her diary, "The drive along the lochside, for ten miles to the hotel of Loch Maree, is beautiful in the extreme...The windings of the road are beautiful, and afford charming glimpses of the lake, which is quite locked in by the overlapping mountains."

Beinn Eighe National Nature Reserve

Shortly after leaving the village of Kinlochewe, Anancaun Field Station is passed on the right. The Station is part of the Beinn Eighe National Nature Reserve which occupies 4,800 hectares of land immediately to the south of Loch Maree. Anancaun provides self-catering accommodation for visiting scientists and students who wish to carry out research in the National Nature Reserve. The name "Anancaun" is an anglicisation of the Gaelic "Ath nan Ceann" which means "Ford of the Heads". This name dates from around 1350 when the MacLeods and the Mackenzies fought a bloody battle on the hillside behind Kinlochewe. The Mackenzies won the day and in triumph cut off the heads of their vanquished foes and threw them into the river. The heads became stuck at a ford which, since then, has been known as Ath nan Ceann.

Please note that dogs are not allowed on the Reserve. Fires are also prohibited. A permit is required for specimen collection. Contact: Scottish Natural Heritage, Anancaun Field Station, Kinlochewe, Ross-shire, IV22 2PD. Tel. (044 584) 244.

Beinn Eighe NNR was established in 1951 and was the first National Nature Reserve to be set up in Britain. Situated within its boundary is a superb remnant of the native Scots pinewood which used to be widespread throughout Scotland. This ancient wood - Coille na Glas Leitire - is the most important feature of the Reserve. It dates back to the Boreal Period (6,000-8,000 years ago), although the oldest existing pines are about 350 years old. During the Second World War, Coille na Glas Leitire was extensively damaged when many trees were cut down to make ammunition boxes. Since then, great effort has gone into regenerating the felled areas and protecting the precious trees which remain. Today the wood contains a variety of animals including red and roe deer, pine marten, common shrew, field mouse and bank vole. If you are lucky, you may catch a glimpse of the rare wild cat. Twenty-seven species of woodland birds also frequent the pine forest, including the willow warbler, coal tit, siskin and the Scottish crossbill - the only bird species unique to Scotland. Above the treeline (c.400m), the NNR contains both mountain and moorland landscapes and their associated flora and fauna. The wild cat, pine marten and golden eagle are all to be seen here, along with rare alpine plants and mosses. The mountain zone is also home to the very rare and beautiful blue hare.

Beinn Eighe has seven main tops. The true summit, Ruadh Stac Mhor (1,010m), lies just outside the boundary of the Reserve. Of the tops which lie within the Reserve, Sgurr Ban (972m) is the highest. Beinn Eighe, like the surrounding mountains, is comprised of a series of ancient Torridonian sediments which were deposited some 800 million years ago. These sediments were originally derived from the ancient base rock of Lewisian gneiss which was easily eroded by fast flowing streams and rivers. The eroded debris gradually became compressed, forming the horizontal beds of hard red sandstone that we see today. During successive earth movements, these horizontal beds became tilted and a new land surface was cut across them. Then, about 600 million years ago, at a time when Scotland lay near the Equator, the entire area was covered by a warm, shallow sea. Grains of sand accumulated in this shallow sea and over time these became compressed to form another series of rocks, known as the Cambrian sequence. The Cambrian sequence consists mainly of hard, white quartzite. Further earth movements tilted the rocks again, moving the underlying sandstone beds back to their original horizontal position and thus setting the overlying quartzite beds at an angle. Finally, about 420 million years ago, the movement of two landmasses from the north-west and south-east resulted in a great buckling and cracking of the rocks. A large piece of Torridonian sandstone was thrust on top of the younger quartzite rocks - a reversal of the usual situation. This piece of red sandstone now forms the upper part of Meall a' Ghiubhais, the mountain just to the north of Beinn Eighe.

The youngest rocks of the Cambrian sequence contain the remains of fossilised worm burrows. These tube forming worms lived in the sand at the bottom of the shallow tropical sea which covered the area during the Cambrian Period. The worms filter fed on the abundant microscopic organisms in the sea water. Today, the fossilised remains of their burrows can be identified as tubes or pipes of rock which differ in colour from the surrounding rocks, or as pock marks which represent the funnel-shaped tops of the tubes. These worms were of a substantial size - tubes with a diameter of 15mm have been recorded. These are some of the oldest fossil remains to be found in Scotland and they represent some of the earliest life-forms on earth. Shales, gritty sandstone and limestone containing various types of fossil shells are to be found on top of the quartzite in places.

The Cambrian sequence also contains rust coloured dolomitic shales known as "fucoid beds". These rocks are rich in lime and potassium - valuable commodities in an area of poor acidic soils. For many centuries, the local people extracted the shales and processed them in kilns to produce a rich fertilizer which was then spread on the agricultural land in the glens. This practice continued until the early part of this century.

During the last Ice Age, this whole area was covered by ice-sheets up to 800m thick. As the ice moved, it cut deep into the Torridonian sandstone, carving out valleys and deep rock basins. The rock debris which resulted from this process was carried along in the glacier and was deposited where the ice finally melted. Loch Maree was formed in this way and in its depths lie glacial deposits of silt and grit which were left behind when the ice melted around 10,000 years ago.

The fantastically shaped peaks of Beinn Eighe show the continued effects of severe frost action. During periods of thaw, water penetrates the holes and fissures within the rock. When the water freezes, it expands in volume and thus exerts pressure on the rock. The rock is eventually shattered by such alternating periods of freezing and thawing, resulting in the distinctive craggy summits which we see today. The quartzite debris which is thus produced forms long sparkling scree slopes which are visible from a great distance.

Aultroy Visitor Centre

About 1/2 mile on from Anancaun, to the left of the road, is the Aultroy Visitor Centre. The Centre is situated within an attractively converted 19th century cottage and is open from May to early September - daily, including Sunday, 1000-1300 and 1400-1700. There is a large carpark. Aultroy contains a wealth of information about the Beinn Eighe National Nature Reserve and a visit is well worth while. There is an excellent relief model of Loch Maree and the Torridon area and also a good geological display which includes examples of the various rock types to be found within the Reserve. There are also colourful displays on the history and management of the Reserve, the flora and fauna to be found there and the work of Scottish Natural Heritage. A small stand sells postcards and a good range of Nature Conservancy Council and Forestry Commission publications. Attractive lithographic prints of An Teallach, Beinn Eighe and Liathach are also on sale, both as small cards and as posters. Lists of the many birds and plants to be seen on the Reserve and in the surrounding area are available free from the Centre.

Toilets: Public toilets are situated to the rear of the Aultroy Visitor Centre.

On The Road To Talladale

As the road continues through the trees at the foot of Beinn Eighe, the southern end of Loch Maree comes into view. The mountain which dominates the scene opposite is Slioch - the Spear. If you look closely at this mountain, you will see that a substantial part of it is comprised of grey Lewisian gneiss. This ancient rock, some

2,500 million years old, forms the base rock of the entire area. As mentioned above, erosion reduced the Lewisian gneiss to a landscape of rounded hills upon which was deposited the sediments which later compressed to form Torridonian sandstone. The grey gneiss which forms the base of Slioch is one such ancient hill. The boundary between the grey gneiss and the overlying red Torridonian sandstone is clearly visible.

About 2 miles on from the Aultroy Centre, there is a carpark to the right of the road. This carpark is situated within the remnant of the old Caledonian Pine Forest mentioned above and is the starting point for mountain and woodland trails which cross part of the Beinn Eighe Reserve. See Selected Walks for further details. A general leaflet about the Reserve is available at the Honesty Box, priced 15p.

Shortly after the road emerges from the forest, Glen Grudie opens up to the left. This glen forms the north-west boundary of the Beinn Eighe Reserve. To the right there is an excellent view of the continuous mountain ridge which runs along the north shore of Loch Maree. To the left of Slioch there are three principal summits - Beinn Lair (860m), Meall Mheinnidh (720m) and Beinn Airidh Charr (791m). The road swings inland and then crosses the Bridge of Grudie before turning back to the lochside. The mountains here are not as precipitous as at the southern end of the loch and the landscape once again has an open feel to it. About half a mile on from the bridge you can see a section of the old road just to the left of the present road. This road continues for 2 miles before it is once again obscured by the new road.

Eilean Grudidh

About 1 1/2 miles on from Bridge of Grudie, there is a large carpark, well signposted, to the right of the road. The vegetation here has grown so high that the view is largely obscured, but it still makes a pleasant picnic spot. Lying just offshore at this point is Eilean Grudidh, a small island which contains the scant remains of an ancient castle. You will have to leave the carpark and make your way through the trees to get a view of the island (the ground here is full of rocky crevasses and it isn't wise to let children wander about unsupervised). Centuries ago, Eilean Grudidh was a stronghold of the MacBeath chiefs and was occupied by seven generations of that clan. In the early part of the 15th century, most of the MacBeaths were driven out of Gairloch by the rival MacLeods and Eilean Grudidh thereafter became a stronghold of Clan MacLeod. The island was originally fortified by building up the natural rocky banks with rough masonry and clay cement. The crude wall thus formed surrounded the entire circumference of the island. Several buildings were then constructed on the level ground in the centre of the island. In one place there is a deep hole which is surrounded by a circular wall. Tradition says that this is the castle dungeon. Unfortunately, not much remains to be seen of the fortification today. Most of the masonry has crumbled and when J.H. Dixon, author of *"Gairloch And Guide To Loch*

Maree", was writing in 1886, the central buildings were nothing more than rough mounds.

On the other side of Loch Maree lies the isolated Letterewe Estate which has been designated a wilderness area and site of special scientific interest. You can make out the estate buildings from across the loch. There are no roads to Letterewe, only a footpath which begins at Incheril by Kinlochewe. Main access to the estate is by boat. Before the Inverness to Kyle of Lochalsh railway was built, the entire mail for the Outer Hebrides was carried on foot along the Letterewe path from Kinlochewe to Poolewe. This path used to be the main track joining the Mackenzie lands in Kintail and Gairloch. The trees on the opposite shore of Loch Maree are oaks - the Letterewe oakwood is the most northerly example of an extensive oak woodland in Britain.

The Furnace Ironworks

Three-quarters of a mile to the south-east of Letterewe lies the area known as Furnace. This was the site of the first industrial iron smelting furnace in Scotland. The brick and sandstone remains can still be seen today by the side of the Abhainn na Fuirneis which flows into Loch Maree. The ironworks at Furnace were built in 1607 by Sir George Hay, a lawyer forced into premature retirement by political circumstances. Hay was born in 1572 and was educated at the Scots College in Douay, France. He was a great favourite of King James VI and was offered a peerage by the monarch. Hay chose to decline this honour and instead turned to the study of law, carving out a career of great distinction for himself. This was cut short when one of his partners, Lord Balmerino, was convicted of high treason and executed. Lest the finger of suspicion should next be pointed at him, Hay retired to remote Letterewe and spent his enforced leisure time in establishing and improving the iron smelting process there. The thickly wooded slopes of Loch Maree and the abundance of local bog iron made Letterewe an ideal site for ironworking. In later years, iron ore was imported by sea from Cumberland and Lancashire. Additional furnaces were built at Fasagh on the north side of Loch Maree, at Talladale and Slattadale on the south side, and at Glen Docherty and Poolewe (see Poolewe and Inverewe Garden). Hay brought skilled miners from Cumbria to supervise the works at his headquarters at Letterewe and the descendants of these workers still live in the region today. At the north-east end of Loch Maree, the area to the left of the Abhainn an Fhasaigh river mouth is known as "Cladh nan Sasunnach" which translates as "Burial Place of the English".

The ironworking industry ran into serious trouble when an Act of Parliament was passed on 27 January 1609 prohibiting the use of natural Scottish woodland in the making of iron. A huge amount of charcoal (mainly from oak and birch) was used in the smelting process: it is estimated that a blast furnace would have consumed over 100 acres of woodland annually. The thickly wooded slopes of Loch Maree were therefore an excellent source of fuel and the Parliamentary Act would effectively have ended the ironworks at Letterewe. At this point however, King James VI intervened on behalf of his favourite. On 24 December 1610, the King granted Hay the sole right to manufacture iron and glass in Scotland for a period of thirty-one years. This grant was ratified by Parliament on 23 October 1612 and so Sir George Hay became a very wealthy man. He stayed at Letterewe, casting guns and cannon, until most of the woodland around the shores of the loch had been cut down and when his lease expired he moved to London where he died in 1634, aged 62. The devastated Loch Maree woodland then became the home of cottars who tried to turn the exhausted areas of bog iron ore into productive arable land.

The Loch Maree Hotel

Shortly after crossing the River Talladale, the Loch Maree Hotel is seen on the right. This fine building was constructed in 1872. Queen Victoria stayed here from 12-18 September 1877 during her visit to Loch Maree and, apart from the modern extension, the exterior of the three storey sandstone building remains much as it was then. The Queen recorded in her diary that the hotel was "...a very nice little house, neatly furnished. To the left, as you enter, are two good rooms - a large one called the coffee-room, in which we take our meals, and the other, smaller, next to it, in which the gentlemen dine. Up the small but easy short winding staircase to the right come small, though comfortable, rooms." While out walking near the River Talladale one day, the Queen met up with some annoying local inhabitants. "The midges are dreadful." she noted later, "...you cannot stand for a moment without being stung." Despite this uncomfortable encounter, Queen Victoria greatly enjoyed her visit to Loch Maree and when the Royal Party departed for Balmoral on Tuesday, September 18, she wrote in her diary, "...at a quarter to nine we left with regret our nice cosy little hotel at Loch Maree, which I hope I may some day see again." To mark the Royal Visit, Sir Kenneth Mackenzie, the 13th Laird of Gairloch, commissioned a commemorative inscription on a boulder of Torridonian sandstone. Today this boulder can be seen on the grass just outside the hotel. The inscription is in Gaelic and translates as follows: "On the 12th day of September 1877 Queen Victoria came to visit Loch Maree and the country round it. She remained six nights in the opposite hotel, and, in her kindness, agreed that this stone should be a memorial of the pleasure she experienced in coming to this quarter of Ross." Note also the beautiful gold embossed Royal Crest on the outside wall of the hotel.

The Loch Maree Hotel has long been a popular destination for both sportsmen and sightseers. Between the years of 1884 and 1913, the steamship "Mabel" cruised the waters of Loch Maree, providing sightseeing trips for hotel guests and other visitors. A small jetty was constructed at the hotel in 1884 to provide a convenient point of departure for guests. Sightseers could also be collected from the mid-day train at Achnasheen and conveyed by carriage to the pier at Rhu Noa to join the steamship there. Circular tours of the loch by coach and steamer could be arranged for the grand price of 10/6.

Eating Out: THE LOCH MAREE HOTEL. Tel. (044 584) 288. The hotel is a pleasant place to stop for morning coffee or afternoon tea. Bar and set lunches are served from 1200-1400. In the evening, a table d'hote dinner menu is available from 1900-2100. Dinner reservations are preferred. The hotel is open from Easter to October and credit cards are accepted. The Loch Maree Hotel holds fishing permits for Loch Maree (see Fishing section).

The Islands On Loch Maree

Shortly after passing the hotel, the many islands of Loch Maree come into view on the right. There are fifty-four islands of varying size on the loch, many of them covered with conifers which are remnants of the native forest which once covered much of Highland Scotland. They are in the care of the Nature Conservancy Council which controls access to them. The principle islands are Isle Maree, Eilean Subhainn ("The Everlasting Island"), Eilean Dubh na Sroine ("The Black Isle Of The Promontory"), Garbh Eilean ("The Rough Isle"), and Eilean Ruairidh Mor ("The Big Island Of Rory" - named after a famous chief of Clan MacLeod). Eilean Subhainn is the largest island on the loch. It is said that the fairy folk gather there every year to pay tribute to their queen. In the centre of Eilean Subhainn is a loch which contains two small islands and on one of these is a large fir tree. It is believed that the fairy queen sits beneath this tree to await the arrival of her people. During the early 19th century, illicit whisky distillation was carried out in bothies on Eilean Subhainn, Garbh Eilean and Eilean Ruaridh Mor.

Isle Maree

Lying close to the Letterewe side, hidden from view by Eilean Subhainn, is Isle Maree. This small island is thickly wooded in oak, holly, hazel, pine, ash, willow and birch. It contains the remains of a chapel which was built in the late 7th century by the Celtic missionary St Maelrubha, a disciple of St Columba. St Maelrubha lived from 642 to 722 and he is responsible for spreading Christianity throughout the western Highlands of Scotland. He left his native Bangor in Ireland in 671 and in 673 he settled at Applecross for several years before moving on to Isle Maree. "Maelrubha" means "Red-haired Tonsured One" and it is from this that the name "Maree" derives. Legend has it that the Saint planted the holly on the island.

Isle Maree was regarded as a holy place long before the arrival of Maelrubha. It was sacred to the Druids and it is believed that they planted the oak as one of their religious symbols. The island was still in use as a pagan meeting place as late as the 17th century. The church records at Dingwall for 6 August 1678 record that a Hector Mackenzie, his two sons and grandson were summoned to appear before the Presbytery for taking part in pagan rites on the island. The rites involved the sacrifice of a bull in an attempt to restore the health of Hector's wife, Cirstane.

Isle Maree also contains an ancient well, now dry and filled in. It was believed that the water from this well had powerful curative properties for people afflicted by mental illness. Until the end of the 18th century, all such people throughout Wester Ross were brought to the well to drink. The procedure for obtaining a cure was recorded by the famous English traveller Thomas Pennant who visited the Gairloch area during his tour of Scotland in 1772. First of all, the patient knelt before an altar while his attendants made an offering of money. The patient then went to the well and drunk the sacred water. This was followed by a second offering, after which the patient was dipped in the loch three times. Pennant noted that this routine could be repeated daily for several weeks in the hope of a cure. Local people believed that cures were most likely to be obtained on St Maelrubha's Day, August 25. It is said that the well dried up after a man washed his mad dog in it.

Close to the well grew an ancient wishing tree. It was believed that a wish made over the well would be granted if an offering was made to the tree. Offerings could be either in the form of copper coins or a scrap of one's own clothing. If you offered money, the coin was hammered edgeways into the bark. Strips of cloth were nailed to the trunk. The practice of nailing or tying cloth fragments to sacred trees is an ancient Celtic custom, still practiced in some areas to this day. The Isle Maree wishing tree was still alive when Queen Victoria visited the island on Sunday, September 16, 1877, and she duly made a wish and hammered some pennies into the trunk.

Legend has it that Isle Maree was the setting of a tragic love story. Towards the end of the 9th century, when the north-west of Scotland was under Viking rule, the local Prince, Olaf, was worried for the safety of his Princess bride. At this time, Isle Maree was the dwelling place of an Irish holy man. The holy man suggested to the Prince that he should bring his bride to the island. Thinking this an excellent idea, the Prince built a tall tower upon Isle Maree and there he dwelt in safety and happiness with his bride. However, the time soon came when Prince Olaf had to go off to fight in a long campaign. The Prince and Princess agreed that, upon his return, they should both sail down the loch to meet one another. If all was well, a white flag was to be flown from the prow of the ship; if ill fate had befallen either one of them, a black flag was to be flown. And so, Prince Olaf went off to war, leaving his bride alone with her thoughts. Before long, the Princess began foolishly to wonder whether Olaf would rather be off fighting on campaign than be with her on Isle Maree and soon she began to doubt his love. In his absence she devised a cruel plan to test his true feelings for her. One day, news arrived that the Prince had returned and was sailing up the loch towards Isle Maree. The Princess immediately set sail on a barge flying a black flag and lay upon a funeral bier, wrapped in a black shroud. When Prince Olaf saw this tragic scene, he was overcome with grief and immediately plunged a dagger into his heart. Only then did the Princess realise how stupid she had been. Full of remorse, she plucked the dagger from the Prince's chest and plunged it into her own heart. The tragic couple were buried on Isle Maree, under the shade of a sacred holly tree. Their graves, marked by smooth stones upon which were carved Celtic crosses, can still be seen today.

The Victoria Falls

The road now begins to turn away from the loch side and enters the Slattadale Forest. Shortly after crossing a little stone bridge, a single storey white cottage (Garbhaig) comes into view on the right. Directly opposite the cottage is the road to the Victoria Falls, named in honour of Queen Victoria who visited them on Sunday, September 16, 1887. There is a carpark on the right a short distance up this road and a well made footpath to the falls enters the trees opposite it. The roar of the water can be heard as soon as you enter the forest and after only a few minutes walk, the waterfall is reached. A wooden platform has been erected to give an excellent (and safe) view. There is a double fall with a small cascade at the bottom, all beautifully framed by the surrounding trees. The path continues up alongside the waterfall. There is a wooden handrail all the way, making it safe for children. At the top of the falls you can walk out onto a wooden bridge which gives a good view up and down the river. This last section of the path can be muddy.

Slattadale Forest Walk and Tollie Path

About 1/3 mile on from the Victoria Falls, a track to the right of the road leads down to the shore of Loch Maree. Here there is a large parking space with uninterrupted views across the loch to the many islands and the hills of Letterewe opposite. There are also several picnic tables. A short walk through the Slattadale Forest begins at the far end of the carpark. For the more energetic, the carpark is also the starting point of the 5 1/4 mile Tollie Path. See Selected Walks for full details.

Toilets: Situated in the Slattadale Forest picnic area, described above. There are separate facilities for the disabled.

On The Road To Gairloch

Shortly after the Slattadale turnoff, the main road begins to climb, giving a spectacular view back down the loch to Slioch. The road turns westwards away from the loch and after a couple of miles emerges from the Slattadale Forest into a bare, rocky landscape. This section of road used to be single track, but rapid improvements are currently underway. Before long, Am Feur-Loch is passed on the left. A 4 1/2 mile footpath to the remote Loch na h-Oidhche begins opposite the small building which lies close to the loch. See Selected Walks for full details. Beyond Am Feur-Loch lies the much larger Loch Bad an Sgalaig. The dominant mountain to the rear of Bad an Sgalaig is Baosbheinn and peeking out behind it is Beinn Alligin. There is a parking spot to the left of the road which has a magnificent view across the loch.

After Loch Bad an Sgalaig, the road follows the course of the River Kerry and begins to descend towards the coast. There are attractive patches of woodland on either side of the deep gorge through which the river flows. This glen used to contain a series of waterfalls which were famed throughout the area for their beauty. Queen Victoria visited the falls on Thursday, September 13, 1877, and in her diary she refers to "...the fine falls of the Kerrie, of which there are two or three successions, with fine rocks and wooded banks, through which the river seems to force its way.". Sadly, the Kerry waterfalls dried up when the head of the river was dammed at Loch Bad an Sgalaig by the North of Scotland Hydro-Electricity Board.

The road now turns northwards and, just after the B8056 junction to Redpoint, it once again becomes double track. The B8056 leaves the main road by way of a picturesque humpbacked stone bridge. It was here that Queen Victoria travelled on Monday, September 17, 1877 to meet up with the many people who had journeyed across from the Isle of Lewis to see her. Around 250 people had made the crossing from Stornoway, hoping to catch a glimpse of the Queen. It had taken them three hours to come over and, after seeing the Queen, they returned to the steamer and headed straight back. A short distance on from the bridge, Kerrysdale House is passed on the right and then the road enters Kerry Wood. In days gone by, this attractive woodland was a well known haunt of the fairy folk. In Gaelic, Kerry Wood was known as "Cathair Bheag" which means the "little seat" of the fairies. Before long, the bustling port of Gairloch is reached.

THE B8056 TO BADACHRO AND REDPOINT

The B8056 to Badachro and Redpoint begins at the picturesque hump-backed stone bridge which crosses the River Kerry 3 miles south of Gairloch. After heavy prolonged rain, the River Kerry can sometimes burst its bank at this point, causing flooding on the section of road immediately after the bridge. The road from Slattadale to Badachro was part of the network of roads which were built in the mid 19th century to provide employment and alleviate the poverty caused by the potato famine.

From the junction, the single-track road winds its way amidst stretches of native forest at the foot of bare gneiss hummocks. After about a mile, the road turns towards the shore of Loch Shieldaig and passes the Shieldaig Lodge Hotel on the right. The hotel is a beautiful building, constructed of attractive red sandstone. It was formerly the Shooting Lodge for Shieldaig Forest and now serves as a base for the many fishermen who come to explore the isolated lochs in the hills behind Badachro. The hotel holds permits for the Aeroplane Loch, Badachro River, Diamond Loch, the Fairy Lochs, Loch Bad Na h' Achlaise and the Spectacles Loch (see Fishing section). If you wish to stop and have a look at Loch Shieldaig, there is a large parking area on the left just after you pass the hotel. This carpark is the starting point of a walk which ascends the hills behind Shieldaig to view the crash site of the U.S.A.A.F. Liberator. The Liberator was returning home to the U.S.A. on the 13th June, 1945, when it became lost and collided with a rocky bluff, killing all 9 crew and 6 passengers. See Selected Walks for full details.

Eating Out: SHIELDAIG LODGE HOTEL. Tel. (044 583) 250. This attractive red sandstone building has a tranquil setting on the shores of Loch Shieldaig. Bar lunches are served from 1230-1330 and morning coffees and afternoon teas are also available. In the evening, a table d'hote dinner menu is offered from 1930-2015. The hotel is open from April to October.

After Shieldaig, the B8056 skirts around the edge of Loch Shieldaig, with only a little stone parapet separating you from the water. From this point, there is a good view back towards the Shieldaig Lodge Hotel. At low tide the bay here is very colourful, with orange-brown seaweed scattered along the shore. Beyond Shieldaig, the countryside opens up again and Loch Bad a' Chrotha is passed on the left. As you cross the little stone bridge, you can see the weir at the foot of the loch. The road now descends to Badachro.

BADACHRO

The little village of Badachro lies strung out along the main road and down a minor road to the right. The minor road takes you down to the Badachro Inn, an attractive white-washed building situated right at the water's edge. From the Inn there are uninterrupted views across the picturesque bay, making this a lovely place to stop for a drink (the Bar is open from 1200-1430 and 1700-2300). There is a little stone jetty next to the Inn which is usually covered in colourful lobster pots. The bay is sheltered from Loch Gairloch by a string of islands which create a safe anchorage, making Badachro popular with both fishermen and visiting yachtsmen. The largest island, Eilean Horrisdale or Thorsdale, is named after Thor, the Norse god of thunder and is a reminder of the Norse domination of this north-west coast many centuries ago.

At the end of the 19th century, Badachro was a bustling fishing centre, with up to 40 boats and 160 men employed in catching cod, herring and ling. The Gairloch cod fishery was carried out by two firms who had curing stations at Badachro, one on the Dry Island and the other on Eilean Horrisdale. These two fish curing stations provided work for 30 men and 10 women. The catch averaged about 40,000 cod per annum and in 1884 the fishermen were paid 4d for each fish. About 2/3rds of the catch was sent fresh by steamer to markets in Glasgow and England while the remainder was dried and sold locally.

Shopping: THE STORE. Tel. (044 583) 265. Open daily, 0730-1930. Situated down the minor road, on the right just before the Badachro Inn. Small shop selling general groceries, bread, milk, fruit, vegetables, frozen foods, pulses, Vegetarian cheeses and dried fruit. Sunday newspapers are available here.
WEST HIGHLAND MARINE LTD. Tel. (044 583) 291. This Post Office and ship's chandlery stocks a range of waterproofs, sweatshirts, T-shirts, fishing tackle, crafts, cool drinks, sweets and ice-cream.

Eating out: THE BADACHRO INN. Tel. (044 583) 255. This attractive white-washed inn is situated right at the water's edge with views over the bay to Eilean Horrisdale. Bar meals are served until 2100 and fresh seafood is often available. The inn is open daily from April to October and on Wednesdays, Fridays and Saturdays from November to March.

Boat Hire: THE BADACHRO INN, Badachro. Tel. (044 583) 255. The Inn has boats available for hire.
WEST HIGHLAND MARINE LTD, Badachro. Contact Iain Thomson. Tel. (044 583) 291. Book at the village Post Office situated on the main road. The booking office incorporates a chandlery shop. West Highland Marine have a range of boats for hire including 14ft and 16ft rowing boats, dinghies, 21ft traditional skiffs, a 21ft 4 berth yacht, sea kayaks and Canadian canoes. Hourly, 1/2 day and day hire is available.

Instruction charts and full safety equipment are provided. Sailing tuition is available by arrangement. You can also book a skippered trip in a traditional skiff or 30ft yacht. Diving air is available for sub aqua parties. If you would like to try your hand at sea angling, West Highland Marine has rods and tackle for hire. There is also a sea taxi service in operation between Gairloch Harbour and Badachro.
WEST HIGHLAND YACHT CHARTER, Badachro. Contact Iain Thomson. Tel. (044 583) 291. Book at the village Post Office situated on the main road. West Highland Yacht Charter offers 1 to 14 day skippered trips on board 30 to 47 foot yachts, visiting some of the many remote islands off the north-west coast. This is a good way to see the puffin colony on the Shiant Isles. If you are an experienced sailor, self-sail charter is also available, allowing you the freedom to plan your own itinerary. For the less experienced, flotilla cruising can also be arranged.

On The Road To Redpoint

Just after the village of Badachro, a minor road on the right leads down to the little coastal settlement of Aird which overlooks Eilean Horrisdale. The main road now skirts along the north shore of Loch Bad na h-Achlaise before arriving in the scattered crofting community of Port Henderson. Several minor roads to the right of the main road wind their way amidst the pretty white cottages dotted about the hillside. It was here in the early 19th century that the local boat-builder, Roderick Mackenzie, had an encounter with a mermaid. Roderick was gathering fishing bait on the rocky coast close to the village when he suddenly spied a mermaid lying asleep among the rocks. He rushed over to her and grabbed her by the hair whereupon the creature let out an unearthly cry. The distraught mermaid then promised that she would grant the boat-builder a wish if only he would let her go free. Roderick agreed and demanded a pledge that no-one should ever be drowned in a boat of his building. He then let go of the mermaid and it is said that the promise was duly kept.

After Port Henderson, the road crosses a windswept peat moor before descending to the village of Opinan. This little settlement of green fields and tidy crofts nestling into the hillside is an unexpected sight after the bleak moorland. Opinan has a beautiful sandy beach and impressive sand dunes which are the haunt of dozens of pied wagtails. There are several flat grassy areas to the right of the road where parking is possible. South Rona, Skye and the tip of Raasay are visible from the beach.

The road turns inland and passes the scattered community of South Erradale, which used to be well-known for its quality tweeds. It then skirts the coast once more and climbs up high over a heather moorland. The distinctive promontory of Red Point with its beautiful sandy beach suddenly comes into view ahead. Shortly after the telephone box, there is a large carpark on the right which must have one of the most magnificent views in the whole area. Out to sea, from right to left, you can see the hills of Harris, the small isles of Sgeir nam Maol, Fladda-chuain and Eilean

Trodday off the northern tip of Skye, the distinctive shape of the Quirang on Skye (you can even make out the striped formation of the Kilt Rock on the coast, just to the left of the Quirang - the waterfall which tumbles over the cliff to the sea below can be seen through binoculars), the islands of South Rona and Raasay, and the Cuillin Hills and conical Red Hills on Skye (the distinct pyramid shape of Marsco is very obvious). Back on the mainland, to the left, rise Beinn Damh, Beinn Alligin and Baosbheinn. There is a viewpoint indicator on the knoll in front of the carpark which identifies the various peaks.

The road now descends to a second carpark from which there is access to the beach and huge sand dunes. As the road begins to dip, look out for the old Victorian post box which is set into the rock on the left. The beach is only a couple of minutes walk from the carpark. Go through the wooden gate on the right and cross the sand dunes. Sheep are usually loose on these dunes - please keep all dogs on a leash. Most people head straight for this first beach but there is a second beautiful sandy beach beyond the Red Point headland from where you can walk to the Redpoint Fishing Station and on along the coast to Craig Youth Hostel and Diabaig. See Selected Walks for full details.

GAIRLOCH

As the A832 descends through Kerry Wood, Loch Gairloch comes into view for the first time. Before long, the visitor arrives at the little settlement of Charleston, now virtually a part of Gairloch.

CHARLESTON

Up until the 19th century, this picturesque area was known as the bay of Ceann an t' Sail which means "The Head of the Salt Water". As more and more houses were built around the head of the bay, the resulting hamlet came to be known as Charleston. Today, this little settlement is generally considered to be part of the village of Gairloch.

The pier at Charleston is the home of the Gairloch fishing fleet. It is worth walking along to the end of the pier when the fleet is in to see the brightly coloured boats bobbing up and down in the water. Gairloch has for centuries been an important centre for cod fishing. In the time of Alexander Mackenzie, the 9th Laird of Gairloch (1721-1766), the estate tenants were bound by law to sell their entire catch of cod and ling to him. The laird kept his own fish curer and sold the catch on to a merchant, Mr Dunbar, for 12/6d per cwt. When the English traveller Thomas Pennant visited the Gairloch region in 1772, between 5,000 and 27,000 cod were caught each year. Most of these were dried and exported to Bilboa in Spain. By 1810, the industry had grown even further, with an average annual catch in excess of 20,000 cod. These were cured by Messrs J. Nicol & Young and were exported, both pickled and dried, to Ireland, Liverpool and London. The large carpark at the pier is a convenient starting point for a short walk to the site of the ancient fort of An Dun. See Selected Walks for full details.

In the woods behind Charleston lies Flowerdale House, the west coast residence of the Mackenzies of Gairloch. The present mansion house was built in 1738 by Sir Alexander Mackenzie, the 9th Laird. In the mid 1800's, Flowerdale was the home of the Dowager Lady Mackenzie of Gairloch. It was Lady Mackenzie who hit upon the idea of building the many "Destitution Roads" in the Gairloch area to help relieve the poverty and suffering caused by the potato famine of 1846-48. The carpark opposite The Old Inn is the starting point of a pleasant walk to Flowerdale House and the waterfalls beyond. See Selected Walks for full details.

Shopping: AMAZON SEAFOODS. Tel. (0445) 2027. Freshly landed seafood is available for sale at a warehouse on Gairloch Pier. The warehouse is usually open to customers from 0815-1800.

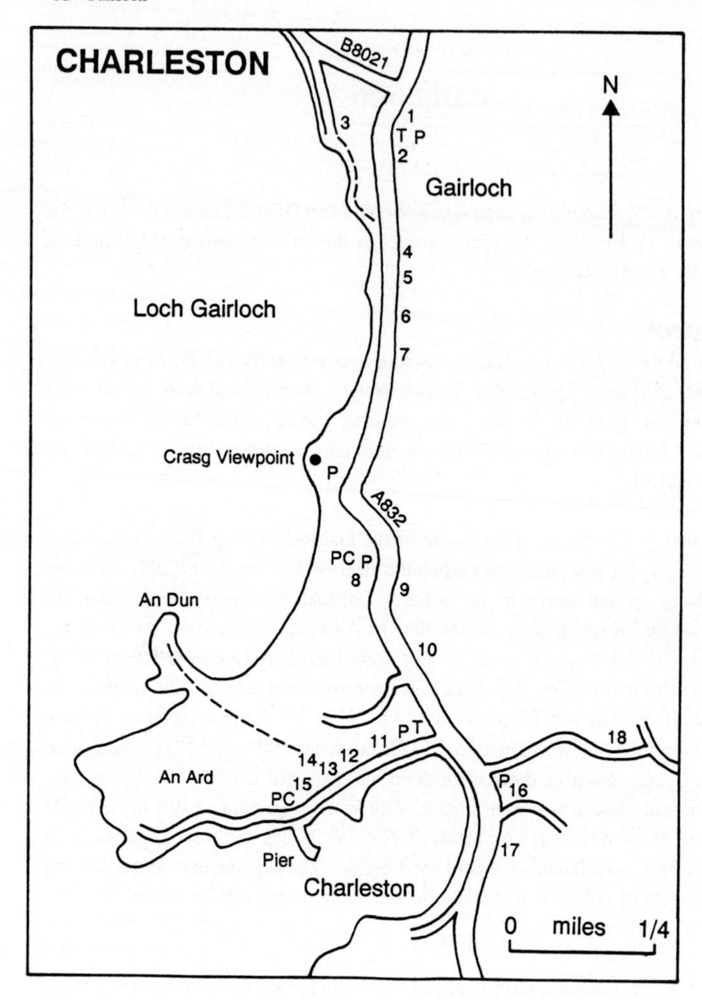

Key

1 - Wildcat Stores
2 - Gairloch Sands Hotel/Watersports Centre
3 - Myrtle Bank Hotel
4 - Library
5 - Doctor
6 - Gairloch Hotel
7 - Gairloch Garage
8 - Gairloch Golf Club
9 - Parish Church
10 - Bank
11 - Boat Club
12 - West Highland Marine Ltd
13 - The Anchorage/Post Office
14 - MV Kerry Cruises
15 - Amazon Seafoods
16 - The Old Inn
17 - Creag Mor Hotel
18 - Flowerdale House
P - Parking
PC - Toilets
T - Telephone

THE ANCHORAGE, Gairloch Pier. Tel. (0445) 2175. This shop stocks a selection of knitwear and fishing equipment including an excellent range of wet flies, dry flies and salmon flies. If you are looking for an unusual gift at a reasonable price, take a look at the huge selection of polished agate slices. The Anchorage holds fishing permits for Loch Bad a Cheamh, Loch Kernsary, Loch Maree, Loch na Curra, Loch na h-Oidhche and Loch Tollaidh (see Fishing section). Complete fly fishing outfits - rod, reel, line and landing net - can be hired for £5.00 per day plus £10 deposit. Sea angling trips can be arranged during the summer season - ask at the shop. Families and large groups are catered for. You can also book here for Highland Trails (see below - All Terrain Vehicles). The Anchorage incorporates a Post Office which is open Monday, Wednesday, Thursday, Friday 0900-1330 and 1430-1730; Tuesday 0900-1300; Saturday 0900-1230.
WEST HIGHLAND MARINE LTD, Gairloch Pier. Tel. (0445) 2458. This shop stocks a range of marine chandlery, waterproof clothing, footwear, T-shirts, outboard engines, sea-angling tackle, sweets, ice-cream and cool drinks. Outboard engines can be serviced by arrangement.

Eating Out: CREAG MOR HOTEL. Tel. (0445) 2068. This quiet hotel on the outskirts of Charleston serves tea, coffee, bar meals and various snacks throughout the day from 0800-2200. There is also a cocktail bar and restaurant which serves table d'hote dinner from 1900-2200. The restaurant specialises in venison, prime Highland beef and fresh local seafood. Dinner reservations are advised. The hotel has a display of original watercolours which are for sale. Credit cards are accepted and the hotel is open throughout the year. The Creag Mor Hotel holds fishing permits for the River Kerry (see Fishing section).
THE OLD INN. Tel. (0445) 2006. The Old Bridge Bistro, situated within the picturesque Old Inn, looks out over the adjacent river and is a pleasant place for a meal. The Bistro is open daily from 1200-2200, May to September. In addition, bar lunches are served from 1200-1415; high teas from 1630-1800 and bar suppers from 1800-2100. In the evening, dinner is served from 1830-2100. Dinner reservations are advised. If you like real ale, this is the place to go. The inn is open all year and credit cards are accepted.

All Terrain Vehicles: If you like trying unusual activities, check out the All Terrain Vehicle guided tours which are operated by HIGHLAND TRAILS. ATV's are like large, robust 4 wheel drive motorcycles and are a novel and exhilarating way to explore the countryside. Full instruction is given before you set off and a safety helmet is provided at no extra charge. All tours are accompanied by an experienced guide and are restricted to persons aged 16 years and over. Tours cover the rugged hills behind Charleston where you may be fortunate enough to see the rare golden eagle, the wild cat or the otter. You will also have a chance to explore the Flowerdale Deer Forest and there are many magnificent mountain and coastal views to be had along the way. 1 and 2 hour tours are available. Highland Trails is based in the old stable block of

Flowerdale House (see Selected Walks), but bookings must be made at The Anchorage on Gairloch Pier. Tel. (0445) 2175.

Cruises and Sea Angling: MV KERRY, a fully equipped modern boat, departs Monday-Saturday from Gairloch Pier for pleasure cruises and sea angling trips in Loch Gairloch. There are no Sunday sailings. Bait and fishing rods are supplied on all sea angling trips. Book at the Post Office on Gairloch Pier. Tel. (0445) 2175. The schedule is as follows:

MAY/JUNE:

Monday-Friday	0930 - 3 hour sea angling trip
	1400 - 2 hour cruise
	1700 - 1 hour cruise
Saturday	1400 - 3 hour sea angling trip

JULY/AUGUST:

Monday-Friday	0930 - 3 hour sea angling trip
	1400 - 2 hour cruise
	1600 - 2 hour cruise
	1800 - 1 hour cruise
Saturday	1400 - 3 hour sea angling trip
	1800 - 1 hour cruise

Toilets: Public toilets are located on Gairloch Pier.

Crasg Viewpoint

As you continue around the coast towards Gairloch proper, it is worth pulling into the large carpark on the left shortly after the Golf Club to take in the panoramic view. The northern tip of Skye can be made out just across the loch while out to sea some 40 miles across the Minch lie Lewis and Harris. An information plaque just in front of the carpark identifies the features of interest which can be seen from this spot. The road now continues along the coast and descends to the village of Gairloch.

GAIRLOCH

This busy fishing port has a magnificent setting at the head of Loch Gairloch with spectacular views to the Torridon mountains, the Isle of Skye and the Outer Hebrides. The immaculate sandy beaches offer safe bathing for people of all ages, making Gairloch a popular choice for family holidays.

The name "Gairloch" comes from the Gaelic "Gearr Loch" which means "Short Loch". The use of the term "Gairloch" to signify a village has really only come about in the present century. Up until the 19th century, the settlement at the head of Loch Gairloch consisted of the separate hamlets of Strath and Achtercairn.

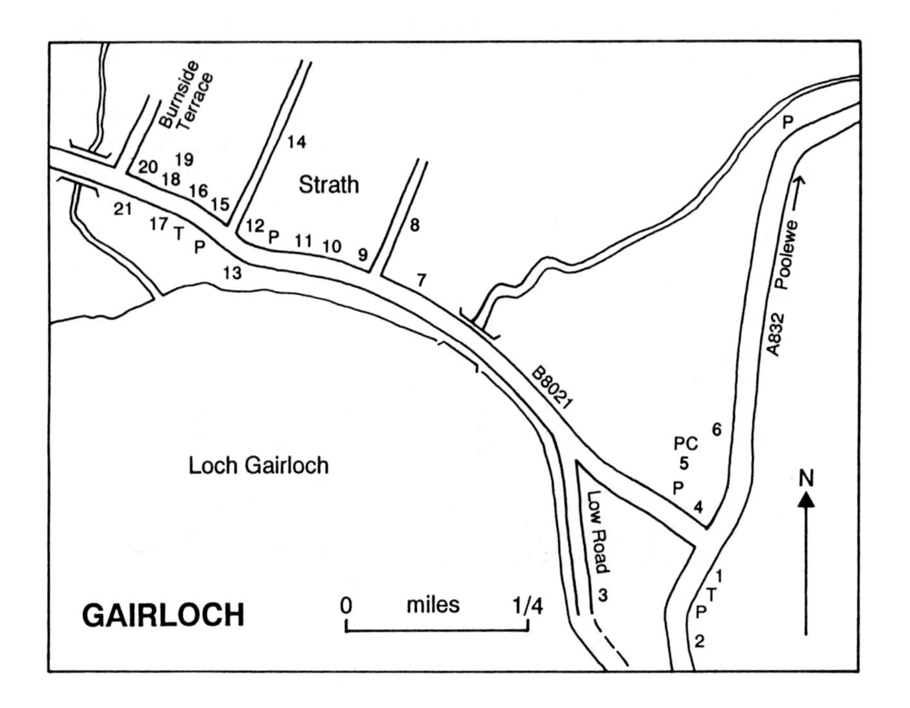

Key

1 - Wildcat Stores
2 - Gairloch Sands Hotel/Watersports Centre
3 - Myrtle Bank Hotel
4 - Police
5 - Tourist Information Centre
6 - Gairloch Heritage Museum/The Steading Restaurant
7 - Kirk Hand Weave
8 - Glebe Park - Pitch & Putt, play area
9 - The Bookshop and Tea Room
10 - Mackenzie Brothers
11 - Sail Gairloch
12 - Millcroft Hotel
13 - Parrys of Gairloch
14 - Gairloch Holiday Park - camp site & launderette
15 - Gairloch Hardware
16 - Strath Post Office
17 - The Nature Shop/Mountain Restaurant
18 - Ewe & Me
19 - Ewe & Me Takeaway
20 - K. Gunn - The Radio Shop
21 - Kenneth Morrison
P - Parking
PC - Toilet
T - Telephone

The fishing village of Strath was as much a centre of commerce in the 19th century as it is today. There were two merchant's shops, a boat-building yard, several shoemakers' shops and a meal mill. In addition to the important cod fishery mentioned above, saythe, ling, salmon and herring were also caught. The hamlet of Achtercairn had its own salmon station. At one time, every household in the Gairloch area grew a small plot of hemp from which the women spun flax to be manufactured into herring nets and fishing lines. There were also abundant oyster beds, some of which were leased to a company in London. Oysters continued to be exported until 1875. Lobsters and crabs were also harvested and were packed in boxes to be sent by steamer to markets in England.

Gairloch has long been renowned as a holiday resort and was popular with Victorian visitors who regularly patronised the magnificent Gairloch Hotel overlooking the bay. The hotel was built in 1872 and enlarged in 1881 to accommodate up to 150 guests. It had everything that the discerning Victorian traveller might require: a coffee room, drawing room, reading room, smoking room, billiard room, several private sitting rooms and a souvenir stall. The hotel had its own greenhouses to ensure a good supply of vegetables, grapes, flowers and decorative plants. A bathing-machine was also kept on the nearby beach for the use of guests. During the height of the tourist season, the hotel even organised Church services for its patrons.

During the 19th century, Gairloch was visited regularly by passenger steamers and was thus very accessible to tourists. In summer, swift passenger steamers from Oban and Portree called every other afternoon and Macbrayne's large cargo and passenger steamer called every Saturday. The busy port was also visited regularly by cargo vessels from Wick and Leith.

Opposite the golf course lies the original Parish Church of Gairloch. This church was built in 1791 on the site of an earlier ecclesiastical building which had existed from at least 1649. The old Churchyard of Gairloch is situated amidst the sand dunes to the right of the golf course and a visit to this interesting place is well worthwhile. Here lie the remains of the old lairds of Gairloch, together with many of the renowned local bards and pipers. Here too can be seen a memorial stone to John Hay, the last manager of the Red Smiddy ironworks at Poolewe (see Poolewe and Inverewe Garden). It is believed that the old Churchyard of Gairloch is the site of an ancient chapel dedicated to St Maelrubha.

Throughout the Highlands and Islands it was once believed that the power of the witch could render milk unwholesome or could even dry up the yield of a herd completely. In the early part of the 19th century, the Gairloch Parish schoolmaster was one Kenneth Mackenzie. Mackenzie lived in the schoolmaster's house at Achtercairn and was always known as the "maighstair sgoil". It is said that he was a

Inverewe House

Poolewe from Inverewe Garden

master of witchcraft and that people travelled from far and wide to seek his advice regarding charms and spells. The maighstair sgoil kept several cows and one day he discovered that his own animals had been placed under a spell which rendered the milk useless. By his own occult powers, Mackenzie was able to determine that the spell was the work of a woman who lived at Strath. Seeking revenge, he lay in wait for her one Sunday morning as the local villagers made their way to church. As the woman passed the maighstair sgoil just by the little burn which runs through Achtercairn, he cast a spell upon her, obliging her to remain behind. As soon as the other villagers were out of sight, Mackenzie caused her to hitch her skirt above her knees and to jump violently back and forth over the burn. This she was forced to do for several hours until the villagers returned from church. Realising that her own powers were no match for those of the maighstair sgoil's, the woman rushed back to Strath and lifted the spell. The milk of Mackenzie's cows immediately returned to normal.

Gairloch Heritage Museum

No visit to Gairloch is complete without a trip to the superb Heritage Museum which was formed by the local heritage society 10 years ago. This award winning museum is open Monday-Saturday, 1000-1700, from Easter to the end of September. During the summer months (July and August) the museum also opens from 1830-2030, Monday-Friday. Admission: Adults £1.00, Children 20p. Between the months of October and March, the museum may be visited by prior arrangement. Telephone (0445) 2287 for further details.

The Gairloch Heritage Museum is situated in a superbly restored farm steading and the fascinating displays include a reconstruction of a croft house interior of 100 years ago, the old village shop from Melvaig (together with a photograph of the original), a schoolroom of days gone by and the light and foghorn mechanism from the Rua Reidh lighthouse. The museum is also packed full of old household and farming implements from the Gairloch area and special sections are devoted to wildlife, fishing and wool processing. Several restored fishing boats can be seen outside the museum. Amongst the many interesting items on display is a letter dated 1877 from Queen Victoria's Private Secretary expressing her delight in all that she saw during her visit to Loch Maree and her satisfaction with the arrangements made for her. Here too can be seen the kitchen table from the old farmhouse at Loch an Draing, Inverasdale (see Poolewe to Cove), fashioned from driftwood over one hundred years ago. There is also a photograph of the wooden pulpit which used to stand in Cove Cave (see Poolewe to Cove). Many museums in Scotland can boast one or two items connected with Bonnie Prince Charlie and the Gairloch Heritage Museum is no exception - in this case there is a plaid which the Prince used as a blanket during his stay at Culloden and a piece of the boat in which he escaped after the battle. A gallery area contains fascinating photographs of the Gairloch district in days gone by and there is also a pictorial exhibition on the history of the Gaels. Here too you can see a display on the local geology and a reconstruction of the earliest blast furnace in Scotland (see Poolewe and Inverewe Garden). A special quiz concerning the various exhibits is available for children - this is both educational and a good way of keeping the kids occupied while you look round. The museum also has a library which contains a good collection of books and archive material (papers and tapes) relating to the area. These are available for perusal by researchers or indeed anyone interested in the Gairloch area. The resident archivist, Mr Roy Wentworth, is available for consultation on Monday mornings and Thursday afternoons, or he can be contacted by phoning (044 583) 204. The small museum shop sells a variety of guides, leaflets, postcards and teatowels. Here you can purchase a reproduction of J.H. Dixon's famous *"Gairloch and Guide to Loch Maree"*. The proceeds of this reproduction have been of great help in establishing the museum, a fact which would no doubt have greatly pleased Mr Dixon. After you have finished looking around the museum, you can pop into the pleasant coffee shop and licensed restaurant which is situated in an adjacent converted farm steading (see "The Steading Restaurant" below). Here you can choose from a range of food from tea or coffee and a selection of cakes to a complete meal. Credit cards are not accepted.

Shopping: THE BOOKSHOP. Stocks a reasonable selection of Scottish and children's books. A few general guide books are available in French and German. You can have a cup of tea or coffee for a nominal price while you are looking round the bookshop.

EWE & ME. Tel. (0445) 2397. This interesting gift shop sells a selection of framed prints, candles, pottery (including Arran Pottery), hand painted glass boxes from the Borders, cards, postcards and a small range of Ola Gorie silver jewellery from Orkney. Credit cards are accepted. Also situated within the shop is Janet's Hair Salon, Tel. (0445) 2397. Ewe and Me is open throughout the year, Monday-Saturday, 0900-1730, with late night opening during July and August.

GAIRLOCH HARDWARE. Tel. (0445) 2499. General hardware and gardening items. There is a good selection of camping gear, walking boots, socks, waterproofs, wellingtons, sports shoes, gloves and torches. The shop also stocks Epigas and carries a range of motoring accessories including oil and emergency fan belts. Barbeque hire is available at £2.00 per day, with £10 deposit. Enquire here also for access to the Pitch and Putt green. Open Monday-Saturday, 0900-1300 and 1400-1730. Closed Sunday.

GAIRLOCH SANDS HOTEL. Tel. (0445) 2131. A small gift and craft shop is located within the hotel.

K. GUNN - THE RADIO SHOP. Tel. (0445) 2400. Newsagents and general store. Sells fishing tackle, various items of pottery and gift ware, a selection of Scottish and hill-walking books, O.S. maps, shoes, wellington boots, waterproofs, cameras, binoculars, compasses, charcoal, Calor Gas and photographic film. A cold drinks cabinet is located in the store. Open Monday-Saturday, 0900-1300 and 1400-1800. Closed

Sunday. The Radio Shop holds fishing permits for Fionn Loch, Loch Tollaidh and more than 30 hill lochs to the east of Gairloch (see Fishing section).

KIRK HAND WEAVE. Tel. (0445) 2375. Outdoor clothing specialists. The shop stocks a variety of locally knitted items, waterproofs, Scottish jewellery and ceramics. They also sell genuine Harris Tweed jackets and tweed skirt lengths. Open Monday-Saturday, 0930-1800. Closed Sunday.

THE MACKENZIE BROTHERS - VG STORES. Tel. (0445) 2483. Grocers, bakers, dairy and newsagents. Also sells wines and spirits. Open Monday-Saturday, 0800-2000. Closed Sunday.

KENNETH MORRISON. Tel. (0445) 2485. Butcher, poulterer and game dealer. The shop also stocks deep freezer supplies and some fruit and vegetables. Open Monday-Saturday, 0730-1730.

THE NATURE SHOP. Tel. (0445) 2316. An unusual gift shop selling a wide variety of items including preserves (Arran Provisions), postcards, O.S. maps, hill-walking and climbing books, jewellery, photographic film and Arran Aromatics gift toiletries and perfumes which are produced without cruelty to animals. There is also a good selection of John O'Groats pottery items. Credit cards are accepted. For overseas customers there is tax free shopping for purchases over £30. The Nature Shop is open daily throughout the year, with late night opening from May to October and at Christmas.

PARRY'S MACE STORE. Tel. (0445) 2236. Licensed grocers. The shop sells bread, milk, groceries, fruit and vegetables and carries a large range of malt whiskies. Enquire here for access to the Pitch and Putt green. Open Monday-Friday, 0830-1830; Saturday 0830-1900. Closed Sunday.

STRATH POST OFFICE. Tel. (0445) 2008. In addition to being a post office, the shop also stocks a selection of hill-walking books, O.S. maps, postcards, photographic film, stationery, greetings cards, Scottish toffee, fudge and tablet. Open Monday, Tuesday, Thursday and Friday, 0900-1300 and 1400-1730; Wednesday 0900-1300; Saturday 0900-1230. Closed Sunday.

WILDCAT STORES. Tel. (0445) 2242. Licensed grocers and newsagents. The shop includes Jan's Deli which has a selection of bread, pastries, quiches, pies and salads. Open Monday-Saturday, 0800-1800. Closed Sunday. Wildcat Stores holds fishing permits for the Dubh Loch, Loch Bad na Scalaig and more than 30 hill lochs to the east of Gairloch (see Fishing section).

Eating Out: EWE & ME TAKE AWAY. There is a take-away shop situated down the lane to the right of Ewe & Me. The Menu includes fish & chips, chicken, burgers, haggis, pies, baked potatoes, sausages, tea, coffee and milk shakes.

GAIRLOCH HOTEL. Tel. (0445) 2001. This grand Victorian hotel overlooking Loch Gairloch serves morning coffee, afternoon tea and bar lunches from 1230-1400. A superb table d'hote dinner is available from 1900-2100. The hotel is open from April to October and credit cards are accepted.

GAIRLOCH SANDS HOTEL. (0445) 2131. The hotel coffee shop serves coffee, tea, snacks and full meals throughout the day from 1000-2100. A special children's menu is available. In the evening there is a take away pizza service. The hotel is open all year.

THE MILLCROFT HOTEL. Tel. (0445) 2376. The hotel is situated in the centre of the village, with fine views over Loch Gairloch to the mountains of Torridon. Bar food is available throughout the day from 1200-2200, all year round. A la carte dinner is offered from 1900-2200, April to October only. Children's meals are available. The menu usually includes a good selection of fresh local seafood and dinner reservations are advised.

THE MOUNTAIN RESTAURANT. Tel. (0445) 2316. Located next to The Nature Shop in Strath, this is a great place to stop for a bite to eat. The restaurant serves a range of food from tea, coffee and light snacks to complete meals. At lunchtime there is a good variety of different types of Ploughman's Lunches, or why not try some of their amazing range of unusual scones which includes peach, pineapple and Orkney Cheese. The restaurant also has a mouthwatering selection of original sweets with enticing names such as the "Torridon Toboggan Run" and the "Northern Lights". At night, you can dine by candlelight. The restaurant is open daily from 0730-2400, Easter until the end of October; and from 0830-2200, November to Easter.

MYRTLE BANK HOTEL. Tel. (0445) 2004. Situated by the sea in the centre of Gairloch, this family run hotel serves bar lunches from 1230-1400 and bar suppers from 1830-2030. Morning coffees and delicious cream scone teas are also available and a table d'hote dinner menu is offered from 1900-2030. The hotel is open all year.

THE STEADING RESTAURANT. Tel. (0445) 2449. This pleasant coffee shop and restaurant is located in an attractive stone farm steading next to the Heritage Museum. The Steading serves a variety of food from tea, coffee and light snacks to complete meals. Main courses begin from around £3.95. The restaurant specialises in local seafood and the menu usually includes Vegetarian haggis. Special dishes are also available for children. The restaurant is licensed, so you can enjoy a drink with your meal. The restaurant is open from Easter to September. Opening hours: Easter to May, Monday-Saturday, 0900-1700; June to September, Monday-Saturday, 0900-2100. Closed Sunday. Credit cards are not accepted.

Tourist Information Centre: Tel. (0445) 2130. During the summer months, the centre is open Monday-Saturday, 0900-1900 and Sunday, 1000-1800. In winter, open Monday-Friday, 0900-1700. The centre sells a selection of local maps and books and also has general information about other parts of Scotland. Staff can offer free advice and information on the local area and a range of useful leaflets are available. The centre also operates a "Book-A-Bed-Ahead" service, which is a good way of ensuring advance Bed & Breakfast or hotel accommodation in this popular area. Staff can locate establishments with vacancies and make reservations for you. Bookings are normally accepted up to 24 hours in advance. A small fee is charged for national

Gruinard Bay

An Teallach and Mellon Udrigle beach

bookings and may also be charged for local bookings. Bureau de Change facilities are available at the centre.

Bank: THE BANK OF SCOTLAND. Tel. (0445) 2015. Open Monday-Friday, 0915-1230 and 1330-1645. Cash advances are available from Visa, Access, Mastercard and Eurocard credit cards. The bank has an outside cashline machine which accepts the following cards: Bank of Scotland, Royal Bank of Scotland, Barkleys Bank and Lloyds Bank.

Bike Hire: Bikes are available for hire from THE MOUNTAIN RESTAURANT, 7 days a week, 0730-2100. Tel. (0445) 2316. The restaurant can supply both mountain and leisure bikes. Mountain bikes cost £12 per day. 1/2 day, evening, daily and weekly hire is available and maps, locks, route suggestions, insurance and trail snacks can be supplied. Group/family and Y.H.A. Member discounts apply. Credit cards are accepted. Mountain bikes can also be hired from the GAIRLOCH SANDS HOTEL. Tel. (0445) 2131.

Cruises: SAIL GAIRLOCH offers skippered cruises on board a traditional 7 berth ketch. 4 and 8 hour cruises are available for groups of up to 5 people at an all inclusive price and it may also be possible to arrange shorter cruises for groups of 2 to 5 people. Overnight cruises are charged per berth. Life-jackets and harnesses are supplied. You can choose to relax on deck and watch the abundant bird and sea life of the Inner Sound and its islands - porpoises and seals are often seen - or you can learn how to skipper the yacht. For full details, telephone (0445) 2326. Credit cards are accepted.

Golf: Gairloch Golf Club. Tel. (0445) 2407. Situated on the left of the A832, between Charleston and Gairloch. There is a large carpark for guests. This is a 9 hole, 3994 yards, par 62 links course. It is open daily, including Sunday, all year round There are teeing off restrictions on Sundays between 1030 and 1115 and also on competition days. The shop and clubhouse are open from Easter to late September. Tea, coffee and various snacks may be purchased from the clubhouse. The current fees are as follows: weekly ticket - £45; daily ticket - £10; Senior Citizens and Under 18's - £5. Clubs can be hired for £5 and trolley hire is also available for £1.

Watersports Hire: Various items of watersport equipment are available for hire from the GAIRLOCH WATERSPORTS CENTRE. Tel. (0445) 2131. The Centre is part of the Gairloch Sands Hotel. Here you can try windsurfing, water skiing, paragliding and canoeing. Tuition is available in all the above sports and a high power rescue boat is always on stand by.

Pitch and Putt: Glebe Park Playing Field. Open 0900-1700 daily, except Sunday, weather permitting. From mid-June onwards. Adults £1.50, children £1.00. Clubs and balls are available for hire for a small deposit. Enquire at Gairloch Hardware or Parry's Mace Store. There is a children's play area adjacent to the putting green.

Library: Gairloch Branch Library. Open Monday, 1500-1700 and 1800-2000; Friday 1500-1700 and 1800-2000. Books may be borrowed by visitors free of charge by arrangement with the Librarian.

Petrol: GAIRLOCH GARAGE. Open Monday-Saturday, 0900-1800. Closed Sunday. Credit cards are accepted for petrol.

Toilets: The main public toilets are located in the Community Hall, adjacent to the Tourist Information Office in the centre of the village. These toilets include facilities for the disabled. There is also a small toilet block just outside Gairloch Golf Club.

GAIRLOCH TO MELVAIG AND THE RUA REIDH LIGHTHOUSE

The original road from Gairloch to Melvaig was partly funded by the Gairloch Destitution Committee which was set up to ease the poverty caused by the potato famine in the mid 19th century. The B8021 branches left at Gairloch and continues westwards along the coast, passing through the hamlet of Strath. A series of small roads on the right lead to the communities of Mial, Smithstown and Lonemore. Directly across Loch Gairloch the cottages of Badachro can be seen, while out to sea there are spectacular views of the Trotternish peninsula on Skye.

The road now skirts the edge of an attractive moor, with a coastline of rocky cliffs to the left, and before long the attractive stone building of Carn Dearg Youth Hostel is seen to the right of the road. The public footpath to Big Sand Beach lies to the left of the road, just past the hostel. The path is marked by a green sign. Unfortunately, there is no carpark and parking on the grass verge can be tricky. Big Sand is an excellent beach for swimming and watersports activities, being protected from The Minch by Longa Island which lies just off-shore. The long expanse of immaculate sand is backed by impressive dunes, making this an ideal place to stop for a picnic lunch. From Big Sand Beach, the road heads inland, passing Sands Holiday Centre on the left.

Shopping: There is a small supermarket at SANDS HOLIDAY CENTRE. Tel. (0445) 2152. Opening hours: Monday-Saturday, 0830-1830; Sunday 1000-1200 and 1500-1700. The shop sells bread, milk, groceries, camping equipment, Calor and Camping Gas, books and fishing tackle.

The road becomes single track at Sands Holiday Centre and continues inland, passing over the River Sand in its little rocky gorge. After rain, a small waterfall is to be seen to the right. Shortly after the river, a minor road on the left leads down to the scattered community of Big Sand. Here, amidst the traditional croft houses, are to be seen many modern bungalows. The road ends in a turning circle with good views across the little channel of Caolas Beag to Longa Island, once a retreat of the Vikings. There is also a good view back down the sweeping line of Big Sand Beach, but access is not possible from this point.

From Big Sand, the main road travels further inland, losing sight of the sea. A pleasant drive across attractive moorland brings you back towards the coast and a minor road on the left leads down to the community of North Erradale. This small hamlet used to be quite a sizeable village with its own school. Fishing was an important part of the local economy and the fishermen's boats used to be kept in the little rocky cove of Port Erradale, just below the village. A short distance along the coast to the north lies Uamh an Oir, the Cave of Gold. Legend has it that long ago twelve crofters led by a piper went into the cave in search of gold. They were never seen again, although the sound of the pipes could be heard at Strath, 5 miles away. As you descend to North Erradale, note the beautiful traditional white croft house on the hill to the left. If you wish to stretch your legs, a pleasant 1 1/4 mile footpath to Big Sand begins just to the rear of this cottage. The path passes between the two knolls behind the cottage and crosses the hills above Rubha Ban, before descending to the crofts of Big Sand.

The main road now climbs high above the precipitous coastline and crosses a peat moor. Out to sea there are good views of the Trotternish peninsula on Skye and the hills of Harris. The crofts of Melvaig suddenly come into view ahead as the road dips. Just beyond the village, the public road ends and there is a small parking area with a good view out to the islands.

Rua Reidh Lighthouse

The road beyond the carpark to Rua Reidh is private and only vehicles on official business are permitted access. The old Keeper's Quarters at the lighthouse have recently been turned into an exploration centre and if you would like to visit Rua Reidh, you can call into the lighthouse tearoom on Thursdays and Sundays from 1100-1700. The beautiful views to be had from the coastal road make the trip well worthwhile. From the carpark, the narrow road climbs steeply and then crosses a windswept heather moor. This 3 1/2 mile undulating road is built directly on top of the peat bog and needs constant attention. It is still maintained by the Lighthouse Board, although the lighthouse is now unmanned. There are some sharp bends and small bridges to negotiate but these should pose no problems. Across the Minch, the view to the Hebridean islands is stunning - from right to left can be seen Lewis, the Shiant Isles, Harris, North Uist, Skye and South Rona. The steep cliffs on the left are the haunt of black guillimots, shags, fulmars and kittiwakes. As the road begins to descend, the white and yellow light tower and square Keeper's cottage suddenly come into view to the left. The light tower is now fully automated and the original light can be seen in the Gairloch Heritage Museum. The road terminates at the lighthouse. You cannot fail to be enchanted by the tranquillity of this beautiful spot. If you would like to spend some time here, B. & B. accommodation is available at the Exploration Centre. There is a cosy sitting room with a log fire where you can spend an enjoyable evening looking through the wealth of reference books. If you do decide to stay B. & B., the Centre can provide reasonably priced packed lunches and evening meals, allowing you to explore this remote and rugged coastline at your leisure. The Exploration Centre also runs a series of activity days throughout the summer months. If you are feeling adventurous, why not try your hand at abseiling, climbing, orienteering or a fully supervised overnight mountain camping expedition. All safety equipment is supplied and all levels of ability are catered for. Group discounts and special family rates apply to some activities. For further details, contact Fran Cree or Chris Barrett on (044 585) 263. The Centre also runs residential activity holidays - see Accommodation for details.

As you drive back to Gairloch, look out for the coastal waterfall on your right at Peterburn farmhouse, shortly after Melvaig. The water tumbles over the high cliffs and plummets to the sea below. It can be quite spectacular after prolonged rain.

GAIRLOCH TO POOLEWE

The A832 from Gairloch to Poolewe follows the line of the old road which was constructed in 1825 by Sir Hector Mackenzie, the 11th laird. In the 19th century, the only public road in the region was that which ran from Achnasheen to Aultbea, with a minor branch from Kinlochewe to Torridon. This highway was known as the county road. All other roads in the region were private estate roads, constructed and maintained by the estate proprietors with contributions from their tenants.

As soon as the A832 leaves Gairloch, it turns inland and begins to climb steeply. At the top of the hill, there is a well-placed carpark to the left which looks down upon the village and gives a panoramic view across Loch Gairloch to the Badachro peninsula and the Isle of Skye.

From the carpark, the road climbs gently over a bleak moorland dotted with bare gneiss and scree. Loch Feur and Lochan nam Breac can be seen to the left. An area of forestry is passed on the right and then the road enters a narrow glen and begins to descend. As the road emerges from the glen, stunning views are to be had across Loch Tollaidh to the hills at the foot of Loch Maree. "Loch Tollaidh" is Gaelic for "Loch of the Hollow".

To the right of the road lies a flat mossy area which is known as Blar na Fala - "The Plain of the Blood". It was here that the local people used to gather their cattle together to be bled. Blood was an important addition to the diet and blood mixed with oatmeal was a common drover's breakfast. This practice was widespread throughout the Highlands and Islands and continued in the Gairloch region until the beginning of the 19th century.

As the road skirts around the north shore of Loch Tollaidh, several small islands can be seen. The island closest to the shore is a crannog, an ancient man-made lake dwelling which was approached by means of a causeway. This artificial island is constructed of stone and rubble raised on a timber platform. The Loch Tollaidh crannog was once a stronghold of the MacBeath clan. When the MacBeaths were driven out of Gairloch by Clan MacLeod in the early 15th century, the crannog became a stronghold of the MacLeods.

The Loch Tollaidh Murders

In 1480, Loch Tollaidh was the scene of a tragic triple murder which was to lead to the establishment of Mackenzie rule in Gairloch. At that time, the Laird of

Gairloch was Allan MacLeod. Allan had three sons by his first wife, the daughter of Alexander Mackenzie, 6th Laird of Kintail.

Allan's second wife was the daughter of MacLeod of Lewis. The Lewis MacLeods had a deep hatred of the Mackenzies and they determined that no-one with Mackenzie blood in them should ever inherit the lands of Gairloch. The two brothers of the second wife therefore plotted to kill Allan and his sons so that the inheritance would fall to them. They sailed across from Lewis and took up residence at Tigh Dige (Flowerdale).

Allan and his family lived on the crannog in Loch Tollaidh. One day, he left the island in his boat and went to fish in the nearby River Ewe. At noon, as the day was hot, he lay down on the hill at Croft and fell asleep. It seems that the MacLeod brothers got word that Allan had left the crannog and so they set out for Loch Tollaidh. When they saw his boat moored at the east end of the loch, they rightly determined that Allan had gone down the river to fish. They sought him out on the hill and killed him where he lay. The brothers then cut off his head and threw it into the river. The hill at Croft was thereafter known as Cnoc na mi-Chomhairle which means "The Hill of Evil Council".

The MacLeod brothers then took the boat and sailed to the crannog. After telling Allan's distressed wife what they had done, the MacLeods grabbed two of her step sons and bundled them into the boat. As fortune would have it, the third step son was not at home on that day and he therefore escaped the gory fate that awaited his siblings. The MacLeods carried the struggling boys to a rocky cliff above Loch Tollaidh and killed them. They then stripped the bloody shirts from the boys and buried their bodies close by the cliff which was thereafter known as Craig Bhadan an Aisc or "The Rock of the Place of Interment". The MacLeods took the shirts back to Tigh Dige as proof of their murderous act.

Meanwhile, Allan's wife had managed to struggle ashore. She hurried to the group of cottages which at that time stood close to the present day Achtercairn. There she sought out an old man who had been a faithful retainer to her husband and told him the terrible story. Under cover of darkness, the old man made his way to Tigh Dige. There, as he peered through a narrow opening in the wall, he saw the blood-stained shirts by the light of the fire. The old man was able to enter Tigh Dige and to take the shirts without being seen. He carried them back to Allan's wife, who in turn took them to the boys' grandfather, Alexander Mackenzie, the Laird of Kintail. Alexander immediately sent his own son, Hector Roy Mackenzie, to the King in Edinburgh. Hector produced the shirts as proof of the terrible deed, whereupon the King granted him a commission of fire and sword for the destruction of the MacLeods. Mackenzie ownership of Gairloch was officially recognised in 1494 when Hector received a grant by charter from the Crown.

It is said that the MacLeod murderers were eventually tracked down and slain by a member of the MacRae clan somewhere between South Erradale and Red Point.

On The Road To Poolewe

After passing Loch Tollaidh, the road crosses a further stretch of moorland. Suddenly, the north end of Loch Maree comes into view and a green sign to the right of the road marks the start of the Tollie Path - a 5 mile footpath which winds its way over the hills to Slattadale on the southern shore of Loch Maree (see Selected Walks). If you wish to admire the view down the loch, there are parking places on both sides of the road, shortly after the green sign. Climb one of the adjacent hillocks for a panoramic view of the mountains on the north shore of Loch Maree. On a clear day you can see all the way back to Glen Docherty at the head of the loch.

If you would like a closer look at the loch, you can take the single-track road to Tollie Farm, an attractive building which is decorated with cartwheels and has a beautiful dovecot filled with white doves. The road continues right down to the water's edge where there is room for several cars to park, but please don't block the turning circle, bridge or launching areas. The little pebble beach here is a good place for a picnic, with views back across the loch to the many islands and, on a clear day, to Glen Docherty.

In the early part of the 18th century, there used to be a turf-built church in Tollie Bay. Turf was once commonly used as a building material throughout Wester Ross. The last turf-built house in Gairloch Parish is believed to have been at Moss Bank in Poolewe. The turf church in Tollie Bay was erected by the Rev. John Morrison who became minister of Gairloch on 1 March, 1711. Rev. Morrison was a Presbyterian and although that system had then been established in the Gairloch area for over twenty years, it seems that some of his parishioners were staunchly Episcopal. These parishioners made life thoroughly miserable for poor Rev. Morrison. He was given no manse and no means of support. Shortly after his arrival in the parish, he was beaten up and held prisoner for three days in a cottage filled with cattle and dung. On another occasion he was even stripped naked, bound to a tree and left at the mercy of the ravenous midges! Rev. Morrison was forced to make ends meet by renting a tract of land at Tollie Bay. Here he built a humble dwelling close to the shore and erected a church of turf next to the shingle beach so that he might continue to conduct his services. While at Tollie Bay, the Rev. Morrison continued to be persecuted. His cattle were stolen and his house was plundered. After six years of misery, including a period in exile in Sutherland, Rev. Morrison's request for transfer was finally approved. On 14 November 1716, the unfortunate clergyman took up duties in another parish.

Beyond the Tollie Farm junction, the main road bends left and descends to the left bank of the River Ewe which flows from the north end of Loch Maree to Loch Ewe. Before long, the quiet village of Poolewe is reached.

POOLEWE AND INVEREWE GARDEN

POOLEWE

The picturesque village of Poolewe lies strung out along the sheltered southern shore of Loch Ewe. The village was formerly called Clive and a document dated 1638 records that it was once a Burgh of Barony. This status entitled the local Baron and his officers to devise local laws and to try criminals and administer justice at the Barony Court. Before the erection of the bridge over the Ewe around 1844, all the crofts on the east side of the river belonged to the separate hamlet of Londubh, which means "the black bog". After the bridge was built, the two communities gradually merged and Londubh is now regarded as part of Poolewe.

Looking at this quiet settlement today, it is hard to believe that at the end of the 19th century it was a bustling port, visited by many small commercial vessels from the Hebridean islands. The importance of the village as a gateway to the Outer Isles is testified by the fact that large sailing packets ran once a week between Poolewe and Stornoway as early as 1756. During the 19th century, Macbrayne's large steamers called into the port once a fortnight and a jetty and large storehouse were erected on the shore of the loch. At this time Poolewe was also an important centre for salmon fishing, the rights being leased to a Mr A.P. Hogarth of Aberdeen under an old charter from the crown. Poolewe was Mr Hogarth's principle station and the salmon handled here was eagerly sought after in London. Early in the season, the salmon would be boiled and then packed in vinegar and sealed in wooden kegs, each keg holding about 32lbs of fish. Throughout the summer, sailing smacks would call twice a week from Aberdeen to transport the kegs, covered in ice, direct to the London markets.

The flat plain between the River Ewe and Cliff Hill to the west of the village was for many centuries the site of a large market known as the Feill Iudha or "Ewe Market". This market was important throughout the district and was even attended by men from as far afield as the Isle of Lewis who would cross The Minch in tiny open boats. The Feill Iudha was discontinued around 1720 when many of the men returning to Lewis were lost amidst a violent storm.

The Church of Scotland at Poolewe is worthy of note, being one of the "Parliamentary Kirks" built by Thomas Telford. Construction was completed in 1828.

From Poolewe comes one of the many strange tales of "Second Sight" to be found in the region. In 1860, the old village smithy and blacksmith's house stood on the east side of Poolewe bridge, close to where the present Pool House Hotel is located. One day, the blacksmith's sickly son returned exhausted from a visit to Gairloch and upon entering the house he sat down on the nearest chair and fainted. When he came to, he was visibly shaken and asked his father to explain why the bridge had been crowded with people. The blacksmith, truly puzzled, told him that there had been no-one on the bridge, but the boy insisted that the bridge had been full of people and that he had had to push his way through them. On the following day, 3 October, there were many small fishing boats out on the water, setting herring nets at the head of Loch Ewe. Suddenly, a storm blew up and a fierce hurricane overturned some of boats and sent others tumbling into the pool under Poolewe Bridge. Anxious friends and relatives rushed onto the bridge to look for their loved ones and so, at the very hour at which he had crossed the bridge on the previous day, the boy's vision came to pass.

Poolewe Ironworks: The Red Smiddy

Poolewe was an important centre for early ironworking. On the banks of the River Ewe, close to the village, lie the remains of the earliest blast furnace in Scotland. This furnace was known as A Cheardach Ruadh, "The Red Smiddy". It seems likely that the Smiddy was built around 1610, some years after the furnace at Letterewe (see Kinlochewe to Gairloch), and that it was probably established not by Sir George Hay himself, but by his factor or manager. The Poolewe ironworks continued in operation until 1670.

Prior to the invention of the blast furnace, iron was produced by simply burning charcoal and iron ore together in a furnace. This resulted in a soft, pasty mass of iron which was high in impurities. By introducing a draught or "blast" of air into the furnace to raise the temperature, a superior molten "pig" iron was produced. The "blast" was provided by bellows driven by a water wheel.

Three natural features determined the siting of the furnace at Poolewe. Firstly, the nearby River Ewe was powerful enough to drive a water wheel. Secondly, the furnace was built at the lowest navigable point of the river so that boats could carry charcoal from the shores of Loch Maree directly to the site (it is estimated that the Red Smiddy would have consumed about 300 acres of trees per annum). Thirdly, the sheltered pool at the mouth of the Ewe was ideal for unloading iron ore and for exporting the finished product by boat.

A visit to the site of the Red Smiddy makes a pleasant evening stroll. Poolewe is also the starting point of an 11 3/4 miles walk to the remote and beautiful Fionn Loch. See Selected Walks for full details of both walks.

Key

1 - Lochewe Service Station
2 - The Chippy Hut
3 - Corriness Restaurant
4 - Taylors of Poolewe
5 - Nirvana
6 - Slioch
7 - Swimming Pool
8 - Poolewe Hotel
9 - Waterside Boat Hire
10 - Pool House Hotel
11 - Community Hall
12 - Inverewe Filling Station
13 - Inverewe Camp Site
P - Parking
PC - Toilets
T - Telephone
PA - Picnic Area

The Tournaig Bard

As you are travelling north through the village, shortly before Inverewe Garden, there is a minor road on the left. Here, by the shore, stands a memorial cairn to Alexander Cameron, the Tournaig Bard, who was well known for his Gaelic songs and poems. Cameron was born at Inverasdale and was the manager of Osgood Mackenzie's farm at Tournaig. The cairn contains an inscription in both Gaelic and English which reads: "Alexander Cameron. The Tournaig Bard 1843-1933 who lived all his long, useful and highly respected life on the shores of Loch Ewe, and whose Gaelic poems and songs earned for him a wide and honoured reputation throughout the north."

Shopping: NIRVANA CRAFTS. Tel. (044 586) 335. This small craft shop has a good range of Scottish books and also stocks beautiful chunky knitwear, wooden toys, framed photographs, jewellery and O.S. maps. In summer, there is usually a small selection of garden plants. The shop has a good range of salmon and trout flies and holds fishing permits for Loch Squod and Loch Tollaidh (see Fishing section). Nirvana is open Monday-Saturday, 1000-1700.

SLIOCH. Tel. (044 586) 412. Located in the new industrial units to the left of the swimming pool. Manufacturers of outdoor clothing. Slioch manufactures a superb range of high quality Goretex and Neoprene waterproofs and polar fleece jackets in a variety of styles. Their robust mountain rescue jackets and salopettes are used by every RAF Mountain Rescue Team in the country and also by many civilian groups. Each garment is available with a variety of optional extras, enabling you to choose the features that suit your individual requirements. Open Monday-Saturday 0900-1200 and 1300-1700. Wholesale and retail sales. Credit cards are accepted and mail order is available.

TAYLOR'S OF POOLEWE. Tel. (044 586) 240. V.G. Stores. Small licensed supermarket stocking general groceries, bread, milk and postcards. There is an in-store bakery which sells freshly baked bread, cakes and pastries. Summer opening hours (June, July, August): Monday-Saturday, 0900-2000; closed Sunday. Out of season: Monday-Saturday, 0900-1800; closed Sunday. The supermarket also incorporates a Post Office which is open on Monday, Tuesday, Wednesday and Friday, 0900-1300 and 1400-1700; Thursday 0900-1300; Saturday 0900-1230.

Eating Out: THE CHIPPY HUT. A takeaway kiosk which has a great selection of fresh fish and chips. Open from 1700-2000 daily (out of season: 1700-1900 daily).

CORRINESS RESTAURANT. Tel. (044 586) 262. This licensed restaurant specialises in seafood and uses only the finest local produce. The mouth-watering range includes lobster, scallops, cod, monkfish, langoustines, crab and mussels. If you are vegetarian, there is usually a vegetarian dish of the day or you could try their delicious broccoli and Stilton quiche. Food is served from noon onwards, Monday-Saturday and from 1230 on Sundays. Last orders are at 2100. The restaurant is open all year and credit cards are accepted. The adjacent bar is a pleasant place for a pre-dinner drink.

POOL HOUSE HOTEL. Tel. (044 586) 272. This attractive white-washed hotel is situated on the edge of Loch Ewe. Bar lunches are served from 1200-1400 and bar suppers from 1800-2030. Morning coffees and afternoon teas are also available. In the evening, a table d'hote dinner menu is offered from 1900-2030. The hotel is open from April to October and credit cards are accepted.

Boat Hire: WATERSIDE BOAT HIRE. Tel. (044 586) 420. Located on the B8057, opposite the Poolewe Hotel. 12ft and 14ft boats are available for hire by the hour or longer. Full safety equipment is provided.

Swimming Pool: POOLEWE SWIMMING POOL. Tel. (044 586) 345. Located at Clifton, just off the B8057. A recently built indoor heated pool, with adjacent carpark. Open Monday-Friday, 0900-2000; Saturday 1000-1600. Closed Sunday. Adults £1.50; Under 5's 60p; Children 90p; O.A.P.'s 60p. Throughout the week there are various sessions for men, women, the general public, adults, parents & toddlers and the over 60's. Contact the pool for current session times.

Petrol: LOCHEWE SERVICE STATION. Tel. (044 586) 239. Open daily 0900-2000, including Sunday. The small shop has a tea and coffee machine and a cool drinks cabinet and also sells bread, milk and sandwiches. Credit cards are accepted. The garage has excellent mechanics and if you are having engine trouble, this is the place to go for efficient and friendly service.

INVEREWE CARAVAN SITE. Tel. (044 586) 249. Open Easter-September only. Petrol is sold Monday-Saturday from 0900-1700 only, although the National Trust shop remains open later. Closed Sunday. Credit cards are accepted. A good selection of shrubs, conifers and heathers are usually on sale next to the shop.

24 Hour Vehicle Recovery Service: LOCHEWE SERVICE STATION. Tel. (044 586) 239.

Toilets: On the B8057, opposite Nirvana Crafts.

INVEREWE GARDEN

No trip to Poolewe is complete without a visit to the world famous Inverewe Garden. The garden is open all year round from 0930 to sunset and there is also a Visitor Centre which is open Monday-Saturday, 0930-1800 and Sunday, 1200-1800. Admission: Adults £2.80, Children £1.40, Senior Citizens £1.40. There are special rates for groups. You can join the National Trust at the Centre and if you do, your entrance fee will be refunded immediately. If you arrive after the Visitor Centre has closed, you can leave your entrance fee in the "honesty box" and enter the garden by a side gate. The Visitor Centre holds fishing permits for Loch A' Bhaid-Luachraich, Loch Ghiuragarstidh and Loch nan Dailthean (see Fishing section).

The Visitor Centre has an informative display on the origins of the garden and here you can purchase the Trust's own reproduction of *"100 Years In The Highlands"* by the garden's founder, Osgood Mackenzie. There is also an excellent shop which has a good selection of Scottish books, postcards, cards, preserves, pottery, fudge and an unusual "wild flower" range of place mats, tea towels, tea cosies, aprons, etc. If you are looking for an unusual gift for a gardening friend, the shop sells a range of wild flower seeds, including some from the garden's own stock. There are also frequent plant sales. Toilets, including a separate toilet for the disabled, are located within the shop.

Eating Out: Inverewe has a pleasant self-service restaurant which looks out over Loch Ewe, so you can happily spend all day wandering around the garden at your leisure. Between 13 May and 1 September, the restaurant is open Monday-Saturday, 1000-1700 and Sunday 1200-1700. From 29 March to 12 May and 2 September to 20 October, the opening hours are Monday-Saturday, 1030-1630 and Sunday 1200-1630. The restaurant is closed during the winter months. You can pop in for a cup of tea or coffee and choose from a range of reasonably priced cakes, scones and sandwiches, or you can have a hot lunch or salad. The restaurant is licensed, so you can enjoy a glass of wine with your meal. A vegetarian option is often available and there are 1/2 price portions for children. The restaurant is non-smoking and toilets are located within the building. A ramp provides wheelchair access.

The Garden

It seems almost a miracle that such an oasis of exotic plants can exist amidst the barren landscape of Gairloch. Inverewe lies close to the 58th parallel, just 4 degrees south of the Arctic Circle. Within the garden, sub-tropical plants flourish at the same latitude as Siberia and as you wander through the lush foliage it is easy to forget that you are on the north-west coast of Scotland. This remarkable garden owes its creation to the ingenuity and foresight of one man, Sir Osgood Mackenzie, a son of the 12th Chief of the Clan, who acquired the Inverewe Estate in 1862 when he was just twenty years old. When Mackenzie came to Inverewe, only one windswept willow tree grew amidst the heather and crowberry on the otherwise barren rocky promontory of Am Ploc Ard (The High Lump). The sparse soil was black acid peat, most of which had been stripped by the crofters for fuel. Mackenzie wanted to build his dream garden in this inhospitable place and he began by erecting a deer and rabbit fence which enclosed the south and west facing areas of the promontory. He then planted a large shelter belt of trees to protect the promontory from the cold north-west winds - only the low-lying northern tip of Lewis lies between Inverewe and Labrador. Next, it was necessary to provide a rich growth medium for his exotic plants and shrubs and Mackenzie therefore imported fertile soil from Ireland by boat The success of the garden owes much to the endurance of the local crofters who carried the soil for the flowerbeds up from the shore in their fishing creels. Similarly, seaweed was also gathered from the rocks and carried to the garden for fertiliser. Aided by the favourable climatic conditions created by the warm tail end of the Gulf Stream, Mackenzie was gradually able to develop a green paradise of rare and unusual plants.

When Osgood Mackenzie died, the work was carried on by his daughter, Mrs Mairi Sawyer, who sometimes used rather unorthodox gardening methods in establishing some of the more temperamental plants. The garden today contains *myosotidium nobile* - beautiful giant forget-me-nots from the Chatham Islands. When these were first planted, they were struggling for survival and all attempts to revive them proved unsuccessful. Then Mrs Sawyer happened to read an article in *The Times* by a sailor who had recently returned from the Chatham Islands. The sailor stated that he had been truly amazed to see giant forget-me-nots flourishing along the shores of the Chathams amidst rotting seaweed and the decaying bodies of sharks. Upon reading this, Mrs Sawyer immediately rushed out and re-bedded the dying plants in seaweed and then gathered pails of herring fry left behind by the tide to use as a mulch. The plants flourished from that day on. It is also said that Mrs Sawyer buried the body of a wild-cat, shot while disturbing a chicken coup, under an ailing *buddleia asiatica*. The bush, which had been 3/4 dead, was covered in blooms the next year and has since gone from strength to strength.

In 1952, only a year before her death, Mrs Mairi Sawyer presented the garden to the National Trust For Scotland. When the Trust took over, Inverewe received around 3,000 visitors a year. That figure has now risen to over 120,000.

Today, the garden contains a wide range of trees, shrubs and flowers. Eucalyptus, Monterey pines, flame flowers, Himalayan lilies, orchids, cabbage palms and Chilean Glory Flowers are all to be found here. March is the month for magnolia trees and in August the pretty flowers of the hydrangeas burst forth. In spring and early summer the garden is awash in a blaze of colour from plants common in Scotland - azaleas, heather, primulas, daffodils and various rock plants. Even when the main flush of summer colour is over there is still plenty to see and the multitude of rhododendrons provide year round foliage interest. There are several viewpoints within the garden which give splendid views over Loch Ewe and the well-stocked greenhouses are also open to the public. The attractive white-walled mansion house may be viewed from the outside only. This was built in 1936 to replace the original house erected in 1865 by Osgood Mackenzie which was unfortunately destroyed by fire. Some of the main paths around the garden are suitable for wheelchairs. It is well worth purchasing a copy of the Trust's excellent guide to the garden. This booklet recounts the history of Inverewe and describes two circular tours which you can take, one lasting 1-2 hours and the other 3/4-1 hour. The guide also includes a detailed listing of the botanical names of the plants to be seen in each section of the garden.

The boundaries of Inverewe extend far beyond the famous garden, encompassing a variety of habitats, including moor, loch, river, woodland and shoreline. During the summer months, the Trust operates a series of guided walks which will enable you to explore these habitats and to learn about their associated flora and fauna. There are a variety of walks to choose from, including a mystery wildlife hunt, the wildlife of moorland and loch, the moors beyond the garden, the 5 lochs walk and a moorland stroll. A fee is charged to help defray the cost of providing the Ranger service. For full details, contact the resident Trust Administrator, Professor Douglas Henderson, on (044 586) 200. During July and August, Inverewe Garden also holds a series of illustrated talks.

POOLEWE TO COVE

The single-track B8057 to Cove forks left from the main road at Poolewe and winds its way northwards along the west shore of Loch Ewe. This is another of the "Destitution Roads" which were built in the mid 19th century to provide employment for the local populace and so relieve the suffering caused by the potato famine.

Just as you are leaving the village, note the first house on the left after the Poolewe Hotel. This three storey grey-harled building, Cliff House, used to be the village manse. Cliff House was erected around 1760 and from then until 1773 it was the home of Reverend John Dounie, the minister of Gairloch. During his incumbency, the famous English traveller Thomas Pennant visited Poolewe and after hearing Reverend Dounie preach in the church at Tollie Croft (now gone), he stayed the night with him at Cliff House. The house remained in use as a manse until 1803. Cliff House takes its name from the rocky bluff behind, Meall a' Cliuth, which translates as "Cliff Hill".

As the road continues along the shore, there are good views across Loch Ewe to the tree covered promontory of Inverewe. From this angle, with the bare windswept hills rising all around, you can truly appreciate the great effort which was needed to establish a sub-tropical garden in such an inhospitable place.

Ewe Salmon Farm is passed on the right, close by the Boor Rocks which lie just offshore. The fish cages belonging to the farm are usually to be seen in the vicinity of the rocks. A short distance on, there is a World War II gun emplacement to the right of the road, from which there is a splendid view down the loch.

The cliffs on the left begin to drop away and the little settlement of Naast comes into view ahead. Naast is a Norse name which means a castle or fort. It is believed that there was once a Viking stronghold here. From Naast, the road continues along the shore to Inverasdale, with its striking red sandstone boulder coastline. The crofts of Brae and Midtown lie strung out along minor roads to the left. Midtown is the starting point of a 10 1/2 mile walk to the deserted farms of Loch an Draing and Camustrolvaig. See Selected Walks for full details.

Shopping: INVERASDALE GENERAL STORES. Located on the left of the main road. Sells general groceries and also stocks Camping Gas.

Shortly after passing through the scattered village of Inverasdale, the beautiful red sand beach at Mellangaun comes into view. This long sweep of sand looks out over the north end of the Isle of Ewe and parking is possible on the firm grassy area at the back of the beach. The rocky headland at the north end of the beach is known as Meallan na Ghamhna. Tradition has it that a large cache of weapons was once hidden in a cave here. The cave was rendered invisible by a charm known as the "sian". The "sian" was effected by means of an incantation and sometimes by use of a magical amulet. The spell had one drawback: any object rendered invisible would reappear briefly once in every seven years. At the end of the 19th century, it is said that the wife of Murdo Cameron of Inverasdale and several other women were collecting lichen from the rocks at Meallan na Ghamhna. Suddenly, the cave filled with weapons appeared before them. They ran back to the village to tell their menfolk, but by the time they had returned with helpers, the cave had disappeared once more.

The road now continues past the crofts of Mellangaun which lie dotted about the headland on the right. On the other side of this headland, in the little bay of Camas Allt Eoin Thomais, lies a smaller sandy beach. Before long, the quiet village of Cove is reached.

Church Cave

On the coast just beyond Cove lies a sea cave which was used by the locals as a place of worship up until the 1920's. Many such natural features were used in this way by the Free Kirk which split from the Established Church in 1843 for the sake of spiritual independence. As you leave Cove the road begins to climb and a traditional white cottage ("Sonas") and several caravans come into view on the left. At this point the road reaches the crest of a little hill and parking is possible for two or three cars on the grass verge to the right. Continue along the road on foot for a short distance until you see a style on the right which contains a yellow marker pointing the way to the cave. Climb the style, skirt around the edge of the farmer's field and then climb a second style. Directly ahead is a small grassy headland from which there is a good view out over the loch. Wild violets, cornflowers, clover and heather are all to be seen here. When the tide is out, a small secluded sandy cove appears just to the left of the headland - an ideal place for a quiet picnic. The cave lies to the right of the headland, down a well worn track. There are a few rock-cut steps to negotiate. The cave is quite large and once your eyes get used to the dim light you can see all the way to the back wall. There used to be a wooden floor, pulpit and pews but these have long since been broken up. In his book *"Gairloch and Guide To Loch Maree"*, J.H. Dixon describes the cave as it appeared in 1886: "It is a romantic place with its old desk, and stones and pieces of wood arranged for seats, the nest of a mavis or thrush on a ledge of rock, and the narrow entrance veiled by a tangle of woodbine and eglantine.". A photograph of the original interior can be seen at the Gairloch Heritage Museum. There is also a small sea-cut cave just to the left of Church Cave.

The Rubha nan Sasan Lookout Station

The road now passes through the village of Cove and terminates at the cliffs of Rubha nan Sasan. The hillside at the end of the road is covered with the remains of a World War II lookout station which was set up to guard the sheltered anchorage of Loch Ewe. From here, a watchful eye was kept on the convoys of ships which departed the loch for America and Murmansk in Russia. The two buildings which housed the large guns remain largely intact and in them you can still see the metal plates and bolts which fixed the guns to the ground. The associated lookout buildings are also intact and dotted about the hillside are the remains of pathways and the bases of many more buildings. The site is a fascinating place to wander around and there are several spots by the side of the road where parking is possible. Resist the temptation to enter the buildings, however, as many of them are now in an unsafe condition. (For further details of wartime activity on Loch Ewe, see Poolewe to Aultbea and Mellon Charles). On the cliffs to the right of the road at this point there is a hydrographic survey pillar. It is well worth climbing up to the pillar to take in the panoramic view of Loch Ewe. Two sea arches are also visible.

POOLEWE TO AULTBEA AND MELLON CHARLES

The road from Poolewe to Aultbea is another of the "Destitution Roads" which were built in the mid 19th century to provide employment for the local populace and so alleviate the poverty caused by the potato famine.

As the A832 climbs north out of Poolewe, it passes a small loch on the left which contains a little island topped by a beautiful rhododendron bush - an escapee from Inverewe Garden. A short distance ahead, the larger Loch nan Dailthean is passed on the right.

Shopping: GARDEN COTTAGE NURSERY. Tel. (044 586) 339. Down a signposted track on the right of the road, just after the loch, lies the Garden Cottage Nursery. If you are a keen gardener or are looking for a gift for a gardening friend, this is worth a visit. The nursery stocks a range of shrubs, heathers, conifers, alpines and herbaceous plants, some unusual. It is open Monday-Saturday, 1200-1900, from mid March to mid October. A mail order catalogue is available.

Shortly after the nursery, the sheltered anchorage of Loch Thurnaig comes into view on the left. This is a sea loch which opens out into the much larger Loch Ewe. By the shore can be seen a tall brick tower and associated buildings which date from the Second World War. The road now climbs high above the shores of the loch and there is a carpark on the right from which there is a spectacular view back across the water to the distant mountains. The ranges of Fisherfield, Letterewe, Flowerdale and Torridon crowd the horizon. An information plaque identifies the peaks which can be seen from this point.

The road continues to climb, giving splendid views across Loch Ewe to the Isle of Ewe, which is said to be the dwelling place of the "wee folk" or fairies. The highest hilltops at the north end of the island are known as the "Sitheanan Dubha" which means "The Black Hillocks of the Fairies". A parking spot on the left looks down upon the village of Aultbea, or Allt Beitha, whose row of white houses hugs the bay to the right of Aird Point. A string of crofting settlements lie scattered along the shore to the left of Aultbea.

Wartime Activity On Loch Ewe

The deep sheltered waters of Loch Ewe were of strategic importance to the Royal Navy as an assembly point in both the First and Second World Wars. During the First World War, the loch was the base of the Tenth Cruiser Squadron which was commanded by Vice-Admiral Tupper. The squadron was comprised of armed merchant-men, most of them great ocean-going liners. The Tenth Squadron was responsible for patrolling up to the Arctic ice to intercept possible German intruders.

During the Second World War, Loch Ewe became the base of the Home Fleet due to the vulnerability of Scapa Flow. Since its heyday in 1919 when it had been home to the Grand Fleet, Scapa Flow had virtually been abandoned and its defences had been allowed to run down. The vulnerability of the base was reinforced when U-Boat U-47 commanded by Gunther Prien entered the Flow on 14 October 1939 and torpedoed HMS Royal Oak, killing 833 of her crew. This disastrous occurrence led to the billeting of the Home Fleet on Loch Ewe. From here, minesweepers patrolled the approaches to Loch Broom and Gairloch and merchant convoys gathered to sail to America and Murmansk in Russia. The Germans, well aware that the British Fleet could no longer use Scapa Flow, employed submarines to mine other possible anchorages around the north-west coast. On the 4 December 1939, mines laid in Loch Ewe by U-Boat U-31 sunk two minesweepers and badly damaged HMS Nelson, forcing the crippled battleship to anchor in the loch to carry out temporary repairs. This event was a major blow to the British. HMS Nelson was one of the two most powerful battleships in the British Navy during World War II. The Nelson and her sister ship, HMS Rodney, were the only new battleships allowed under the terms of the Washington Treaty and both were heavily armoured and fitted with nine powerful 16in guns. Each gun weighed over 100 tons and could fire a 2,000lb shell a distance of 40,000 yards.

The tranquil scene today belies the fact that this sheltered coast is still of great value to the military, receiving regular visits by N.A.T.O. warships and their auxiliary vessels. As the road descends to Aultbea, note the entrance to the N.A.T.O. Oil Field Depot on the right, at the hairpin bend. If you look back as you pass the depot, you can see the landscaped hillside which contains the oil storage facilities. The grey pier jutting out into the loch also belongs to the military.

AULTBEA

Situated down a minor road to the left of the A832, the little village of Aultbea lies strung out along a sheltered bay, overlooking the Isle of Ewe. Aultbea is an anglicisation of the Gaelic "Allt Beitha" which means "The Burn of the Birches". In 1893, an ambitious proposal was put forward to extend the railway from Achnasheen to Aultbea but this plan was shelved in favour of cheaper lines to Mallaig and the Kyle of Lochalsh. During the Second World War, the increased naval activity in the area brought great prosperity to the Aultbea community and gave rise to several fine hotels.

If you follow the road through the village and turn left at Pier Road and then right, you will arrive at a picnic area which has good views up the loch and across to

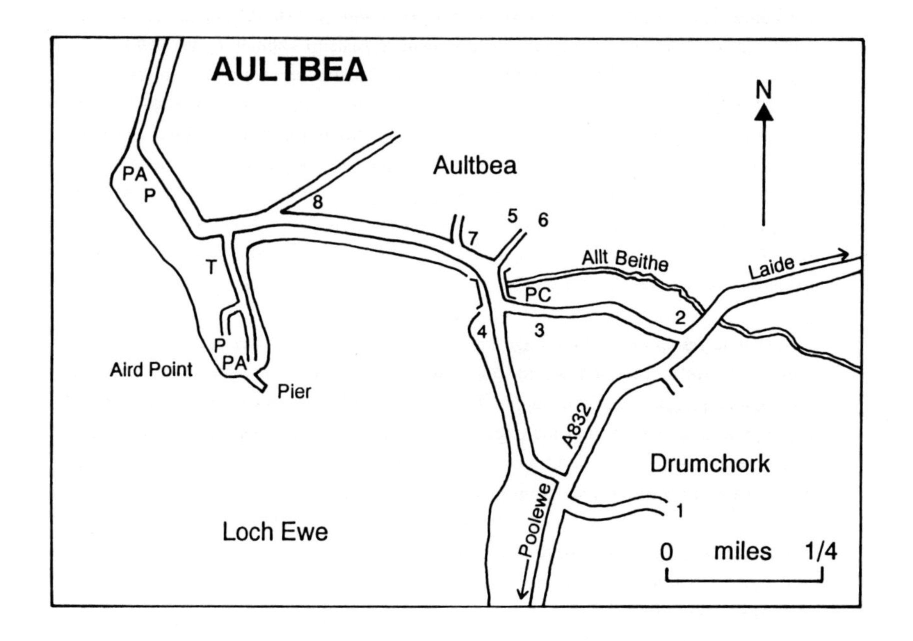

<u>Key</u>

1 - Drumchork Hotel
2 - Aultbea Butchers Company
3 - Aultbea Woodcraft
4 - Aultbea Hotel
5 - Bridgend Stores/Petrol
6 - A. Forbes & Sons Garage
7 - Post Office
8 - Aultbea Stores
P - Parking
PC - Toilet
T - Telephone
PA - Picnic Area

the Isle of Ewe. From this point, the two types of land use on the island can be seen quite clearly. The left (south) side of the island consists of undulating farmland while the right (north) side consists of hilly moorland. This difference is due solely to the underlying rock types. The farmland on the south of the island overlies Permo-Triassic sandstone which breaks down to form a calcium-rich soil which is easily cultivated. The north side overlies Torridonian sandstone which breaks down to form acid moorland soils which are useless for agriculture. Centuries ago, the Isle of Ewe was largely covered by woodland. Dean Monro, writing in 1549, states that the dense woodland on both the Isle of Ewe and Gruinard Island provided a good hiding place for thieves and other criminals.

If you rejoin the main village road and take the first left after the football pitch, you will arrive at a second picnic spot which has several picnic tables. The remains of a building dating from the Second World War can be seen adjacent to the carpark. It is possible to skirt around the edge of the football pitch and walk between the two picnic areas. Both of these sites are part of the Ross and Cromarty Naval Trail, but unfortunately, the descriptive plaques are currently missing.

Shopping: AULTBEA BUTCHERS COMPANY. Tel. (0445) 731 357. Situated on the left of the A832, just after the second turn-off to Aultbea. Suppliers of Scotch beef, lamb and pork. The shop carries a range of their own sausages, pies and black puddings and also sells game, freshly baked bread, dairy products, fresh fruit and vegetables. There is also a large stock of frozen foods and fresh fish is often available. Open Monday-Saturday, 0830-1300 and 1400-1730. Closed Sunday.
AULTBEA STORES. Tel. (0445) 731 203. Mace Supermarket. Licensed Grocers and Newsagents. The shop stocks bread, milk, dairy produce, fruit, vegetables and frozen foods. Fresh and locally smoked fish is also sold. Diving air is available. Open Monday-Thursday, 0830-1730; Friday & Saturday, 0830-1900. Closed Sunday.
AULTBEA WOODCRAFT. Tel. (0445) 731 422. This craft shop has an unusual range of beautifully made wooden items including vases, thimbles, lace bobbins, needle cases, house signs, children's toys and decorative fruit. The shop also stocks sheepskins, greetings cards, clocks and barometers and there is a nice selection of framed photographic prints, drawings and paintings. Open April to October, Monday-Friday, 1000-1300 and 1400-1730; Saturday 1000-1230. Closed Sunday.
BRIDGEND STORES. Tel. (0445) 731 204. Licensed Grocers. Also sells petrol, Calor Gas, toys, fishing tackle and camping equipment. Credit cards are not accepted. Open Monday-Saturday, 0900-1300 and 1400-1730. Closed Sunday.

Eating Out: AULTBEA HOTEL. Tel. (0445) 731 201. This is a pleasant place to stop for a snack or a full meal. The hotel is situated right at the water's edge with fine views over Loch Ewe. The Waterside Bistro is open daily from 0900-2100 and here you can enjoy a cup of tea or coffee, home-baking, Danish pastries and various snacks and grills. Children are welcome and there is a special children's menu. On Sundays,

why not try a delicious roast lunch from the Carvery Trolley, which is available from 1230-1500. If you are looking for somewhere special for an evening meal, the Zetland Restaurant offers full silver service table d'hote, a la carte and carvery dinners from 1900-2100. The fine selection of seafood includes local salmon, Loch Ewe lobster, crab and prawns. The hotel is open all year and credit cards are accepted.
DRUMCHORK LODGE HOTEL. Tel. (0445) 731 242. Bar lunches are served from 1230-1400; bar suppers from 1830-2000 and dinner from 1900-2000. Morning coffees and afternoon teas are also available. The hotel is open all year and credit cards are accepted.

Toilets: Turn right just after the Aultbea Hotel. The small toilet block is situated on the left, just after the junction.

Petrol: BRIDGEND STORES. Tel. (0445) 731 204. Pumps are located next to the shop. Petrol and Calor Gas. Credit cards are not accepted. Open Monday-Saturday, 0900-1300 and 1400-1730. Closed Sunday.

24 Hour Vehicle Recovery Service: A. FORBES & SONS. Tel. (0445) 731 200.

On The Road To Mellon Charles

As the road leaves Aultbea, note the ancient raised beach on the right. The beaches of the current coastline are formed of attractive red sandstone pebbles. There are good views across Loch Ewe to the hills opposite and, after rain, the waterfall on the Abhainn Ur can be seen behind the village of Inverasdale. The road continues to wind its way along the coast, passing the settlement of Bualnaluib which is situated up a minor road on the right. Beyond Bualnaluib lies the crofting community of Ormiscaig and here is to be found the base of the Aultbea Salmon Farm which has cages out on Loch Ewe.

The villages along this stretch of coast lie close to the Sitheanan Dubha at the north end of the Isle of Ewe and many tales are told of the power of the local fairy folk. The great 19th century piper William Maclean was born at Ormiscaig. It is said that as a boy he was employed in herding cattle on a hill above the village. One day he returned home with a bagpipe chanter and to everyone's amazement, he could play to perfection. Maclean said that he had been given the chanter and the ability to play from the fairy folk. William Maclean later emigrated to Chicago where he won many piping competitions. This belief in the power of the fairy folk to confer skill in bagpipe playing is common throughout the north-west Highlands and Islands.

The road now continues on to the strangely named village of Mellon Charles. The word "mellon" is an anglicisation of the Gaelic "meallan" which translates as "hillock". In the 19th century, villagers here often reported seeing eerie lights and hearing strange music emanating from the nearby Sitheanan Dubha. Beyond Mellon Charles, the road terminates in a turning circle. From this point, a distinct peat track heads towards the deserted village of Slaggan (see Aultbea to Laide and Mellon Udrigle) which lies some 1 1/2 miles distant. The peat track disappears after 3/4 of a mile and the rest of the way is over rough moorland, but there are good views across to the Inverasdale Peninsula and to the islands of Lewis and Harris. If you decide to do the walk in this direction, parking can be tricky. There is a small quarry cutting on the left, just before the end of the road where there is room for one car to pull off.

AULTBEA TO LAIDE AND MELLON UDRIGLE

The A832 continues past Aultbea and climbs up over a high moorland which is beautiful in August when the purple heather is in full bloom. It is worth pulling into the carpark which is situated on the right at Druim Breac Summit, the highest point on the road. From here there are panoramic views of the surrounding countryside and the distant mountains. An information plaque on the knoll behind the carpark identifies the peaks which can be seen from this point. The road now descends past an area of forestry and a sign for "Old Smiddy Holidays" is seen to the right. Fishing permits for 22 hill lochs in the Aultbea area are available from the Old Smiddy (see Fishing section). Shortly after the Old Smiddy, a minor road branches left at the petrol station to Laide and Mellon Udrigle.

LAIDE

The village of Laide looks out across the quiet water of Gruinard Bay which is protected from The Minch by the peninsula of Rubha Mor or "Big Point". From this tranquil spot there are spectacular views to the mountains of Coigach and Assynt. Close to the shore lie the picturesque ruins of the ancient Chapel of Sand. This site has a long association with Christianity - local tradition says that the chapel was constructed by St Columba back in the 6th century. A small road on the right descends to the chapel and there is room to turn and park by the graveyard gate. Part of the intricately carved window arches of the chapel are still intact and a large remnant of arch can be seen on the left, just as you walk in the door. The walls are cemented with lime manufactured from burnt shells.

Shortly after the chapel, the next road on the right leads down to the village jetty. About half way down there is a small parking space with a picnic table which has a spectacular view out over Gruinard Bay to the hills of Assynt and Beinn Ghobhlach on the Scoraig peninsula. Close to the village jetty can be seen the remains of the old salmon station. In the 19th century, this station was part of the important Gairloch salmon industry which was leased by Mr Hogarth of Aberdeen (see Poolewe and Inverewe Garden for further details).

Shopping/Petrol: R. MACLENNAN GENERAL STORES. Tel. (0445) 731 252. Access and Visa Cards are accepted for petrol. The small shop sells general groceries and fishing tackle and also incorporates a Post Office. Open Monday-Saturday, 0830-1300 and 1400-1730. Closed Sunday.

On The Road To Mellon Udrigle

From Laide, the single-track road continues along the coast and crosses a beautiful moorland. Before long, the houses of Achgarve can be seen dotted about the hillside on the left. Shortly after passing the junction to Achgarve, another road, marked by a blue metal sign, branches left. This is the road to the deserted village of Slaggan. The sign states that the road is suitable for rough terrain vehicles only, but it is used frequently by fishermen and the road surface is kept in a reasonable state of repair and should pose no problems for most vehicles. The biggest difficulty is that there are very few places where you can pull off the road to let other vehicles pass. If you would prefer to walk to the village, there are two parking areas in quarry cuttings on the right of the main road, just past the Slaggan turn-off. There is also a large pull-off on the right, about 100 yards down the Slaggan road. The round trip to Slaggan is a good expedition for walkers and mountain bikers. See Selected Walks for full details.

The main road continues past the turn-off to Slaggan and a small loch is seen on the left. This is Loch na Beiste or "The Loch of the Beast". Legend has it that this loch was once the home of a fearsome kelpie or water-horse. One Sunday morning in 1840, as the village elders were on their way to church, the beast rose out of the water to terrify them. The elders, frightened for their lives, approached the laird and asked for permission to drain the loch. This was granted but, despite repeated attempts, the loch remained full to the brim. The elders next decided to kill the monster in its lair, which they believed to be in the deepest part of the loch. Soundings were taken from a boat and a deep hole was located in the middle of the loch. The elders ferried fourteen sacks of lime to this spot and tipped them in. The beast was never seen again.

The road now descends to Mellon Udrigle. The word "mellon" is an anglicisation of the Gaelic "meallan" which means "hillock". Just before the village is reached, another road branches left to the scattered community of Opinan. A short distance after this junction, there is a small carpark on the right which has room for about a dozen cars. From here there is access to the beautiful white sand beach of Camas a' Charraig. This broad sandy bay with its sparkling blue-green waters looks across to the mountains of Coigach and Assynt. From left to right can be seen Quinag, Suilven, Canisp, Stac Pollaidh, Cul Mor, Ben Mor Coigach and Beinn Ghobhlach on the Scoraig peninsula. At the far end of the beach lies a small rocky promontory which is excellent for birdwatching.

The beach at Mellon Udrigle is the starting point of a leisurely coastal walk around the Rubha Beag or "Little Point". See Selected Walks for full details.

LAIDE TO DUNDONNELL

From Laide, the A832 continues around the coast, giving good views across Gruinard Bay to Gruinard Island.

Eating Out: OCEAN VIEW HOTEL. Tel. (044 582) 385. Signposted; situated down a minor road to the right, shortly after the Laide junction. Bar meals are served from 1200-2130 and morning coffees are also available. The hotel restaurant specialises in fresh local seafood and a table d'hote dinner is offered from 1930-2130. Dinner reservations are preferred. The hotel is open from March to December.

Church Cave and Old Woman's Cave

Shortly after you pass the road to the Ocean View Hotel, you will see two houses on the right. The road then bends sharp right and a carpark comes into view on the left, just by the "Sheep" roadsign. Park here and walk along about 1/2 way to the next carpark, looking out for a small wooden post on your left. This post marks the beginning of the path down to the caves. The short track is quite distinct and there are several steps towards the bottom. When you reach the shore, the caves are just to your left. The first cave is quite small now, the floor being considerably raised by decades of accumulated sheep dung. The remains of a rough sandstone wall can be seen stretching across the mouth of the cave. This is the Old Woman's Cave. When William Jolly visited the cave in 1886 in the course of research for Dixon's *"Gairloch and Guide to Loch Maree"*, it was home to a seventy year old woman and a young girl. The front of the cave had been crudely enclosed by a wall of stones, turf and cloths. A peat fire burned close by the door on the left, while to the right lay the old woman's bed, protected from the sky above by the overhanging rock. She declared that the place was more comfortable than it looked. Jolly writes, "As she drank her simple cup of tea from the top of a box, after putting some clothes to dry upon the shore, with her wrinkled but intelligent face, her Gaelic Bible her only literature, the wild rocks round, and the splash of the restless waves in the ear, this simple, solitary old woman looked as picturesque and pathetic an object as I had ever seen, much more so than the wildest of gipsies at a camp fire."

A short distance further on lies Church Cave, a much larger cave, and similarly popular as a sheep shelter. It is surprisingly warm and dry inside. Like the cave at Cove, this was once used regularly by members of the Free Kirk. The pews were constructed of boulders from the adjacent beach. The remains of a well built dry stone wall stretch across the entrance, protecting the cave from the elements. This wall once contained a door and the cave was kept under lock and key. When you have finished looking at the caves, the rocky shoreline at this point is full of interesting nooks and crannies to explore.

On The Road To Gruinard

The A832 continues past the scattered crofts of First Coast and Second Coast. In Gaelic, these settlements are known as Bad an t'Sluig and An t'Eithire Donn which mean "The Grove of the Miry Puddle" and "The Brown Shore". The road now climbs up over a bleak landscape of bare rock hummocks. Just as you begin to descend, there is a small parking area on the left from which there is a spectacular view of Gruinard Beach and the hills beyond. The low-lying ground towards the sea is comprised of a mass of rounded gneiss hillocks which contrasts markedly with the red Torridonian sandstone beyond. From this point, the raised beach in Gruinard Bay can be clearly seen. Raised beaches mark the positions of ancient shorelines which were formed as the land rose after the end of the last Ice Age.

The road now descends steeply and crosses first the Little Gruinard River which flows down from Fionn Loch and then the Inverianve River which flows from Loch a' Mhadaidh Mor. Just after the Inverianve River, there is a large parking area on the right. Directly opposite lie the steps which lead down to the beautiful red sand beach of Gruinard. Here, if there are not too many people about, you may see the heads of inquisitive seals bobbing up and down in the water. The name Gruinard comes from the Norse "Grunna Fjord" which means "Shallow Fiord".

The carpark at Gruinard is the starting point of a 3 3/4 miles walk which follows the Inverianve River to its headwaters, passing several attractive waterfalls along the way. See Selected Walks for full details.

Gruinard Island

After the carpark, the road cuts inland and crosses the Gruinard River which flows out from Loch na Sealga. You have now entered the Parish of Lochbroom which has as its capital Ullapool. Shortly after re-emerging at the coast, there is a parking area on the left. This is the closest mainland point to Gruinard Island and from here you have an excellent view to the shore opposite. This small island, lying barely 3/4 mile offshore, was used during the Second World War by the Ministry of Defence for an experiment in germ warfare. Intelligence reports suggested that the Germans were investigating the use of biological toxins as offensive weapons and government scientists were instructed to determine whether such weapons were possible. To do this, sheep were tethered around the island and a cannister of the deadly virus "Bacillus anthracis" was exploded remotely to gauge the effect on the animals. Within a few days, all the sheep were dead. Further trials with the anthrax virus proved beyond all doubt that biological weapons were indeed possible. These macabre experiments ceased after the war, but that was by no means the end of the story. Relations between the Government and the local people were not improved when local sheep became infected with the virus. The island was visited frequently by Government scientists and it soon became clear that the anthrax spores could live on in the soil for anything up to 1,000 years. Gruinard was therefore declared unsafe and warning signs were placed at regular intervals around the shore. This situation continued until recently, the Government being unwilling to spend the money necessary to clean up the island. Continual protests eventually resulted in the organisation of a clean-up operation in 1987 and in 1990 Gruinard Island was declared safe by the Ministry of Defence.

On The Road To Dundonnell

The road swings inland and climbs up over heather moorland, passing an area of conifers to the left. A short distance after the conifers, there is a large parking area on the left from which there are spectacular views of the Summer Isles. A mobile tea and snack kiosk is often to be found here. The carpark also gives a splendid view across Little Loch Broom to the remote Scoraig peninsula opposite. This peninsula is dominated by the distinctive shape of Beinn Ghobhlach and the smaller crag of Cnoc a' Bhaid-rallaich. The scattered crofts of Scoraig near the tip of the peninsula can be reached only by a 4 1/2 mile footpath which winds its way along the coast opposite. There is also an infrequent passenger ferry service across Little Loch Broom from Badluarach. The native inhabitants of Scoraig deserted their homes because of the hardships of crofting in such an isolated spot. The village has since been repopulated by English incomers seeking an "alternative" way of life. Several years ago, one of the new inhabitants caused uproar throughout the Highlands when he burnt the village church to the ground - an incident which is still talked about to this day.

Windmill Tour: Most of the electricity used at Scoraig is generated by windmills and you can learn all about these fascinating mechanisms and see them in action by taking a tour of the village. Tours cost £20 which includes the return ferry from Badluarach and lunch or tea for up to four adults. Visits by larger groups may be made by prior arrangement. For further details, telephone Hugh Piggott on (085 483) 286.

The road descends towards the coast, giving good views across Little Loch Broom. A minor road branches left and passes through the communities of Badcaul and Durnamuck before terminating at Badluarach, from where the ferry to Scoraig can be joined.

Shopping: DUNDONNELL STORES. Situated on the right, a short distance down the minor road to Badluarach. General grocery supplies. Open Monday-Saturday, 0830-1800. Closed Sunday.

The main road continues along the shore of Little Loch Broom. To the right, the scene is dominated by the many peaks of An Teallach - The Forge. It is said that the mountain acquired this name on account of the smoke-like clouds which usually wreath its summit. This huge massif of Torridonian sandstone has as its highest point Bidein a Ghlas Thuill (1,062m). Its eastern spurs are capped by Cambrian quartzite and these form distinctive grey screes similar to those found on Beinn Eighe. In places, the red sandstone weathers to form strange stepped pinnacles which resemble stacked pancakes. These provide excellent scrambling and climbing.

At Ardessie, the road crosses a bridge over the Allt Airdeasaidh and it is worth stopping here to have a look at the waterfalls. The main waterfall can be seen from the bridge itself and you can also follow a track up the left side of the river to view the waterfalls further upstream. Ardessie is the base of Ardessie Fisheries, whose farm cages can be seen out in the loch. The road now passes through Camusnagaul and arrives at Dundonnell at the head of Little Loch Broom. The name "Dundonnell" derives from the fact that Lochbroom Parish was once owned by Clan Donald.

Dundonnell is the starting point of a circular walk which climbs the flanks of An Teallach to view a series of waterfalls. See Selected Walks for full details.

Eating Out: THE DUNDONNELL HOTEL. Tel. (085 483) 204. The hotel is situated on the right of the main road, at the head of Little Loch Broom. The Broombeg Bar within the hotel serves bar lunches from 1200-1430 and bar suppers from 1730-2030. A variety of home baked items are served with morning coffee and afternoon tea. Table d'hote and a la carte dinner menus are offered between 1900-2030. Dinner reservations are advised. The hotel is open between April and October and credit cards are accepted.

Petrol: DUNDONNELL SERVICE STATION. Situated opposite the Dundonnell Hotel. The small shop sells O.S. Maps, photographic film, Camping Gas and Calor Gas. Access and Visa are accepted. To obtain petrol, call in to the hotel bar. Open Sunday-Wednesday, 0900-2000; Thursday-Saturday, 0900-2300.

DUNDONNELL TO BRAEMORE JUNCTION

From Dundonnell, the A832 follows the edge of broad, tree-lined Strath Beag. On the left is the Dundonnell River which flows into Little Loch Broom. This river used to be known as the Little Broom. After some 2 miles, a minor road branches left, heading for Badrallach on the other side of the loch. A short distance along this road is to be found Dundonnell House which was built in 1769. The attractive grounds of this house are planted with oak, sycamore, lime, beech and chestnut and there are beautiful Oriental gardens which are occasionally open to visitors during the summer months. The minor road now crosses the head of Strath Beag and climbs up through an area of forestry, before following the line of the steep crags below Beinn nam Ban. At a hairpin bend, a 1 1/2 mile footpath branches right and descends to Allt na h-Airbhe on the shore of Loch Broom, where a passenger ferry to Ullapool may be joined. From the hairpin bend, the minor road descends steeply towards the community of Badrallach, which nestles at the foot of Cnoc a' Bhaid-rallaich. The 4 1/2 mile footpath to Scoraig begins at the end of the road (see Laide To Dundonnell).

From the Badrallach junction, the A832 continues through Strath Beag and after a short distance, Corrie Hallie Craft Shop is reached.

Shopping: CORRIE HALLIE. Tel. (085 483) 229. Situated on the left of the A832, just after the Badrallach junction. Well signposted. There is a small pull-off adjacent to the shop and a large parking area on the left about 100 yards further on. If you wish to sample the local salmon, Corrie Hallie is the place to go. Here you can purchase both fresh and smoked locally caught salmon. If you want to send some as a gift to friends (or mail some home to yourself!), a mail order service is in operation. The shop also sells various items of craftwork and knitwear. Corrie Hallie is open Monday-Friday, 0930-1800; Saturday 0900-1700. Closed Sunday.

The large parking area just beyond Corrie hallie is the starting point of a strenuous 12 mile walk to the remote Strath na Sealga. See Selected Walks for full details.

The main road now enters an area of attractive natural woodland and follows the course of the Dundonnell River which lies just to the left. Trees to be seen here include birch, hazel, alder, oak and rowan. After heavy rain, torrents of water gush down from the crags opposite and tumble into the river below. There are several parking spots on the left of this stretch of road where you can pull off to have a closer look at the river. As the crags on the left begin to diminish, a pretty cascade is seen in the river and it is possible to pull off by the side of the road to admire the fall. There is a larger waterfall a short distance ahead and it is also possible to park here by the left of the road.

The hills on either side now begin to drop away and the landscape changes dramatically. The Dundonnell River flows along a broad, treeless glen and a desolate heather moorland opens up ahead. The road climbs up over the moor, passing a lonely ruin on the far side of the river. This was once a wayside inn. A short distance ahead, another ruin with an iron roof is seen to the left of the road. The rounded lump of Meall an t-Sithe dominates the scene on the right, while ahead lie the mountains of Fannich. A series of glacial mounds lie scattered across the moorland to the right.

This startling change in landscape is due to a change in rock type. The distinctive peaks of Torridonian sandstone have been left behind and in their place are rounded peat moor hills of schist, a thermally altered rock which has a banded appearance. This metamorphic rock is known as Moine Schist, from the Gaelic word "moine" which means "peat-moor". It was originally derived from the sediments of an ancient sea floor which were compressed and folded and then altered by intense heat and pressure. The Moine Schist dates from between 800 and 1,000 million years ago. Around 420 million years ago, during a period of earth movements known as the Caledonian orogony, the schist was pushed westwards over the top of the sandstone and gneiss on an incline called the Moine Thrust Plane. The Plane is marked by a zone of crushed rock, up to 12 miles wide in places, which runs for 120 miles from Skye to the north coast of Sutherland.

As you continue along the A832, you can see sections of the old road winding back and forth alongside the current road. This is another "Destitution Road" which was built in 1851 to provide employment for the local populace. This helped relieve the poverty and suffering caused by the potato famine and the Highland Clearances in the late 18th and early 19th centuries. Around 1,000 people were involved in the construction of this road.

As the road begins to swing left, Loch a' Bhraoin comes into view on the right. Loch a' Bhraoin is Gaelic for "Loch of the Showers" and it is from Bhraoin that the word "Broom" derives. Lochbroom Parish is surrounded by several large mountain masses. Behind An Teallach rise the ranges of Fisherfield, south lie the hills of Fannich, to the east rise the many tops of Inverlael and to the north are the hills of Coigach. As you continue in towards these mountains, the average rainfall figures increase dramatically and it is this phenomenon that has given Lochbroom its name. The A832 now follows the course of the Abhainn Cuileig and passes two conifer plantations on the right. Behind the trees rise the hills of the Braemore Forest. There are plenty of parking areas on this stretch of road.

Just after the patch of forest on the left, pull into the large carpark for a spectacular view down Strath More to the head of Loch Broom. Strath More is a good example of a "U"-shaped glaciated valley. The broad flat bottom and steep sides were formed when a glacier scoured its way through a pre-existing valley, deepening and widening it. The debris left behind by the glacier creates a fertile plain which is ideal for agriculture, as the patchwork of fields below testifies. For several months each year, Loch Broom becomes a rendezvous point for fleets of trawlers and large factory ships which come here mainly from eastern Europe to fish for herring and white fish. The rich herring fishing to be found in the loch was originally discovered by the Dutch in the 18th century and this led to the construction of curing stations on Isle Martin and Tanera Mor. Despite a decline towards the end of the 19th century, the fishing industry boomed once again during the Second World War when Loch Broom provided a safe alternative to fishing in the mine-laden North Sea. An information plaque in the carpark describes the formation of Ullapool and names the peaks which can be seen from this viewpoint.

Corrieshalloch Gorge

About 1/2 a mile on from the viewpoint carpark, to the left of the road, lies the footpath to the Corrieshalloch Gorge. The path is signposted and there are parking areas on both sides of the road. This footpath involves a steep descent to the gorge below and there are 79 steps to climb on the way back up. This route therefore tends to be quieter than the other footpath which descends from the A835. Whichever way you decide to go, the gorge is well worth seeing. A seemingly precarious suspension bridge spans the rocky cleft and as you gaze down upon the river which gushes far below you, its hard not to feel a little dizzy. The suspension bridge is an amazing piece of engineering and was built by Sir John Fowler, the joint designer of the Forth Road Bridge. Fowler was once the owner of the Braemore Estate in which the gorge is situated.

The statistics of Corrieshalloch are impressive. The gorge is 1.6km long and 60m deep. The Falls of Measach which tumble over a rocky ledge and plunge into the gorge below are 45m high. The Gaelic name "Corrieshalloch" translates as "Ugly" Gorge, which seems most inappropriate for this attractive natural feature. The top of the gorge is lined by a forest of native trees - rowan, whychwood, hazel, birch and alder - while further down, ferns cling to the damp rocky walls. At the very bottom of the gorge, the dim and humid conditions create an ideal environment for colonies of mosses and liverworts. Corrieshalloch Gorge was formed some 13,000 years ago, when the ice was retreating from Scotland at the end of the last Ice Age. As the ice melted, the resulting water gushed down towards Loch Broom with such force that it cut a channel through solid rock. Local legend has it that Corrieshalloch is haunted by a spectral stag and hound which fell into the cleft as one tried to chase the other across the Falls of Measach. Today, the gorge is managed by the National Trust for Scotland.

The A832 continues on to Braemore Junction and here you can see the orange snow gates which are closed when the road behind is impassable. The high moorland between Dundonnell and Braemore experiences severe blizzard conditions in winter and is frequently blocked by drifting snow. At the junction we reach the end of our guided journey. From Braemore, you can either follow the A835 north to the bustling town of Ullapool or south-east to Inverness, the capital of the Highlands.

Part III

Heritage and Environment

SELECTED WALKS

The Gairloch/Torridon region is a walker's paradise. The area includes some of the finest mountain and coastal scenery in Britain with a variety of crags, ridges, peaks and glens to delight people of all abilities. Although most walkers enter the hills adequately prepared, many others are inappropriately equipped and each year the Mountain Rescue Teams have to be called out to locate walkers who are suffering from exposure. There are several important points to remember to minimise your risks in the hills. Weather in the Scottish mountains can change suddenly. What starts out as a warm sunny day at the foot of the mountain can often turn into arctic conditions at the top - snow storms have even been known at the height of summer. Wear strong hill-walking boots and carry with you warm clothing and waterproofs. The wilderness areas of north-west Scotland are on a vast scale and it is often difficult to estimate distance. This can be very dangerous for the walker, leading him or her to over estimate their capabilities. Always carry a map and compass and know how to use them. Take an ample supply of high-energy food with you (e.g. chocolate, fruit, nuts) and eat small amounts frequently - fatigue is often caused by insufficient food rather than over-exertion. When climbing on the high tops, it is also a good idea to take a hot drink. Additionally, you should carry a small first-aid kit, whistle and torch. Ideally, you should leave details of your route and estimated time of return with a responsible person. The Northern Constabulary produce a useful form for you to complete and leave with the police, your landlady or warden etc. Please remember to report your safe return, otherwise you could be the subject of a rescue search!

Weather Forecast: For an up-to-date guide to mountain conditions in the West Highlands, telephone (0898) 654 665.

Country Code: When walking in the hills, please observe the Country Code: Guard against risk of fire; Keep dogs under control (no dogs are allowed on the Beinn Eighe National Nature Reserve); Leave gates as you find them; Keep to paths across farmland; Do not damage hedges, fences or walls; Leave no litter; Do not contaminate water supplies; Do not harm animals, plants or trees; Be careful on country roads; Respect the life of the countryside.

Cairns: Please resist the temptation to build cairns. Existing cairns have been erected for good reason. Some have historical significance, being built by mourners as a mark of respect for the dead as they carried a coffin to its burial place. Others have been strategically placed to mark a division of the path or to guide walkers over indistinct ground in mist. Adding to them can be confusing and is certainly unsightly. Several areas of Britain have been spoiled by indiscriminate cairn building.

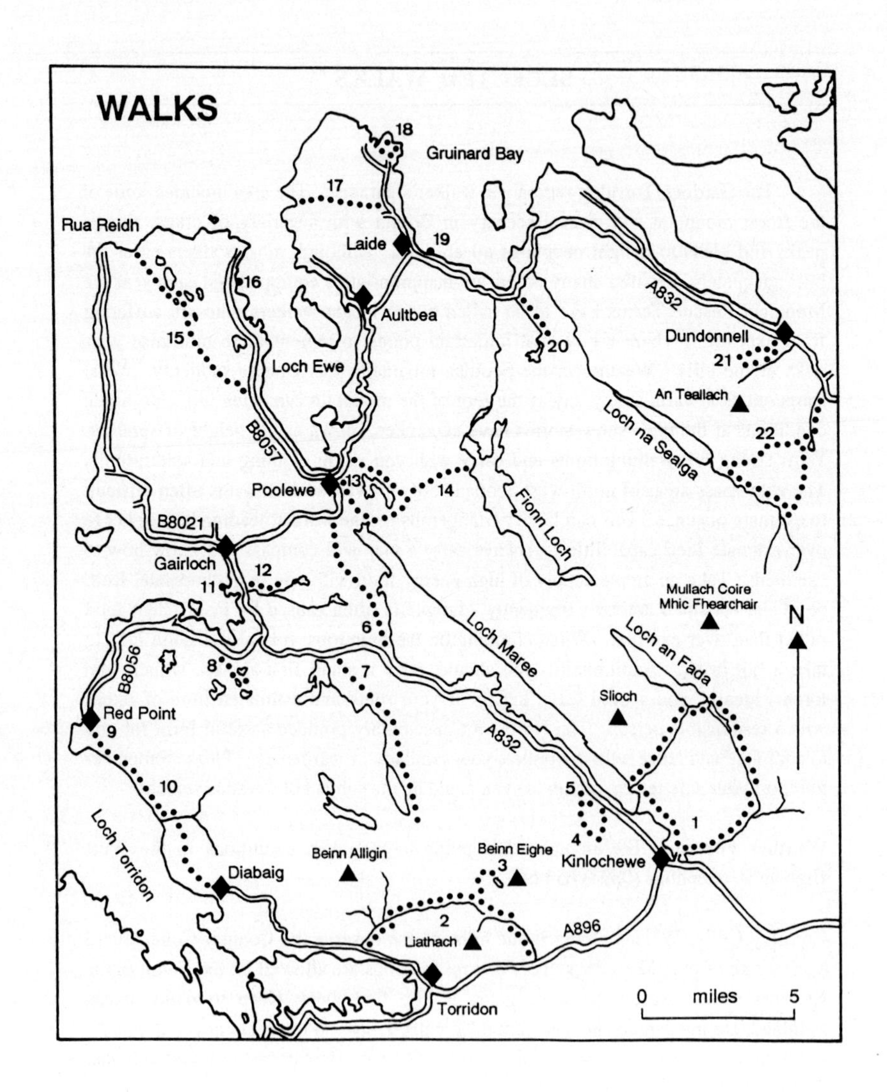
WALKS
Gruinard Bay
Rua Reidh
Laide
Aultbea
Loch Ewe
B8057
A832
Dundonnell
An Teallach
Loch na Sealga
Poolewe
Fionn Loch
B8021
Gairloch
Mullach Coire
Mhic Fhearchair
Loch Maree
Loch an Fada
N
B8056
Red Point
Slioch
A832
Loch Torridon
Diabaig
Beinn Alligin
Beinn Eighe
Kinlochewe
Liathach
A896
Torridon
0 miles 5
1
2
3
4
5
6
7
8
9
10
11
12
13
14
15
16
17
18
19
20
21
22

Stalking Restrictions: Many of the estates in the Gairloch/Torridon area derive a large part of their income from deer shooting. This is an important part of the local economy and gives employment to many local people. The autumn cull takes place between 1 September and 30 November and if you are planning a high moorland walk during this time, please contact the warden nearest to the area you wish to visit for advice on "no-go" zones. Telephone numbers are as follows:

The Manager, Shieldaig Lodge Hotel, Badachro. Tel. (044 583) 250.
Mr I. MacKenzie, Post Office House, Diabaig. Tel. (044 581) 220.
The Ranger, National Trust For Scotland, The Mains, Torridon. Tel. (044 587) 221.
The Warden, Nature Conservancy Council, Anancaun. Tel. (044 584) 254 or 244.
Mr J. Wills, Grudie House, Kinlochewe. Tel. (044 584) 259. If no reply, telephone (044 584) 254 or 244.
The Forester, Loch Maree. Tel. (044 584) 203. If no reply, telephone Achnashellach (052 06) 273.

Selected Walks: The following selection of walks contains itineraries to suit people of all ages and abilities. In addition to strenuous hill walks, attractive coastal and waterfall walks are also included. Each individual entry gives details of the distance and time required for each route, together with an indication of the state of the paths and a recommendation on footwear. Although a general location map is included here, it is strongly advised that the appropriate 1:50,000 Landranger map should be carried on the moorland and hill walks. O.S. Sheet 19 covers most of the walks detailed here. The Coire Dubh Mor walk is split between Sheets 24 and 25 and the Coire Mhic Fhearchair walk is split between Sheets 19 and 25.

1. LOCHAN FADA

This strenuous walk passes through magnificent mountain scenery to reach the remote Lochan Fada on the north side of Slioch. Much of the way is along rough tracks and the ground can be extremely boggy, particularly in the middle section around the edge of the loch. There are several burns to be crossed and these can prove tricky when in spate. After prolonged rain, it may be impossible to cross the Abhainn an Fhasaigh at Lochan Fada. It is therefore better to choose a dry spell if you wish to do the complete circuit via Gleann na Muice. Hill-walking boots are essential. **Distance:** 14 1/2 miles (23 km) for the complete circuit. **Time:** Allow 8 hours for the round trip.

Step By Step: Take the road to Incheril which branches north from the A832 just to the east of Kinlochewe. Turn left at the crossroads and continue until you reach the farm gates. Park by the roadside (Map Ref. NH 033 624), taking care not to block the gates. Follow the road past the farm and take the left hand footpath which cuts north-west through the fields toward the Kinlochewe River. After a short distance, the footpath passes through an attractive woodland on the banks of the river. About 3/4 mile beyond the woodland, a spectacular waterfall is seen plummeting over the crags of Meallan Ghobhar to the right.

The footpath continues on to the south-eastern shore of Loch Maree, passing several patches of attractive deciduous woodland. Beyond the last patch of woodland, Gleann Bianasdail suddenly opens up to the right. This dramatic gorge nestles between the crags of Slioch on the left and Beinn a'Mhuinidh on the right. Magnificent views are to be had down Loch Maree from this point. The Abhainn an Fhasaigh is crossed by means of a small footbridge and thereafter the path splits. Take the right hand branch and follow the course of the river up through the glen.

The footpath through Gleann Bianasdail is distinct for most of the way, but can be marshy in places. There are several burns to be negotiated on this stretch and care should be taken when the path begins to climb high above the banks of the river. Some 3 miles on from the footbridge, the path descends to the shore of Lochan Fada. This beautiful loch is surrounded by spectacular mountains. To the south lies Slioch and to the north-west are the hills of Letterewe and Fisherfield. The great mass of Mullach Coire Mhic Fhearchair rises straight ahead.

Following periods of prolonged heavy rainfall, it may prove impossible to cross the Abhainn an Fhasaigh at Lochan Fada. If this is the case, retrace your steps to Incheril. If you are able to cross, follow the shore of the loch. The path is indistinct here and the ground can be very boggy. There are also several streams to negotiate. After about 3/4 mile, the stepping stones at the eastern end of Lochan Fada are reached. These stones give relatively easy access to the far side of Loch an Sgeireach where a distinct footpath is once again joined. Follow the footpath to the south-east, keeping Loch an Sgeireach and Loch Gleann na Muice just to your right. About 2 1/2 miles on from the stepping stones, the path becomes a track which follows the course of the Abhainn Gleann na Muice and descends to cross the river by a small bridge. Gleann na Muice means "The Glen of the Pig" and it is believed that wild boar were once hunted here. A short distance ahead, the buildings at the Heights of Kinlochewe are reached. From here, it is an easy 2 1/2 miles level walk back along the Abhainn Bruachaig to Incheril. When you reach the road end, follow the footpath to the right which will bring you back round past the farm to your parking spot.

2. COIRE DUBH MOR

This attractive and popular walk passes through National Trust For Scotland land on the north side of Liathach and ends in the vicinity of Torridon House on Upper Loch Torridon. You must either arrange for a car to meet you at the bridge by the waterfall above Torridon House or be prepared to retrace your steps back to the starting point. (It is also possible to begin the walk at the Torridon end - see Torridon to Diabaig). The path follows the course of several waterways and involves only gentle climbing. It is an excellent route for those who wish to experience wilderness walking. The path is distinct for most of the way, becoming vague only in the middle section, but this should pose no problems for the experienced walker. Some sections can be very marshy, particularly after rain, and hill walking boots are essential. **Distance:** 7 1/2 miles (12 kms) each way. **Time:** Allow at least 4 hours in each direction.

Step By Step: Park in the carpark just beyond the bridge over the Allt a' Choire Dhuibh Mhoir in Glen Torridon (Map Ref. NG 958 568). The distinct path begins at the bridge and follows the left bank of the Allt a'Choire Dhuibh Mhoir upstream. On the left tower the crags of Stuc a Choire Dhuibh Bhig and on the right lie the scree slopes of Beinn Eighe. As you climb upstream, the steep hills on either side begin to close in and after some 2 miles you pass through the narrow neck of land between Liathach and Beinn Eighe and cross via a ford to the right bank of the stream. You are now on the hidden north side of Liathach, with splendid views ahead to Beinn Dearg and Beinn Alligin. To the north lies the pass between Beinn Dearg and Beinn Eighe which leads into Glen Grudie.

The path now levels out somewhat and begins to bend left, heading for a small lochan. At the lochan there is a fork marked by a large cairn - keep left (the right branch bends around the shoulder of Beinn Eighe and climbs to Loch Coire Mhic Fhearchair - see below). The path skirts to the right of several small lochans and then the larger Loch Grobaig, before following the course of the Abhainn Coire Mhic Nobuil. This section is usually waterlogged and the path non-existent, but if you keep the river just to your left, you can't go wrong. You now follow the river downstream between the sides of Beinn Dearg and Liathach. About 2 3/4 miles on from Loch Grobaig you will come to the Allt a'Bhealaich stream which flows between the flanks of Beinn Dearg and Beinn Alligin. A path joins from the right and descends to a small bridge which will enable you to cross the main river. From here, a good path follows the left bank of the river to the main road above the woodland of Torridon House. There are several waterfalls on this section of the river, but viewing is difficult. The best waterfall is to be seen from the bridge over the main road, right at the end of the walk.

3. COIRE MHIC FHEARCHAIR

If you love breath-taking wilderness scenery, this walk is not to be missed. Coire Mhic Fhearchair on the north side of Beinn Eighe is one of the most beautiful corries in the Highlands. The walk involves a steep uphill pull but the spectacular destination makes the journey more than worth while. The path is distinct all the way to the corrie and should pose no problems. Hill-walking boots are essential. **Distance:** 10 miles (16 kms) return. **Time:** Allow 5 hours for the round trip.

Step By Step: Park in the carpark just after the bridge over the Allt a' Choire Dhuibh Mhoir in Glen Torridon (Map Ref. NG 958 568) and proceed as for the Coire Dubh Mor walk described above. Follow the distinct path up the left bank of the Allt a' Choire Dhuibh Mhoir and after about 2 miles cross to the right bank via the ford. Continue until you reach the fork in the path marked by a large cairn. Follow the right hand path around the flank of Sail Mhor, one of the heels of Beinn Eighe. This path remains relatively level for about 1 1/2 miles, skirting high above Loch nan Cabar and giving spectacular views into the lochan strewn moorland between the hills of the Torridon and Flowerdale Forests. The path then bends to the right and climbs steeply uphill towards the corrie.

The scene which confronts the walker is truly spectacular. The floor of the corrie is filled by the dark water of Loch Coire Mhic Fearchair which spills out over the lip creating a series of sparkling cascades. The corrie is encircled by a huge cliff which contains three massive buttresses, split from each other by gullies. The lower halves of the buttresses are of red sandstone while the upper halves are of white quartzite. This remarkable feature is appropriately known as the Triple Buttress. The encircling arm on the right is Sail Mhor (981m) which means "Big Heel". The arm on the left is Ruadh-stac Mor which, at 1010m is the true summit of Beinn Eighe. As you look back out from the corrie, Baosbheinn, Beinn an Eoin and Beinn a' Chearcaill can be seen from left to right. Now retrace your steps to the carpark.

4. BEINN EIGHE MOUNTAIN TRAIL

This superb circular trail begins at the Beinn Eighe lochside carpark, just to the north-west of Kinlochewe (Map Ref. NH 002 650). The path climbs to a cairn above Loch Allt an Daraich from which there is a panoramic view of the surrounding landscape. This is an ideal outing for those who wish to experience mountain walking without actually ascending any of the peaks in the area. The cairn is situated only 550m above sea level and yet the views obtained from the top are suggestive of a far greater height. On a clear day, thirty-one Munros can be seen, from Sgurr nan Ceathramhnan 40 kilometres (25 miles) to the south in Kintail, to Ben Wyvis 48 kilometres (30 miles) to the east. The outward section of the trail involves a steep ascent over rock and scree but the descent is both gentler and less strenuous. The path is well marked with cairns. The top can be very exposed, so dress sensibly. Hill-walking boots are essential. An excellent guide booklet which describes features of interest to be seen on the trail is available by the Honesty Box in the carpark, priced 75p. **Distance:** 4 miles (6 1/2 kms) return. **Time:** Allow 4 to 5 hours for the round trip.

5. BEINN EIGHE WOODLAND TRAIL

The Beinn Eighe Woodland Trail begins at the lochside carpark on the A832, just to the north-west of Kinlochewe (Map Ref. NH 002 650). This attractive trail passes through the remnant of ancient Caledonian Pine Forest which is the most important feature of the Reserve. The path is distinct, but is rough and somewhat steep in places. Wellington boots or stout shoes should be worn. The circular route winds its way through Coille na Glas Leitire (Wood of the Grey Slope) and climbs to a height of 110m where there is a viewpoint which looks out over Loch Maree. The path then descends through the forest to the road below. An informative guide booklet which describes the history of the forest and points out features of interest is available by the Honesty Box in the carpark, priced 75p. **Distance:** 1 mile (1 1/2 kms) return. **Time:** Allow 50 minutes for the round trip.

6. THE TOLLIE PATH

This attractive path passes through the Slattadale Forest on the shore of Loch Maree and then climbs up onto the open moorland below the crags of Creag Mhor Thollaidh. The Tollie Path follows the line of the old Contin to Poolewe Military Road which was constructed around 1760 by Major William Caulfield (see Achnasheen to Gairloch for further details). Spectacular views are to be had back across the loch and its many islands. The path is distinct for most of the way but can be boggy in places. The last section crosses high moorland which gives easy walking. There are several small burns to cross en route but these should pose no problems. Hill walking boots are essential. You must either arrange for a car to meet you on the A832 1 1/2 miles south of Poolewe or be prepared to retrace your steps back to the starting point. If you wish to do the walk in one direction only, better views are to be had by starting from the Poolewe end (see Gairloch to Poolewe). **Distance:** 5 1/4 miles (8 1/2 kms) each way. **Time:** Allow 3 hours in each direction.

Step by Step: Park in the Slattadale Forest carpark on the shore of Loch Maree (Map Ref. NG 888 722). The path begins on the shore of the loch and then passes through the edge of the forest, the oldest part of which was planted in 1922. After about 1 1/4 miles, the path emerges onto open hillside . This first section of the walk involves very little climbing and after you have emerged from the trees there are spectacular views back down the loch. After a further 3/4 mile walk across fairly level ground, the path turns inland and climbs steeply to the crags above Tollie Bay at the north end of Loch Maree. After passing several lochans the path descends across the rocky moor to the east of Loch Tollaidh, emerging on to the A832 some 1 1/2 miles south of Poolewe.

7. LOCH NA H-OIDHCHE

Nestling amidst the hills of the Flowerdale Forest lies the remote Loch na h-Oidhche, well known to fishermen for its excellent brown trout. A clear path leads all the way to the bothy of Poca Buidhe at the southern end of the loch. This path is rough in places and can be extremely wet after heavy rain. Hill walking boots are essential. This fairly level walk gives magnificent views of the Flowerdale and Torridon hills. **Distance:** 12 miles (19 1/4 kms) return. **Time:** Allow 5 1/2 hours for the round trip to Poca Buidhe bothy.

Step By Step: Park next to the small building which lies close to Am Feur-Loch on the A832 (Map Ref. NG 856 721). Cross the footbridge opposite and follow the distinct track. This first section of the path passes between the crags of Meall Lochan a' Chleirich on the left and Meall a' Ghlas Leothaid on the right. It then climbs up over the low pass between Meall a' Ghlas Leothaid and Meall na Meine. For the final 2 1/2 miles, the path follows the course of the Abhainn a' Gharbh Choire and descends gently to the shore of the loch. There are several streams to cross on this section and these can prove tricky after prolonged heavy rain. Loch na h-Oidhche has a spectacular setting between the steep flanks of Beinn an Eoin on the left and Baosbheinn on the right and is popular with fishermen seeking the native brown trout. If you wish to extend your walk, the path continues for a further 2 miles along the east shore of the loch and passes the bothy of Poca Buidhe before terminating amidst a group of smaller lochs to the south. From here, retrace your steps to the carpark.

8. U.S.A.A.F. LIBERATOR CRASH SITE

In the hills behind Shieldaig lies the wreckage of a United States Air Force plane which crashed on the 13th June, 1945, with the loss of all on board. The B-24-H Liberator Bomber (Serial No. 42-95095) became lost while travelling home and collided with a rocky bluff, killing the 9 crew and 6 passengers. Most were between the ages of 20 and 25. The crew belonged to the 66th Bomb Squadron, 44th Bomb Group (H). Today, the site is a war grave and the wreckage of the plane has been left exactly as it was discovered all those years ago as a reminder of the bravery of the passengers and crew who were returning home to the U.S.A. after a long and brutal war. Access to the site is by an estate road and then a footpath which winds its way up the hill behind Shieldaig. The footpath can be very muddy in places and wellington boots or hill-walking boots are recommended. **Distance:** 2 1/2 miles (4 kms) return. **Time:** Allow 1 hour 20 minutes for the round trip.

Step By Step: Park in the carpark just after the Shieldaig Lodge Hotel on the B8056 (Map Ref. NG 806 725). Walk back along the road for a short distance until you reach an estate road which branches right. Follow this road over the burn and past the old steading buildings on the left. After about 5 minutes walk, a small cairn marks a footpath which branches left from the road. Follow this distinct path up the hill. Height is quickly gained and the view back towards Gairloch begins to open up.

Shortly after crossing a small burn, a rusty sign for the "Fairy Lochs" is seen on the left. Keep right, following the direction of the arrow. After climbing up a small rise, the first Fairy Loch comes into view on the left. Follow the distinct path which skirts around the loch and climbs over another rise before passing between two rocky knolls. As the path turns left, the crash site comes into view. With the loch on your right, the wreckage lies strewn down the hillside ahead and to the left. Pieces of twisted metal are scattered over a wide area and some sections of the aircraft, including part of the propeller, lie within the loch. The path now descends to a memorial which was set up by the families and friends of the deceased. Today, even after so many years, the place has an air of tragedy and great sadness. Please remember that this is a war grave and on no account should any of the wreckage be removed.

If you wish to have a view of the surrounding countryside, climb up onto the little knoll above the wreckage. From here you can see Baosbheinn in the Flowerdale Forest, Beinn Alligin, the Isle of Skye and Gairloch. Retrace your steps to the carpark.

9. REDPOINT FISHING STATION

The beautiful sandy beach at Redpoint lies at the end of the B8056. Most people head straight for this first beach, which is easily seen from the road above. If you are looking for somewhere quieter, there is a second beach hidden on the other side of the promontory, from where you can walk on to the Redpoint Fishing Station. The route follows a farm track and cuts across grassy fields, suitable for any type of footwear. This level coastal walk gives magnificent views across the Sound of Raasay to Skye and Rona and down Loch Torridon to the remote Applecross peninsula. **Distance:** 2 1/2 miles (4 kms) return. **Time:** 40 minutes return.

Step By Step: Park in the beach carpark at Redpoint on the B8056 (Map Ref. NG 732 688). Go through the wooden gate at the left of the carpark. This is also the start of the 7 mile public footpath to Diabaig. The isolated Craig Youth Hostel is 5 miles from this point. Continue down the farm track past Redpoint Farm, go through the gate and then follow the faint track over the grassy fields. You can either head straight down to the beach or keep left to emerge at the Redpoint Fishing Station. Total walking time from the carpark to the Station is 20 minutes. The Fishing Station is still in use, the main catch being salmon. Behind the buildings are the tall poles between which the nets are hung out to dry. On the beach, just to the left of the Station is an interesting collection of rusty anchors. The long stretch of red sand beach is beautifully clean and is an excellent spot for birdwatching: herring gulls, black backed gulls, oystercatchers, ringed plovers, pied wagtails, gannets, rock pipits, eider ducks, herons and cormorants can all be seen here. If you are lucky, you may also spot the rare red-throated diver. Lying just off-shore are three small islands. Two of these are intermittently covered by the sea but the largest, Eilean Tioram, has a grassy top and can be reached at low tide. Out to sea there are beautiful views to the Isle of Skye and South Rona. To the left lies the Applecross Peninsula and Loch Torridon. You can just make out the rocky headland which encircles Loch Diabaig. If you have binoculars, scan the coast ahead and you will see two old crofts at the foot of a tree-lined gorge. The isolated Craig Youth Hostel lies hidden further back in the gorge. Retrace your footsteps to the carpark.

10. REDPOINT TO DIABAIG

If you wish to extend the above walk beyond the fishing station at Redpoint, the public footpath continues on to Diabaig. You must either arrange for a car to meet you at Diabaig or be prepared to retrace your steps to Redpoint. The rough path keeps close to the shore and gives level walking for most of the way, but it can be very muddy after rain. There are also several major streams to cross and these can prove tricky when in spate. Hill walking boots are essential. **Distance:** 7 miles (11 1/4 kms) each way. **Time:** Allow 4 hours in each direction.

Step By Step: Park in the beach carpark at Redpoint on the B8056 (Map Ref. NG 732 688). Go through the wooden gate at the left of the carpark and continue down the track past Redpoint Farm. Go through the farm gate and follow the faint track across the fields to the Fishing Station. Beyond the station, the path crosses a large stream and then heads towards the Craig Youth Hostel, keeping close to the shoreline. There are a further six streams to cross on this stretch of the walk. This coastal path gives panoramic views across the Sound of Raasay to Skye and South Rona.

The path turns inland and follows the course of the Craig River uphill, eventually crossing it by means of a bridge close to Craig Hostel. It is 5 miles from Redpoint to Craig. From here, the path continues up the hill behind the hostel, passing close to Lochan Dubh on the left. It then crosses the high moorland behind Diabaig. There are three streams to negotiate on this section of the walk. Keep a look out for the wild goats which frequent the hills above Diabaig. These goats are descended from domestic herds which were once kept for their milk. The path eventually emerges by the Post Office hut in Diabaig. The section of path from Craig Youth Hostel to Diabaig is 2 miles in length.

11. AN DUN

Gairloch Pier is the start of a short pleasant walk to the site of the ancient fort of An Dun and the broad sandy beach beyond. The path is sealed for most of the way and is suitable for any type of footwear. **Distance:** 1 1/4 miles (2 kms) return. **Time:** Allow 40-50 minutes for the round trip.

Step By Step: Park in the carpark at Gairloch Pier (Map Ref. NG 808 752). The path begins further down the pier, just to the left of the M.V. Kerry Cruises office. Climb the concrete steps and follow the winding path which is sealed for most of the way. The first section involves a steep pull up the little promontory of An Ard but the path soon levels out and gives good views across the harbour to the Shieldaig-Badachro coastline beyond. The path descends to the beach and arrives at a small grassy headland which juts out into the sea.

This headland is known as "An Dun". A dun is a small fortified homestead of thick dry-stone wall construction. Although not much remains to be seen of the fortification today, a few interesting facts may be determined from the scant remains. The dry-stone wall enclosed a roughly circular or oval area about 65 feet in diameter. The natural gullies on the eastern side of the headland were artificially deepened to increase the defensive capabilities of the dun. Excavations from similar sites suggest that within the dun, small timber structures would have been built against the inner face of the wall to provide shelter for the inhabitants. It is likely that the site would have been further fortified by several lines of outer stone walls which restricted access to the headland. The tumbled remains of the walls which flank the entrance on the southern side show traces of vitrification. Vitrification (the fusing together of rocks and boulders through intense heat) occurs when timber lacing within a dry-stone wall is set on fire. Dry-stone walls were sometimes laced with timber to give additional strength but it is not known whether the timber was fired deliberately to further stabilise the structure or whether the firing was the act of an aggressor. The use of timber lacing within the wall may date the dun to as early as the 7th century B.C. and occupation may have continued until the 2nd century A.D. The dun was probably home to several inter-related family groups.

In common with many other duns, An Dun was reoccupied at a later date. The site became a stronghold of the MacBeaths, probably sometime in the 13th century shortly after their arrival in the area from Assynt. When the MacBeaths were driven out of Gairloch by the MacLeods in the early 15th century, the fortification became a stronghold of Clan MacLeod. The "Castle of Gairloch" as it was known, remained in the possession of the MacLeods until the middle of the 16th century when they were driven out by the Mackenzies. Nothing remains to be seen of the fortification today. Back in 1886 however, low banks of loose stones could still be distinguished on top of the rocky knoll and these may have been the remains of the castle walls.

From this headland there are good views across Loch Gairloch to Gairloch and Strath. The immaculate sandy beach beyond is a good place for a picnic. From here you can either retrace your steps or continue along the beach until you reach the obvious path which is lined by pine logs. This path takes you past the Golf Club and on to the main A832 road, from where you can walk back along the pavement to Gairloch Pier. If you wish to visit the beach and fort without climbing An Ard, park in the Golf Club carpark and follow the short path just to the right of the toilet block.

12. FLOWERDALE HOUSE AND WATERFALLS

Charleston is the starting point of a private road which takes you past the old mansion of Flowerdale to view two waterfalls on the upper reaches of the Flowerdale River. The road is sealed as far as Flowerdale Mains Farm. The track beyond the farm can be very muddy and wellington boots are recommended for this section. **Distance:** 3 miles (4 3/4 kms) return. **Time:** Allow 1 hour 20 minutes for the round trip.

Step By Step: Park in the public carpark opposite The Old Inn (Map Ref. NG 811 752). The beautiful old red sandstone footbridge which leads across to the Inn used to be much wider - if you look over the right hand side of the bridge you can see the original stone piers which supported the road. The original bridge was badly damaged in floodwater and this is a reconstructed version. The main Gairloch road used to pass over this bridge and run between the Inn and the white cottage on the right.

Proceed on foot down the minor road marked "Private Road". This is the road to Flowerdale House and although cars are not permitted, pedestrians are welcome. After a short distance you will see two small reed filled lochans on the right. When the river is in spate, these two lochans merge into one. This is the favourite haunt of a grey heron and if you are quiet you may spot him fishing in the shallows. By the left of the road, built into the hillside, is the old ice house belonging to Flowerdale House. Ice houses acted as primitive refrigerators. Towards the end of the winter, ice would be collected from shallow man-made ponds and placed within the ice house. If the house was well built and packed correctly, the ice would remain frozen for several months and blocks could be chipped off when required.

The road now continues past the large white mansion of Flowerdale. Flowerdale is the ancient seat of the Mackenzies of Gairloch. This beautiful house was built in 1738 by Sir Alexander Mackenzie, the 9th Laird and it was the first house in the area to have a slated roof. Flowerdale was damaged by cannon fire in 1746 when a Government naval vessel was sent to Gairloch to punish the Highland people for the popular uprising which culminated in the Battle of Culloden. This seems to have been a totally cruel and unjust act on the part of the Government as Sir Alexander had taken no part in the rising. It is said that one of the cannon balls, an 18lb shot, remained stuck in the seaward gable end of the house for many years after this event. In the mid 1800's, Flowerdale House was the home of the Dowager Lady

Mackenzie. It was Lady Mackenzie who hit upon the idea of building the many "Destitution Roads" in the Gairloch area to help relieve the poverty and suffering caused by the potato famine of 1846-48. Flowerdale was restored and extended to its present form in 1904.

Up until the 19th century, Flowerdale House was known as "An Tigh Dige", which means "The Moat House". This name refers to the original home of the Mackenzies which stood in a field below the present house. The Tigh Dige was built by Hector Roy Mackenzie, the 1st Laird, who succeeded to his title in 1494. It was a "black house", built of turf with a roof of sticks and divots and surrounded by a moat. This remained the family home until the middle of the 17th century when the 6th Laird, Kenneth Mackenzie, built a more substantial building on the same site. This second building continued in use until the present house was erected in 1738. Both of the earlier houses have been completely destroyed by agricultural operations.

In the field below Flowerdale, just to the left of the old driveway, can be seen a raised circular plot of land. This is known as the "Island of Justice" and it was here that the Laird used to preside over the trials of local criminals. The island was once surrounded by a deep moat and access to it was by means of a small wooden foot-bridge. The Laird stood at a large tree at the centre of the island, while four of the principal clansmen stood at trees around the perimeter. The clansmen acted as the jury. The suspect, accuser and witnesses all stood at trees close to the island. If a criminal was condemned to death, the sentence was carried out on a small hill overlooking the old Gairloch Churchyard. This place was known as "Cnoc a Croiche" which means "Gallows Hill". This form of justice continued until the 18th century.

The road turns left by the beautiful old stone stable block of Flowerdale House, now used by Highland Trails (see Gairloch). This stable block was known as the "Sabhal Geal" which means "The White Barn". It was built in 1730 by Sir Alexander Mackenzie, the 9th Laird, and it is the earliest dated barn in northern Scotland. The Mackenzie coat-of-arms can be seen above one of the windows. One of the figures on the coat-of-arms (wearing tartan trews) is Donald Odhar, the great MacRae archer. An example of his great skill with the bow is given in the following story. It is said that one day a boat manned by the MacLeods sailed into the bay at Charleston with the intention of attacking the Mackenzies. Donald Odhar was on a hill behind Flowerdale House known as Craig a Chait, "The Rock of the Cat". With his keen eyesight, he spied one of the MacLeods climbing the mast of the ship for a better view of the surrounding country. Taking careful aim, Donald let fly an arrow and pinned the unfortunate MacLeod to the mast. The arrow had travelled a distance of a 1/2 mile! The Latin motto "Fidelitatis Proemium" on the Mackenzie Coat-of-Arms means "Loyalty Above All" and refers to the faithfulness of Donald Odhar.

As the road continues, a large white house is passed on the left. Note the traditionally built crow-stepped gables. Just as the road turns right, a small track leads to a building which is known as The Temple House. This used to be the residence of Flowerdale's head gardener. Although now much altered, the style of the original entrance and windows suggest that this building dates to before the 16th century Reformation. It may have been the residence of the priests of the early Gairloch Church.

The road now crosses a burn and continues on to Flowerdale Mains Farm. At this point the tarmac road ends. If you wish to continue, cross through the wooden farm gate and follow the well made farm track. Just after you go through the gate, look across the burn to the hillside on your right. Here, immediately behind the stone farm wall, the land rises to form a low ridge. This ridge is comprised of an extremely rare rock type, known as a banded iron formation, and this is the only one known in Britain. The rock is made up of stripes of grey quartz and a black iron oxide called magnetite, which is magnetic. This formation was deposited on the ocean floor by hot springs some 2,200 million years ago at a time when the earth's atmosphere did not contain oxygen.

The path now continues through an area of devastated forest and eventually reaches a fork in the river. This last section of the walk can be very muddy. Each branch of the river contains a spectacular waterfall and both are seen to best advantage by crossing over to the neck of land between them. This can be tricky when the river is in spate. If you wish to extend your walk you can climb above the waterfalls by following the steep path up the left side of the river. After rain this muddy path can be treacherous and care is needed. Now retrace your steps to the carpark.

13. POOLEWE IRONWORKS: THE RED SMIDDY

In the 17th century, Poolewe was an important centre for ironworking. The site of the earliest blast furnace in Scotland lies on the bank of the River Ewe, a short distance from the village. A visit to this important archaeological site makes a pleasant stroll. (For more details of the Red Smiddy, see Poolewe and Inverewe Garden). The walk follows a sealed minor road, suitable for any type of footwear. **Distance:** 1 3/4 miles (2 3/4 kms) return. **Time:** Allow 35 minutes for the round trip.

Step By Step: Park in Poolewe village carpark (Map Ref. NG 856 808). Walk back to the A832 and cross the bridge over the River Ewe. Now take the minor road opposite the Pool House Hotel and follow it along the bank of the river. Go through the gate marked "Londubh Common Grazing". The road is private from this point on and cars are not permitted. Continue along this road until you pass a beige harled cottage on your left. The driveway of the cottage is marked by painted white bricks and there are topiary bushes flanking the gate. About 250 yards further on, as the road bends left and just before the power lines cross your path, you will see a large area of ferns to the right. Take the grassy track between the ferns and continue down to the river bank. Turn left and follow the bank for a short distance until you come to a pile of white stones. Amidst these stones you can still see the remains of an oval building. Immediately to the left of this (i.e. away from the river) lies a rectangular hole set into a knoll. This is all that remains of the furnace. It is constructed of sandstone and in 1852 the chimney was still standing to a height of 8-10 feet. An archaeological excavation carried out in 1980 revealed that the furnace building was 20ft square with a thatched roof and originally stood about 20ft high. The furnace would have been loaded by shovelling in charcoal and iron ore at the top. At the base of the structure there were two openings. Into one was inserted the nozzle of the bellows which provided the air for the "blast". The other was kept closed during firing and was then opened to let the molten iron flow out.

Small pigs of cast iron were discovered in a flat area to the north of the furnace and this may have been deliberately formed to give a level surface on which to mould the iron. Several other iron articles and pieces of rough clay bricks have also been found in the vicinity of the furnace. Note also the stone structure in the river ahead. This is all that remains of the weir which originally spanned the river from bank to bank, maintaining the water power needed to drive the bellows of the blast furnace. It is said that the weir also acted as a bridge, giving access to the furnace from the other side of the river. The weir was broken up and rebuilt as salmon cruives sometime prior to 1830 and these were subsequently demolished in 1852 to lower the water level and drain an area of land at the head of Loch Maree. As you retrace your steps, just as you pass the oval building, look out for a large mound on your right which is devoid of ferns. This is a huge heap of slag. If you wish to extend your walk, you can continue along the track to Fionn Loch (see below). A full reconstruction of the Red Smiddy can be seen at the Gairloch Heritage Museum.

14. FIONN LOCH

Poolewe is the starting point of a circular walk to the isolated and beautiful Fionn Loch which lies between the hills of Letterewe and Fisherfield. Much of the walk is along a well made vehicle track, but if you decide to return via Loch Kernsary be prepared for a badly eroded and very muddy footpath. Hill walking boots are essential. **Distance:** Complete circuit via Fionn Loch: 11 3/4 miles (19 kms). Shorter circuit: 6 1/4 miles (10 kms). **Time:** Allow 5 hours for the complete circuit and 3 hours for the shorter route.

Step By Step: Park in Poolewe village carpark (Map Ref. NG 856 808). Walk back to the A832 and cross the bridge over the River Ewe. Now take the minor road just opposite the Pool House Hotel. This first section of the walk is on a metalled road which runs alongside the River Ewe, passing the Free Kirk on the left. Continue through the gate marked "Londubh Common Grazing". From this point on, the road is private and cars are not permitted. The banks of the River Ewe are dotted with patches of natural woodland while to the left lie fields and heather moorland with areas of peat cuttings. The road now begins to climb and swings left, bringing the mountains of Letterewe into view for the first time.

A second gate is now reached and beyond it lies a stretch of beautiful natural woodland. A fisherman's path on the right leads down to a pleasant spot on the riverbank which would make an ideal place for a picnic. The metalled road forks a short distance ahead. The right fork leads to Inveran Lodge only. Take the left track, now unsealed, which climbs up through a forest of oak, birch, alder and rhododendron. The white walls of the lodge can be glimpsed through the trees to the right. Inveran was once the home of J.H. Dixon, author of the well known *"Gairloch and Guide to Loch Maree"*, first published in 1886 and still in print today. Before long, an old cottage is passed on the right and the track begins to swing further left, giving a view of the north-west end of Loch Maree. After rain this scene is spectacular, with lots of silvery burns tumbling down the steep sides of the mountains to the loch below. To the right of the track, the scene is dominated by Beinn Airigh Charr.

A large wooden gate is reached. This marks the start of the Kernsary Forest which is part of the Letterewe Wilderness. Letterewe has been designated an Area of Special Scientific Interest and camping, fishing, fires and mountain bikes are not permitted. The road climbs up over a grassy moorland, passing Loch an Doire Ghairbh on the right and then a conifer plantation on the left. The large expanse of Loch Kernsary now opens up to the left - the lush green horse pastures on the shore are an unexpected sight. The road swings sharp right and continues along to the estate cottages.

Go through the farm gate just beyond the cottages. From here, you can either return to Poolewe via Loch Kernsary (see * below) or continue on to Fionn Loch. To continue, follow the road to the right, which now climbs up through an area of forestry and then over high moorland, giving beautiful views of the Letterewe hills. Just to the left of these lie the hills of the Fisherfield Forest. This road was constructed around 1875 by Osgood Mackenzie, the founder of Inverewe Garden. After crossing through the metal gate on the high moorland, the road begins to descend, passing Loch na h-Airigh Molaich on the right and then the larger Loch an Eilean. The last stretch of road passes through the aptly named Bad Bog and terminates by the boat house on the shores of Fionn Loch.

This beautiful loch has long been a popular destination for fishermen and is famed for the size and quality of its trout. In the last century, Osgood Mackenzie recorded a catch of twelve trout weighing a total of 88lbs. Fionn Loch still abounds with large fish today. This unusual fertility is caused by a band of lime-bearing rock which runs beneath the loch, releasing calcium and other alkaline salts into the water. These salts have given rise to a large population of molluscs and crustacea which require calcium to build their shells and these in turn provide an abundant source of food for the trout. Fionn Loch means "The Fair Loch" in contrast to the darker body of water at its eastern end, the Dubh Loch, which means "Black Loch".

To return, retrace you steps to the gate by the estate buildings. Instead of going through, turn right (* turn left if doing shorter circuit) and follow the muddy track down to the stream, keeping the farm fence on your left. There are two large steady stepping stones a few yards to the left, where you can cross without getting your feet wet. Make for the pile of clearance stones and, keeping these on your left, look for the faint track which passes between two clumps of trees.

The path now climbs high above Loch Kernsary and crosses a peat moor. From this point on, it becomes very muddy and is badly eroded in places, which makes for very slow going. About 3/4 of the way along the lochside, it is possible to descend to a small pebble beach, from where you can make out a small island in the loch. This island is the site of an ancient crannog, although there is nothing to be seen today. This last section of the walk is through National Trust For Scotland land and is part of the Inverewe Estate which also includes Inverewe Garden. After crossing the burn at the head of the loch, the path ascends a small hill and Poolewe comes into view. The final section of the walk takes you across farmland and through a large wooden stock gate. The path eventually emerges round the right hand side of a single storey white cottage onto the A832 between the Londubh turnoff and Inverewe Garden. At this end, the path is marked by a blue "Footpath" sign.

15. LOCH AN DRAING AND CAMUSTROLVAIG

Midtown on the B8057, close to Inverasdale, is the starting point of a strenuous walk to the deserted farms of Loch an Draing and Camustrolvaig. There is a fairly good path across the moorland for most of the way, but the middle section of the walk skirts around several areas of woodland and here the ground can be very boggy. On one section of moorland, the path disappears completely but the way ahead is obvious and should pose no problems for the experienced walker. Good walking boots are essential. **Distance:** 10 1/2 miles (17 kms) return. **Time:** Allow 6 1/2 hours for the round trip.

Step By Step: As you are driving through Inverasdale, take the small road on the left immediately after the distinctive stone building of the Free Kirk. Continue through the crofts of Midtown until you reach the end of the road. There is space for one car to pull off in a small quarry cutting on the right (Map Ref. NG 815 860). Parking elsewhere can be tricky. Take care not to block driveways or farm gates.

The obvious track begins around the left side of the last house on the road. Go through the gate and follow the track across the field. There are several beautiful rowan trees growing here. The path passes in front of an old deserted croft and then heads out onto the open moor. This first section of the walk gives glorious views across Loch Ewe to Beinn Ghobhlach on the Scoraig peninsula, An Teallach and Beinn Airigh Charr at the foot of Loch Maree. To the south lie the mountains of Torridon. Loch Sguod appears on the right and behind it, from left to right, lie the crofts of Mellangaun, Firemore, Coast and Inverasdale. After about twenty minutes, the beautiful waterfall on the Abhainn Ur is reached. This stream flows into Loch Sguod and can be tricky to cross after prolonged heavy rain. It used to be spanned by a small bridge, the concrete piers of which can still be seen amidst the cascades above. As the path continues, the moor gradually rises on the right, cutting off the view of Loch Ewe. Several lochs now come into view ahead.

Before long, the first patch of natural woodland is reached. This woodland is particularly beautiful in August and September when the rowan trees are fully laden with bright red berries. Another large stream, the Allt a' Cham Loin Mhoir, is crossed at this point and just after it, to the left of the path, lie the remains of an old croft house. This is a pleasant spot for a picnic. If you are feeling tired, this is a good point at which to turn back as the track ahead deteriorates rapidly.

The path now weaves in and out of several patches of woodland and then skirts around the right shore of Loch Ceann a' Charnaich. This section can be very boggy and the track is indistinct in places. Immediately after the loch there is a beautiful woodland of ancient pine trees. The path continues along the fringe of the trees and the tip of Loch an Draing comes into view ahead. Just before the water is reached, the path cuts left into the trees, entering just after two huge lichen covered pines, one of which has tumbled to the side. This area of woodland used to be the haunt of a fairy known as the Gille Dubh, so called because of his black hair. The "Black Lad" clothed himself in garments made of tree leaves and green moss. He was said to be a genial fairy and generally kept himself to himself. On one occasion, he came to the aid of Jessie MacRae, a little girl who lived at Loch an Draing. Jessie had become lost in the woods and the Gille Dubh looked after her and took her home the next morning. In the latter part of the 18th century, the Gille Dubh was seen by many people over a period of more than 40 years. In the early 19th century, five Mackenzie chieftains set out to shoot the harmless fairy. They did not find him and the poor creature has never been seen since!

Before long, the small pebble beach on the shore of Loch an Draing is reached. In still weather the surface of this beautiful loch is like a huge mirror. The path now becomes indistinct and the best way forward is to follow the edge of the loch until you reach open moorland and then cut diagonally left across the moor, making for the end of the clump of trees ahead. Once you have rounded the tip of the trees, cut diagonally left across the next area of moor and cross the small burn. A sheep enclosure is now visible and a distinct path runs along the left side of the fence.

The strip of land which separates Loch an Draing and Loch nan Eun is reached before long. The first ruined croft house is seen to the left of the path and a short distance ahead, also on the left, is a second, more substantial farmhouse. This is the farmhouse of Loch an Draing. The doors, windows and fireplaces of this building can still be made out. Some of the stones have fallen away from the outer wall on one of the gable ends revealing the intricate construction of the chimney flue. The farmhouse kitchen table, fashioned from driftwood over 100 years ago, can be seen on display in the Gairloch Heritage Museum. To the right of the path, next to the modern sheep pens, lie the farmhouse outbuildings.

The path now continues across the moor, giving beautiful views to Loch nan Eun and the coast beyond. The houses of Camustrolvaig lie towards the end of the path, close to the precipitous sea cliffs. "Camustrolvaig" is an unusual Norse/Gaelic hybrid which means "Goblin or Troll Bay". The first ruin, on the left, has been rebuilt as a fisherman's bothy. The remains of two other houses lie just to the right of the path. According to local gossip, these houses used to belong to a family of stonemasons. The mother was fed up with living in such an isolated place and longed to move, but the rest of the family were quite content with the situation. In her desperation to be rid of the place, the woman burnt down the farmhouse in a fit of rage.

Beyond the ruins, a narrow track winds its way down the cliff to the beautiful white sand beach of Camas Mor. An impressive waterfall tumbles down into the bay from the rocky bluff above and along the coast to the left is a sea arch which can be reached at low tide. As you wander along the beach you may spot the heads of inquisitive seals who have swum in to meet you. This tranquil bay has a strange other-worldly feel about it and is an ideal place to pause for thought before you retrace your steps to Midtown.

16. CHURCH CAVE, COVE

This short stroll takes you to view a natural sea cave near Cove which was used by local people as a place of worship until fairly recent times (Map Ref. NG 813 913). See Poolewe to Cove for full details.

17. THE DESERTED VILLAGE OF SLAGGAN

The deserted village of Slaggan on the Rubha Mor peninsula was once a thriving crofting community. Today, only the walls of the croft houses remain, but the beauty and tranquillity of the place make a visit to the site well worthwhile. The going is easy along a fairly level, well made road which is sealed for most of the way. Any stout footwear would be suitable. Vehicles can also negotiate this road, despite the warning sign (see Aultbea to Laide and Mellon Udrigle for further details). From Slaggan, a track leads down to the beautiful sandy beach at Slaggan Bay which is an ideal place for a picnic. The walk can be extended to the cliffs of Gob a' Gheodha. **Distance:** 5 3/4 miles (9 1/4 kms) return; 7 1/4 miles (11 1/2 kms) return including the extension to Gob a' Gheodha. **Time:** Allow 1 hour 40 minutes for the round trip; 2 hours for the round trip including the extension to Gob a' Gheodha.

Step By Step: Park in one of the large quarry cuttings just past the turn off to Slaggan which is marked by a large blue sign (Map Ref. NG 887 941). Walk back to the junction and take the road to Slaggan. This first section of road is sealed and crosses an attractive heather moorland, passing Loch na h-Innse Gairbhe on the left. This small loch is ringed by water lilies and reeds and is particularly beautiful in summer when the lily flowers are in bloom. A much larger loch, Loch an t-Slagain, is passed on the left, just before the final descent to the village. This attractive loch contains several small tree-covered islands. The last stretch of road is unsealed, but the surface is in good condition and provides easy walking.

Ahead and to the left lie the ruins of Slaggan. The most obvious house is a two storey building of fairly modern type, with both gables completely intact. Just before this is reached, in the field to the left, are the remains of eight traditional croft houses and their associated outbuildings - byres, storehouses and field and garden walls. A couple of the croft houses are fairly well preserved. They have no roofs, but the doors, fireplaces and small windows can still be made out. In the 1860's, Slaggan was a thriving community and had what was known as a "side-school" - a school for children who lived outwith travelling distance of any School Board establishment. A room in the village was set aside for the use of the Reverend Ronald Dingwall, a Free Kirk minister who visited the community on occasion. Slaggan was also the home of Alexander Grant, Bard mor an t'Slaggan - The Great Bard of Slaggan. Grant was born at Mellon Charles c.1742 and lived most of his life at Slaggan, moving to Tournaig shortly before his death in c.1820. It is said that the title of "Great Bard" referred to his height and strength rather than his ability to compose poems and songs. He apparently stood more than 7ft tall in his stockings and was one of only two men in the country (the other being Sir Hector Mackenzie of Gairloch) who could crush a handful of black periwinkles. The Bard was also reputed to have second-sight and could discover the whereabouts of items that had been lost or stolen. Being a canny Scot, the Bard put this reputation to good use whenever the opportunity arose, as the following story illustrates. One day, there was a man in Loch Carron who had some cheeses stolen from him. Upon discovering his loss, he immediately sent for the Great Bard of Slaggan, requesting that he discover the identity of the thief. The man who had stolen the cheeses heard that the Great Bard had been summoned and, terrified of discovery, he walked out on the road each day, hoping to meet up with Grant. Eventually the thief spied a stranger and, upon hearing that he came from Slaggan, knew that this was the Great Bard. "I am the man that stole the cheeses, and I'll give you fifteen shillings if you will not tell that I am the man." said the thief to Grant. The Bard replied "Of course I know it was you that stole the cheeses, but where did you put them?". "I put them in a peat-stack at the back of the township." said the terrified thief. "Yes, I know that," said the Bard, "but which stack did you put them in?". "The one that's farthest from the township altogether." replied the thief. "Are you sure you put all the cheeses there?" asked the Bard. "Yes, I put them all there," the thief replied, "but one cheese is out of count.". The Great Bard, now having all the information he needed, took the fifteen shillings from the man and promised that his identity would not be revealed. He then continued on to the house of the man who had summoned him to Loch Carron. When asked to state the whereabouts of the cheeses and the identity of the culprit who had stolen them, the Great Bard first demanded a fee of twenty-five shillings. "I will not tell you who stole them, but I will tell you where they are." said Grant. Upon receipt of his fee, the Bard continued, "When tomorrow comes I will tell you where the cheeses are; but I must warn you that there will be one cheese missing.". The next day the cheeses were indeed discovered, just as Grant had said, and the Great Bard returned to Slaggan with the grand sum of forty shillings in his pocket and with his reputation still intact.

From the village, you can get down to the white sand beach at Slaggan Bay. Go through the gate and follow the track to the beach. Please keep dogs on a leash as there are always sheep on the hill. This tranquil bay looks out to the Shiant Isles and the hills of Harris and is a pleasant spot for a picnic. If you wish to extend your walk, you can follow the rough track around the cliffs on the right to the rocks of Gob a' Gheodha, where you can also get down to the shore. This is a popular spot with sea anglers. Allow another 20 minutes walking time for the extension to Gob a' Gheodha. Retrace your steps back to the main road.

18. RUBHA BEAG CIRCUIT

The beach at Mellon Udrigle is the starting point of a pleasant coastal walk around the Rubha Beag or "Little Point". The terrain covered is mainly short, springy grass and heather moorland, with easy walking on a well formed peat track in the latter stages. Stout shoes or wellington boots are suitable for this walk. **Distance:** 2 1/2 miles (4 kms) return. **Time:** Allow 1 hour 25 minutes for the round trip.

Step By Step: Park in the dune carpark at Mellon Udrigle (Map Ref. NG 891 959). Cross over to the left bank of the stream and follow it down to the beach. As you skirt left around the beach, you will pass a large white house with a boat ramp. Note the old ship's bell on the gable end of the house. Continue around the coast, following the sheep tracks over short, springy grass. There are splendid views back to the sandy bay of Camas a' Charraig and ahead to the Summer Isles. This stretch of coast is excellent for birdwatching. Rock pipits, ringed plovers, oystercatchers, herring gulls, black backed gulls and shags are all to be seen here. If you are lucky, the rare black throated diver may also put in an appearance.

After walking for about 5 minutes, look out for the large sea cave in the cliffs to your right. About 2 minutes further on, note the area of ridge-and-furrow strips on your left, followed by several heaps of clearance stones. The remains of an old road lie just behind the clearance cairns. The ridge-and-furrow method of cultivation improved land drainage and so enabled marginal boggy areas to be brought into use. The strips are known as "feannagan". This method of agriculture continued until the mid 19th century. If you climb up a short distance to the left, Loch Dubh na Maoil and the beautiful heather moorland behind it come into view. Back across Gruinard Bay, from left to right, can be seen Beinn Ghobhlach on the Scoraig peninsula, the great mass of An Teallach and the broad sandy beach at Gruinard. The waterfall on the Inverianvie River can just be made out directly above Gruinard beach.

Proceed through the gap in the old stone wall. You are now walking on the surface of the old road. The neat construction of the pebble base can be clearly seen. As the old road begins to make its way uphill, follow the sheep tracks to the right. After walking for a few minutes, note the area of ancient peat cuttings to the right. A little further on, you can descend to a long, narrow pebble bay which is a good spot for a picnic on a hot summer day. Out to sea, on the left side of the bay, is a long, narrow rock which is a favourite fishing perch for shags and other divers.

Strike left above the bay, following the sheep tracks. This will bring you closer to the diving rock and you can get a good view of the birds from the nearby grassy headland. Fulmars and gannets may also be seen out to sea at this point. The next bay along contains an impressive detached sandstone stack. The island which can be seen directly out to sea is Priest Island, one of the largest of the Summer Isles. Continue around the coast until you come to an area of ancient peat cuttings on your left. Note the old peats which have been thrown back into the trench and abandoned. Follow the sheep track to the right of the peat cuttings and ascend the headland, avoiding the steep gully. Cross the moorland of springy heather and make directly for the crest of the hill. At the top is a small boulder cairn and a cross inscribed "Ceol Na Mara". From this vantage point, there are views back to the scattered communities of Mellon Udrigle and Opinan. Loch Dubh na Maoil and Loch Dubh Geodhachan Tharailt lie amidst the moorland below.

Now head for the strip of land between Loch Dubh Geodhachan Tharailt and the sea and join the distinct sheep track. Follow this path around the coast, past several rocky inlets. The path becomes indistinct in its latter stages and you must then make your own way across the short heather. A grassy headland is reached after about 20 minutes walk. This is the northernmost tip of Rubha Beag and from here, the coast curves back towards Opinan. Turn inland and climb the hill directly in front of you. From the sandstone cairn at the top there are panoramic views of the mountains and islands. Now head for the sandstone cairn on the adjacent knoll. Across the rocky estuary ahead lie the crofts of Opinan while to the north-east can be seen the tip of Loch Broom, the Summer Isles and the mountains of Assynt. In the estuary below, you can see the long sandy channel which has been cleared to give access to the fishing boats. The old crofts of Opinan, now in ruins, are located on the low-lying grassy area at the back of the estuary. The modern houses are built on higher, drier ground. You may see a heron fishing in the crystal clear waters of the estuary. Watch also for the unusual spectacle of sheep grazing on seaweed at low tide.

Descend to the estuary, keeping to the left of the old stone wall. On the other side of the wall lie the remains of several stone bays which would have been used by the fishermen of old for storing their boats. Just as you pass the pile of tumbled stones, look back to the left to see the large area of ridge-and-furrow strips. Watch also for the many pied wagtails which frequent the sand dunes at this point. Now cut up left across the heather to attain the old peat road which runs between the long, low rocky hill to the left and the marshy area on the right. The road gives an easy walk back to Mellon Udrigle, passing several ancient peat cuttings on the way.

19. CHURCH CAVE AND OLD WOMAN'S CAVE, SAND

This short walk takes you down to the shore at Sand to view two sea caves (Map Ref. NG 913 916). In the latter half of the 19th century one was used as a place of worship by members of the Free Kirk while the other was the home of a seventy year old woman. See Laide to Dundonnell for full details.

20. INVERIANVE WATERFALLS AND HIDDEN GLEN

The carpark at Gruinard Beach is the starting point of an attractive walk which follows the course of the Inverianve River to the hidden glen at its head, passing several spectacular waterfalls along the way. The distinct path can be very muddy, particularly after rain and wellington boots are recommended. The middle section of the walk involves some scrambling along a steep sided gorge and is therefore not suitable for small children. Distance: 3 3/4 miles (6 kms) return. Time: Allow 1 hour 50 minutes for the round trip.

Step By Step: Park in the carpark at Gruinard Beach (Map Ref. NG 953 899). Walk back towards the Inverianve River and enter the farm gate on the left, just before the bridge. A very distinct path follows the river upstream, along the bottom of a fairly broad glen whose steep craggy sides are studded with heather. As far as mud is concerned, this first section of the walk is by far the worst. Ahead, the first large waterfall can be seen, encouraging the walker ever onwards. The rounded lump of Beinn Dearg Bheag in the Fisherfield Forest is framed in the gorge above the waterfall. Looking back downstream, the view out to sea is dominated by the Rubha Beag headland on the Aultbea peninsula.

The first large waterfall is reached after about 20 minutes walk. Here the river gushes out over a rock ledge and falls 50ft into a deep plunge pool below. From this point on, the walls of the glen narrow considerably and the path becomes a broad ledge winding its way high above the river. The water once again becomes turbulent as a series of cascades are reached. Here the path splits into two: the left hand path climbs high up the gorge, whereas the right hand path descends to the water's edge, close by the cascades. This latter path doubles back on itself by an old holly tree and climbs up to rejoin the other track. This section of the walk involves some easy scrambling over rock and extra care is needed in a couple of places, but there should be no real problems.

At the top of the cascades, the path takes a slight turn to the left and the hidden glen comes into view. This attractive broad, flat-bottomed glen with gently meandering river comes as something of a surprise after the steep, rocky gorge below. The path once again becomes muddy and continues along the glen and through an old walled field. This fertile area is a striking island of emerald green amidst the surrounding crags and heather. Such fields are called "achadhs". They remained in cultivation until the middle of the 19th century.

At the end of the glen, the walls narrow and suddenly the river bends sharp right. This crazy angle is caused by an area of faulted rock. Another spectacular waterfall can be seen in the river ahead, with a smaller fall just above it. From this point you can either follow the faint track up the left side of the river for a closer look at the waterfalls or you can climb up the knoll directly opposite the waterfalls for a panoramic view of the surrounding landscape. From the knoll, to the north-east, can be seen the long straight ridge of Ben Mor Coigach and, next to it, the striking profile of Beinn Ghobhlach on the Scoraig peninsula. To the south-east lies the An Teallach massif and to the south are the hills of the Fisherfield Forest. Looking back towards the waterfalls, the tip of Loch a' Mhadaidh Mor can be seen disappearing behind a knoll on the left. This loch is the source of the Inverianve River. The lochans at the foot of Creag-mheall Beag can also be seen. Now retrace your steps to the carpark. Gruinard Beach is an ideal place for a refreshing paddle after your walk.

21. AN TEALLACH WATERFALLS

This short but strenuous walk takes you up to view the waterfalls on the lower flanks of An Teallach. The path is fairly rough and wet in places and some steep climbing is involved. Hill-walking boots are essential. **Distance:** 2 miles (3 1/4 kms) return. **Time:** Allow at least 2 1/2 hours for the round trip.

Step By Step: Between the Dundonnell Hotel and the telephone box, there is a Mountain Rescue Hut by the left of the road. Leave your car in the small parking area next to the hut (Map Ref. NH 093 879). Cross the road and climb the fence directly opposite. From here, a distinct path winds its way up the hill behind a wooden house. It climbs steeply and zig-zags up a series of rocky bluffs. After about 40 minutes, the path forks by a small cairn. Follow the left hand branch and continue to climb until you reach a series of flat sandstone platforms. A broad glen now opens up and a series of waterfalls can be seen in the river ahead. On the left side of the glen rises the huge mass of Glas Mheall Mor, one of the buttresses of An Teallach, while on the right is the lesser hill of Meall Garbh. Glas Mheall Mor is particularly attractive after heavy rain when silvery torrents of water gush down its steep sides. Looking back down the glen, the many lochs on the heights of the Scoraig peninsula can be seen.

From this point, continue up the glen and make for the large isolated boulder on the flank of Meall Garbh to your right. The path is indistinct here and the ground can be very boggy. At the boulder, strike right and climb to the top of the broad stony ridge of Meall Garbh. From here there is a spectacular view down the entire length of Little Loch Broom. Now make your way to the right (east) and join up with the path which makes its way down the rocky shoulder of Meall Garbh. This too can be indistinct in places and a certain amount of care is needed, but the way down is fairly obvious. At a small cairn, this path joins up with the path taken on the ascent. From here, retrace you steps to the carpark.

22. STRATH NA SEALGA

This strenuous walk takes you in to the hidden southern side of An Teallach to view the beautiful and remote Loch na Sealga and the mountains of the Fisherfield Forest beyond. The walk begins along a well-defined vehicle track, but this gradually deteriorates and after about 2 1/4 miles a rough footpath is joined. Some sections are marked by cairns. The final 5 3/4 miles of the walk are again along a vehicle track. Walking boots are essential. **Distance:** 12 miles (19 1/4 kms) return. **Time:** Allow 7 1/2 hours for the round trip.

Step By Step: Park in the lay-by just to the south of Corrie Hallie Croft (Map Ref. NH 114 852). The vehicle track begins on the opposite side of the road, passing through a gate and following the left bank of the Allt Gleann Chaorachain. The track climbs steadily and cuts through an attractive birch wood. On emerging from the wood, the track crosses to the right bank of the stream and climbs up above Loch Coire Chaorachain. To the left there are good views over the loch studded moorland of the Dundonnell Forest. Shortly after passing Loch Coire Chaorachain, the track splits at a point which is marked by cairns. Take the right-hand footpath and follow it over the shoulder of Sail Liath, the southernmost summit of An Teallach. Keep a look out for the rare golden eagle which frequents the crags above. The path now descends to the bothy of Shenavall.

You are now in the flat green strath of Sealga. To the north-west lies the beautiful Loch na Sealga - the Loch of the Hunts - from which the Gruinard River flows. This area was named in antiquity from its fame as a hunting ground. Today, red deer still populate the strath at the head of the loch. From this point, the entire southern aspect of An Teallach is to be seen and across the strath rise the twin peaks of Beinn Dearg Mor and Beinn Dearg Bheag.

From Shenavall, cut left and follow the footpath which now makes its way along the floor of the strath beside the meandering river. After about 1 3/4 miles the bothy at Achneigie is reached and just beyond this the path once again becomes a rough vehicle track. The track continues along the strath and turns sharp left, cutting northwards across the bleak moorland of the Dundonnell Forest. Loch Coire Chaorachain is reached once again and from here simply retrace your footsteps down through the birch wood and back to your car.

LANDSCAPE

The landscape of the Gairloch-Torridon area is one of the most dramatic and beautiful in Scotland. How was this landscape formed? There are two factors which exercise a dominant control on the formation of mountains, lochs and the landscape in general - the rock formations and glaciation. The creation of the modern Gairloch-Torridon landscape is part of the geological history of the area. Superimposed on this is the influence of man and his domestic, industrial and agricultural practices. Although often maligned, these can add to the attraction and scenic beauty of an area - as in the creation of Inverewe Garden in Poolewe.

This section concentrates on describing the formation of the present landscape through geological forces. This involves a trip through time to an age when the coastline of Scotland was nothing like it is at present, and when Scotland as we know it today did not exist.

ANCIENT LANDSCAPES

The oldest rocks in the area are part of the Lewisian Gneiss Complex, which includes rocks 2,900-2,000 million years old. These rocks were originally sediments laid down in ancient oceans at a time when there was little or no oxygen in the atmosphere. At this time the earth's crust was hotter and more active than today, and these rocks were baked and crushed ("metamorphosed") several times by burial to great depths in the crust. As a result, they now look nothing like the original sediments and have a distinctive banded or striped appearance formed by white, pink and black minerals. This rock type is called a gneiss, and the minerals can sometimes form attractive large crystals several centimetres long.

Over many millions of years these rocks formed the valleys and mountains of the land, throughout this time, the Lewisian gneiss was considerably eroded to form a low-level hummocky terrain with occasional hills which rose to 600 metres above the ancient valley floors. Finally, around 1000 million years ago parts of this landscape were buried under sediments which now form the Torridonian Sandstone. This sequence is well exposed in cross-section in Slioch and can be seen from car parks off the main road. In the body of the mountain, ancient gneiss hills can be distinguished beneath the Torridonian sandstone, which also infills the ancient valleys. This buried Lewisian hill is part of a fossil landscape over 1000 million years old - a landscape which existed before life on earth and which was formed in an atmosphere with no oxygen.

The Torridonian sediments which covered this ancient landscape were derived under desert-like conditions from a landmass which once existed in what is now the north Minch. Rivers flowed from this landmass to the SE through valleys and lakes eventually reaching estuaries. As they flowed, the rivers deposited sediments in the river channels, in shallow lakes, and on plains forming fan-shaped deposits. Additionally, the river valleys were also infilled with scree from the surrounding mountains. The rocks of Torridonian Sandstone in the Gairloch-Torridon area were formed from these river sediments. They were deposited during a time when the area was subsiding and built up to form a sedimentary sequence which was originally over 7km thick.

It may seem unlikely that it is possible to describe what the landscape of this area was like a thousand million years ago. The clues to reconstructing the environment lie in the rocks themselves. Ripple marks in the sediments show the flow direction of the ancient rivers and mud cracks indicate dry periods when the rivers or lakes dried up. The red-brown colour of the sediments and markings on the surface of the grains are signs of a desert-like climate, indicating that Scotland at this time lay close to the equator. This conclusion is supported by magnetic measurements on the rocks, which indicate that the land lay at a latitude of 15°N at the start of the Torridonian deposition.

The age of the Torridonian sequence as a whole ranges from 1000-750 million years. However, most of the rocks in the Gairloch-Torridon are around 800-750 million years old and represent the younger part of the sequence. Some of the older rocks are found in the area notably north of Poolewe and a small outcrop near the Rubha Reidh lighthouse. Remarkably for rocks of this age, none of the Torridonian rocks have been metamorphosed.

Two hundred million years passed after the Torridonian rocks were formed. During this time the Torridonian and Lewisian strata were tilted westward by earth movements, and were extensively eroded. Eventually, after hundred of millions of years, the land subsided and was submerged in a warm, shallow sea. In this sea sediments which now form the Cambrian Quartzite were deposited on the eroded, tilted surface of Torridonian rocks. The Quartzite is a distinctive white rock which in this area is most conspicuous and spectacular on Beinn Eighe where it forms dramatic screes which are clearly seen from Kinlochewe. Worms lived in the sands of the Cambrian shallow sea and traces of their burrows have been preserved in the upper sections of the quartzite. These appear in the rock as infilled vertical tubes or pipes up to 15mm in diameter and 1m in length. The quartzite formation which contains these trace fossils is known as the Pipe Rock. Following deposition of the Pipe Rock, the supply of sediment from the land to the sea declined, possibly as a result of a more arid climate. This allowed different rocks to form in the sea. These rocks contain less sediment and more carbonate minerals and form what is now known as the Fucoid

Beds. This sequence is composed largely of carbonate-rich siltstones and shales with abundant fossils, including trilobites and braciopods. Early geologists mistakenly identified trace fossils, now known to be flattened burrows, as the marks of seaweed (fucoids). Although the original interpretation was not correct, this name for the sequence has been retained. The Fucoid Beds are interesting however, in that they are naturally enriched in potash and phosphate in some areas, and the crushed rock is a natural fertiliser.

After deposition of Cambrian sediments around 570 million years ago, the whole sequence was again tilted, this time to the east, returning the Torridonian strata close to their original position. Looking at the mountains of Torridonian Sandstone today, the older strata forms near-horizontal steps whereas the Cambrian rocks capping some hill-tops are now tilted.

The Lewisian Gneiss, Torridonian Sandstone and Cambrian Quartzite together account for most of the rocks found in the Gairloch-Torridon area. There are however, smaller outcrops of much younger sediments which are part of the New Red Sandstone sequence. Like the Torridonian these are also river sediments deposited under arid, desert-like conditions. At this time, about 240 million years ago, Scotland lay at about 25°N of the equator and the rivers flowed from the land northwest into what is now the Minch. The largest remains of these sediments are found in a strip from Gruinard Bay to Aultbea and on the Isle of Ewe. Small outcrops also occur at Big Sand, Red Point and at Camas Mor on the Rubha Reidh peninsula. This latter outcrop extends into the Minch along the submarine Rubha Reidh Ridge. The soils overlying the New Red Sandstone rocks tend to be more fertile than the other rocks in the area, because of their higher lime content. This difference can be clearly seen on the Isle of Ewe as described in the "Poolewe to Aultbea and Mellon Charles" Section of Part II.

One rock series which has not been covered lies largely to the east of the area dealt with in this book. It does however, make an appearance between Achnasheen and Kinlochewe, and to the east of An Teallach and therefore deserves some description. This is the Moine Series or the Moine Schists, a group of highly deformed metamorphosed rocks which cover a large part of northern Scotland east of a line known as the Moine Thrust. These rocks are considered to be 1000-800 million years old, but the oldest formations have been dated at 1500 million years. They are thought to have been derived from erosion of the Lewisian gneiss and deposited in an estuarine or shallow sea environment. As there is some overlap in the ages, it is possible that the rocks of the Moine Series were deposited in the sea at the same time as the Torridonian sediments were deposited on the adjacent continent. The range of rock types in the Moine Series is quite variable. Some do form mountains, but a knolly, peaty, boggy landscape is more typical of Moine terrain. The name for the series is actually derived from a boggy area in northern Sutherland known as a'Mhoine ("the peat bog").

The Moine Thrust, which separates the Moine Series from the other rocks in the area, is a zone composed of a complex series of folded Lewisian, Torridonian and Cambrian sediments thrust over one another. Over a long period of time, earth movements used planes of weakness, such as shale layers, to push rocks to the WNW. When this first started is uncertain, but it is known that a period of great activity occurred 450-420 million years ago during which older rocks were thrust WNW over younger series, so that the older rock now lies on top of the younger.

Another major structural feature of the area is the Loch Maree Fault. This can be traced from Camas Mor on the Rubha Reidh peninsula through the loch and on past Kinlochewe and Achnasheen. It is responsible for the line of Glen Docherty, the steep sides of the hills on the north shore of Loch Maree and on the south-west shore of Loch Ewe, and for the scarp which extends from Poolewe to Camas Mor. The fault is an ancient zone of shearing or movement in the Lewisian rocks. Although this has not been active for over 1000 million years, the fault penetrates deep into the earth's crust and remains a line of weakness which is exploited by rivers and glaciers to form lochs, valleys and cliffs.

THE ICE AGE

About 4 million years ago global temperatures started to fall, marking the start of a period of fluctuating cold-warm climatic changes which the world is still experiencing. There have been at least seven Ice Ages in the 4500 million years of earth history. The last ice sheet developed around 27,000 years ago, and survived for 14,000 years. During this time the Scottish Highlands were covered in ice up to 1000 metres thick and in the Gairloch-Torridon area, glaciers moved north-westwards from the land out to sea. Ice filled the Minch and extended over Lewis out into the Atlantic, although it did not reach St Kilda.

As the ice sheets moved, they scoured the land, widening, deepening and straightening valleys, scraping rocks clean of soil and cutting spectacular corries in the mountains and rounding off the tops of hills they covered. Through the action of the ice, the pre-existing land was dramatically changed and moulded into the landscape of today.

The end of the Ice Age started 13,000 years ago and was caused by a period of global warming. The ice gradually melted, retreating to the highest, coldest mountains. A sudden period of cooling 10,500 years ago did cause the ice to return to parts of Scotland, including Gairloch and Torridon. However, this was only a brief interlude and by about 10,000 years ago the entire ice sheet had melted.

When ice sheets melt, they leave behind the material gathered as they scraped over the land surface. These deposits often create distinctive features in the landscape, and it is through them that geologists can work out the history of glaciation in an area. The deposits are generally of two types: boulder clay or till, which is a mixture of pebbles, boulders, silt and mud, and moraines. It is moraines which form the more obvious landscape features. They are made up of boulders, gravel and sand which, after being dropped by the glacier, are moved about, or re-worked, by the melt waters and streams. This action creates distinctive hummocky features in the landscape, and at its most spectacular can look like hundreds of miniature hills. One of the best examples of this to be found in Scotland is the Valley of a Hundred Hills in Glen Torridon (see the KInlochewe to Torridon Section). Re-working of the gravels can form terraces now located high above the level of the present-day streams. Two large flat-topped terraces lie just outside Achnasheen on the road to Kinlochewe and are described in the Travel Guide (Achnasheen to Kinlochewe Section). The railway line is actually built on a lower terrace.

The weight of ice up to one kilometre thick acting on the land caused it to sink. Once the ice melted, this weight was removed and the land slowly started to rise towards its original level, a rise which is still continuing today. This process has not always been steady and consistent, and the land has sometimes risen in irregular "jumps". These jumps are marked by the presence of raised beaches around parts of the coastline. Today raised beaches can be recognised as flat, often grass covered areas, several metres above the level of the present beach, which extend inland often towards a bank or cliff. They mark the position of an ancient shoreline which was raised out of the water as the land rose. Often two or three raised beaches can be seen at the same location. However many raised beaches there are, the highest is the oldest (up to 15,000 years old) and the lowest the youngest (usually around 6,700 year old). As the ice melted so the sea level rose, however in this area the land rose faster than the sea, lifting the old beaches out of the water and preventing them from being flooded. Only once did the rise in sea-level overtake the rise in the land, and this happened 6,700 years ago. The rate of uplift then increased and raised the land out of the sea once again, leaving the 6,700 year-old shoreline as the last, and lowest, of the raised beaches. Several examples of raised beaches exist in the Gairloch-Torridon area, though some are more obvious than others. Gairloch village is partially built on a raised beach and others exist at Poolewe, North Erradale and at Big Sand and Red Point where they are covered in part by blown sand. However, one of the best views of a raised beach can be had overlooking Gruinard Bay from the pull-off on the A832 road (see the Laide to Dundonnell Section).

THE ARCHAEOLOGY OF GAIRLOCH AND TORRIDON

As the visitor explores the beautiful landscape of the Gairloch/Torridon region, he may be forgiven for thinking that the area has only recently been settled by man. There is a noticeable absence of dramatic monuments such as castles, stone circles and brochs which are found in abundance elsewhere in Scotland. However, closer examination reveals a range of interesting sites which give a fascinating insight into the life of the early inhabitants of this remote area.

Mesolithic Hunters and Fishermen

When the ice finally retreated from Scotland around 8,000 B.C., it left a landscape totally devoid of soil and vegetation. Over a period of several thousand years, this harsh environment was slowly recolonised by plants, trees and game animals and gradually the landscape became capable of supporting human occupation. The first recognisable traces of human activity date to around 5,000 B.C. These invariably take the form of huge mounds of discarded shells and other food debris such as fish and bird bones. Such "midden" sites are usually recognised in coastal locations. A possible Mesolithic cave shelter and associated midden has been found in the hills between Red Point and the Craig Youth Hostel. This site may be seen as the temporary winter or spring camp of a group of nomadic hunter-gatherers. Wester Ross would have been particularly attractive to such groups, offering sheltered bays with abundant fish and shell-fish and a forested hinterland filled with herds of deer and wild boar. It is likely that plant food, fish and shell-fish formed the most important part of the diet of these early inhabitants, with meat playing only a secondary role. During the summer months, the hunters would certainly have followed the herds of deer inland to obtain skins and bone and antler for tool making. Venison would have been a welcome addition to the diet at this time. Small mammals and birds would also have been hunted. From the excavation of similar sites elsewhere, we know that these early inhabitants were skilled hunters with a surprisingly elaborate tool kit well suited to their nomadic way of life. Wood, bone, antler and stone were expertly fashioned into spears, harpoons, bows, arrows, knives and scrapers. The Mesolithic way of life continued relatively unchanged until around 3,500 B.C. when an influx of new settlers arrived in Scotland from northern Europe. These Neolithic peoples, the first farmers, lived side by side with the hunter-gatherers for some time before both groups merged to lead a settled way of life. To date, no trace of these first farming communities have been found in the Gairloch/Torridon region.

Bronze Age Settlers

Around 2,000 B.C., the archaeological record in Scotland reveals a marked change in burial customs. The Neolithic practice of collective burial in chambered tombs is replaced by individual burials, often in stone cists, both with and without above-ground cairns. Burials begin to be accompanied by richly decorated pottery vessels known as "Beakers" which were probably intended to hold food and drink to sustain the deceased during his journey into the afterlife. This change coincides with the arrival of new groups of peoples from the European continent who brought with them knowledge of copper and bronze working. Several other interesting elements appear at this time, including the many standing stones which are to be found throughout Scotland. One such stone occurs close to Badrallach on the Scoraig peninsula (Map Ref. NH 081 915). Several possible functions have been suggested for such monuments: calendrical or astronomical indicators; memorial stones; route or boundary markers. Careful investigation has revealed that many standing stones are clearly related to the movements of the sun, moon and stars. Many appear to mark the passing of the seasons, in particular mid-summer and mid-winter. Such monuments are indicative of an agricultural community to whom the turning of the seasons would have been of great importance. Calendrical and astronomical observations were probably associated with ceremonies of a religious nature and this suggests an advanced society capable of supporting a priestly class.

It is not until the later part of the Bronze Age, around 800 or 700 B.C., that the first identifiable remains of houses and field systems are to be found in Wester Ross. An excellent example of the type of farming community which existed at this time is to be found close to the River Sand, just north of Gairloch (centred on NG 788 808). Here, there are at least twenty-four hut circles, two large enclosures, traces of field walls and heaps of clearance stones in an area covering nearly 50 acres of hillside. The hut circles represent the ruined walls of substantial domestic dwellings. These circular houses would once have had an inner circle of strong upright posts, perhaps with a ring beam. A roof of thatch would have rested on the uprights and sloped down to the outer stone wall. Inside, the hut may have been divided by a wall of wickerwork which stretched between the timber uprights. Evidence from similar sites elsewhere suggests that there was probably a porch or baffle-wall just outside the doorway to give some protection from the elements. The inhabitants of this site would have followed a settled farming way of life similar to that established by their Neolithic predecessors. Sheep, cattle and pigs would certainly have been raised. Barley and oats may have continued to be grown, although the deterioration of climatic conditions and a dramatic rise in peat formation in the late Bronze Age may have reduced the amount of land available for cultivation. Scattered amongst the remains of the Bronze Age settlement at the River Sand are to be found the abundant remnants of later dwellings, indicating that the site continued to provide favourable conditions for settlement until comparatively recent times.

A similar settlement site also occurs at Gleann Crom, just above the A832 Poolewe to Aultbea road (NG 876 863). Here, three hut circles can be seen amidst the moorland. Although originating in the Bronze Age, this type of settlement site continued to be built and occupied well into the ensuing Iron Age and it should therefore be broadly dated to the 1st millennium B.C.

Warrior Celts

The centuries between 900 B.C. and 500 B.C. saw a major expansion in the Scottish bronze industry. New forms of weapons and tools appeared and the presence of exotic imports such as elaborate vessels of beaten bronze suggests close contacts with continental Europe. It is during this period that many valuable items were deliberately gathered together and buried. That such hoards were never recovered suggests that there was considerable unrest in the country and it is not surprising that the first defensive forts make their appearance at this time. A new building technique known as timber lacing appears in Scotland around the 7th century B.C. This method of construction may have been introduced by groups of migrants from north-east Europe. Timber-lacing involved the building of substantial dry-stone walls in and around a framework of pegged timbers. This had the effect of binding the walls together, creating a strong, substantial structure. Many of these early fortifications show traces of vitrification, that is the fusing together of rocks and stones through intense heat. This occurred when the timbers within the walls were set alight. Whether this was done deliberately to improve the strength of the walls or whether it was the act of an aggressor, we do not know. One such vitrified fort occurs on the little knoll of An Dun in Gairloch (NG 803 754). The term "dun" is used in Scotland to indicate a class of small fort with a thick dry-stone wall enclosing a roughly circular or oval area. At An Dun, the dry-stone wall enclosed an area approximately 65 feet in diameter. The natural gullies on the east of the knoll were artificially deepened to give added protection to the dun and there may also have been several lines of outer walls to further restrict access to the site. Within the dun itself, timber ranges may have been erected against the inner face of the wall to provide shelter for the inhabitants. Duns are usually to be found on sites which afford some degree of natural protection, such as rocky knolls, promontories and isolated rock stacks, and An Dun is no exception. From this little headland, a clear view is to be had across the sandy beach to Gairloch. An Dun may be seen as the fortified homestead of several inter-related family groups who had banded together for added security in troubled times. Such vitrified duns may have continued to be occupied until as late as the 2nd century A.D.

Another dun is to be found at Loch Thurnaig, just north of Inverewe Garden (NG 863 833). This appears to be of solid-wall construction, a technique which dates to the second and third centuries A.D. It is around this time that the peoples of Scotland are first mentioned in the written records. In his account of Britain written around 120 A.D., Ptolemy of Alexandria states that the area approximating to modern day Wester Ross was inhabited by a tribe called the Carnonacae.

Crannogs are a fascinating form of defended homestead which first begin to appear in Scotland in the latter half of the 1st millennium B.C. A crannog is a timber house which is built on an artificial or partly artificial island. These small islands were constructed close to the shores of lochs and consist of layers of timber and brushwood consolidated by vertical wooden poles and rubble. Many could be reached only by boat while others were linked to the adjacent shore by winding causeways of timber or stone set below the water to confuse hostile visitors. Two examples occur close to Gairloch. One, in Loch Kernsary (NG 882 803), is associated with an unusual boat-shaped building on the adjacent shore. The other, in Loch Thollaidh (NG 845 786), was recently investigated by a team of archaeologists and their findings are awaited with great interest. It is obvious that such sites could have been very easily defended. Even in times of siege, abundant supplies of fresh water and food could be obtained from the surrounding loch. In more peaceful times, the adjacent shore could be used for agricultural purposes. So successful was this defensive design that crannogs continued to be built, or at least used, until the 17th century.

The Picts

The Picts or "painted ones" are first mentioned by the classical writer Eumenius in 297 A.D. The term "Pictland" appears to refer to a political alliance of several quite different tribal groups who were held together by an aristocratic class. This probably accounts for the fact that archaeology has been unable to recognise any element from day-to-day life which can be said to be characteristically "Pictish". The only cultural aspect which can be said to be truly Pictish is the fine artwork in the form of sculptured stones and metalwork which flourished under the patronage of the aristocracy. In 1964, a Pictish sculptured stone was built into the new cemetery wall in Gairloch (NG 807 756). This can now be seen in the Gairloch Heritage Museum. The roughly prepared slab contains a fish symbol and part of a goose. It has been suggested that stones such as this one which bear only one or two animal symbols might represent territorial markers. Stones which bear more complex series of symbols may be memorials to the deceased or may commemorate political and marriage alliances between different family groups. The Gairloch stone is the only example so far discovered in Wester Ross and this suggests that Pictish influence and rule was far less established here than in the east.

The only other evidence in Wester Ross for Pictish settlement comes from the use of the Pictish word "aber" which means "confluence". Applecross (NG 711 445) was formerly known as Abercrosan - the confluence of the Crosan. In all probability, the Gairloch/Torridon area once contained many more names of Pictish origin which have since been replaced by Gaelic and to a lesser extent Norse.

The Pictish kingdom formally came to an end in 843 A.D. when the Picts were united with the kingdom of Dalriada to the south under the Scottish king, Kenneth MacAlpin.

The Early Celtic Church

The historian Bede, writing in the 8th century, records that the northern Picts were converted to Christianity by the Irish missionary St Columba around 563 A.D. In 673 A.D., another Irish missionary, St Maelrubha, founded a monastery at Applecross. This establishment soon became second only to Iona in terms of its importance as a centre for Christian teaching. The rise of Christianity did much to spread the Gaelic language which was spoken by the missionaries and by the inhabitants of the kingdom of Dalriada to the south which had been founded by families from Antrim in Northern Ireland. Gaelic soon came to absorb and replace the Brythonic or Welsh form of Celtic language which had been spoken by the Picts.

The influence of the early Celtic Church in the Gairloch/Torridon region can be seen in the use of Gaelic place-names which identify early religious sites. The word "cill" meaning "church" occurs in Kildonan - "Donan's Church" - on the shore of Little Loch Broom (NH 077 908). Several interesting features can be seen at this site. Lying close to the stream which runs through the deserted village of Kildonan is a small graveyard of roughly oval shape. Although largely overgrown with bracken, several graves can be made out. These consist of flat slabs laid end to end on either side of shared headstones. No marks can be discerned on these headstones. There are also traces of what appears to be an open paved area and it has been suggested that this may have been the site of a preaching cross where open-air services were conducted in the absence of a church building.

The little settlement of Annat in Torridon (NG 896 545) is named from the Irish "annoid" which means "a church containing the relic of its founder". Although no church is visible at Annat today, the hill behind the village is known as "Beinn na h-Eaglaise" - Church Hill.

Close to the shore at the village of Laide lie the ruins of the ancient Chapel of Sand (NG 902 920). Part of the intricately carved window arches of the chapel are still intact and a large remnant of arch can be seen on the left, just as you walk in the door. The walls are cemented with lime manufactured from burnt shells. This site has a long association with Christianity - local tradition says that the chapel was constructed by St Columba back in the 6th century. Although the present chapel is undoubtedly several hundred years old, an examination of the construction techniques suggests a date considerably later than the 6th century. It is possible however that the small chapel replaced one or more earlier buildings which may indeed have dated back to the time of St Columba.

The Vikings

After an initial foray along the south coast of England in 789 A.D., the Vikings sacked the church of St Cuthbert on Lindisfarne in 793. Thereafter, Viking attacks on Britain increased dramatically and during the 9th century, the Norwegian Vikings carried out many raids in the Highlands. On one occasion the church at Applecross was violated. These savage attacks certainly reinforce the traditional picture of the Vikings as a race of blood-thirsty marauders, but archaeological evidence suggests that this was not always the case. It seems that in some areas, the intention was to settle down amongst the native inhabitants and to co-exist peacefully.

No Viking remains have been found in the Gairloch/Torridon region, but the abundance of Old Norse names indicate that there was certainly Norse activity and influence in the area. Most of the names refer to natural features and this possibly suggests that most visits to the area were of a temporary nature. One such word which falls into this category is "dalr" which means valley. In its slightly altered form "dale" it is to be found in the following place-names: Erradale - Gravel Beach Valley (NG 743 811 and 744 714) ; Inverasdale (Inveraspidill) - Aspen Valley (NG 82 86); Slattadale - Even Valley (NG 888 719) and Talladale - Ledge Valley (NG 916 703). The term "dalr" was often used to signify a small valley situated off a main strath. The word "aig" is also indicative of Norse influence. This is the Gaelicised form of the Old Norse "vik" which means "bay". This term was applied to sheltered bays where boats could be anchored or pulled up on to the beach. The following names contain this element: Diabaig (diup-vik) - Deep Bay (NG 795 604); Melvaig - Bent Grass Bay (NG 743 864) and Shieldaig (sil-vik) - Herring Bay (NG 803 726 and 816 540). The Norse word "gil" which means "ravine" occurs in the place-name Udrigil - Outer Ravine (NG 892 961).

More permanent settlement is suggested by the use of the word "skiki" which means "cultivated strip". This can be seen in its Gaelicised form "scaig" in the place-name Ormiscaig which means "Orm's Strip" (NG 85 90). Another place-name which falls into this category is Mial (NG 797 779) which comes from the Old Norse "mjo-vollr" meaning "Narrow Field".

Norse power in the Northern Highlands and Western Isles was broken on 3 October 1263 when Haco, King of Norway was defeated at the Battle of Largs. In 1266, Haco's successor Magnus ceded all Norwegian territory in Scotland, with the exception of Orkney and Shetland, to the King of Scotland.

Fortifications In The Early Clan Period

In common with many similar sites, the vitrified dun at Gairloch (NG 803 754) was reoccupied at a later date. The site was refortified in the 13th century by the MacBeaths who had probably arrived in the area from Assynt. The MacBeaths were driven out of Gairloch by the MacLeods in the early 15th century and the fortification thereafter became a stronghold of Clan MacLeod. The "Castle of Gairloch" as it was known, remained in the possession of the MacLeods until the middle of the 16th century when they were driven out by the Mackenzies. Nothing remains to be seen of the fortification today. Back in 1886 however, low banks of loose stones could still be distinguished on top of the rocky knoll and these may have been the remains of the castle walls.

The crannog on Loch Thollaidh (NG 845 786) was also occupied by the MacBeaths and then the MacLeods. It was from this crannog that the two sons of Allan MacLeod were abducted and subsequently murdered, an event which was to bring about Mackenzie rule in Gairloch (see Gairloch to Poolewe for full details). When J.H. Dixon was writing in 1886, only a pile of loose rubble remained of this crannog. Dixon also mentions that another stronghold of the MacLeods was situated on the headland between Port Henderson and Opinan (NG 743 738). This site was known as Uamh nam Freiceadain.

Eilean Grudidh (NG 952 693) was occupied from the 13th century onwards by seven generations of MacBeath chiefs. In common with other sites in the area, the island subsequently became a stronghold of Clan MacLeod. Eilean Grudidh was fortified by means of a crude wall of rough masonry and clay cement which was built up around the natural rocky banks of the island. This wall encircled the entire circumference of the island, enclosing a flat central area in which several buildings were erected. In one place, there is a deep hole surrounded by a circular wall. Tradition says that this is the castle dungeon. Most of the masonry work has now crumbled and not much remains to be seen of the old "Castle of Grudidh". When J.H. Dixon was writing in 1886, the central buildings were nothing more than rough mounds.

17th-19th Century Settlement Remains

The hills and glens around Gairloch and Torridon contain abundant remains of farming settlements of a fairly recent date. The deserted villages of Camustrolvaig (NG 762 917), Innis Bhuidhe (NG 78 80), Kildonan (NH 078 908) and Slaggan (NG 845 940) are all well worth visiting. At these sites can be seen many houses of varying ages, together with associated farm buildings and walled enclosures.

As you explore the hillsides in the region, keep a look out for the old walled hill-fields or "achaidhnan". These are often very easily spotted, as the land inside the wall is strikingly green and fertile compared to the surrounding hillside. A good example of an achadh occurs close to the Inverianve River (NG 966 882) and this may be visited on the Inverianve Waterfalls walk (see Selected Walks). Several more examples are to be seen close to the deserted village of Innis Bhuidhe (see above). The achadh was a clever way of enriching a plot of land for improved cultivation.

First of all, an area of dry sloping ground was chosen. This was then surrounded by a stone and turf wall sufficiently high enough to keep cattle in. Into this enclosure, the cattle would be driven every night after milking and there they remained until morning. This routine would be continued for several weeks until the achadh contained a good amount of manure. The cattle would then be taken to another walled enclosure. The following spring, the manured achadh would be turned over by means of the "caschrom" or foot plough and would then be sown with black oats. Sometimes it was possible to derive two or three crops of oats from the same plot and sometimes the oats were rotated with field peas. When the achadh became completely exhausted, the wall was allowed to tumble into ruin and the plot returned to the wild. When it was deemed that the plot had recovered sufficiently, the walls were rebuilt and the whole process was repeated. This method of cultivation dates to the early 17th century and it was practiced until the mid 19th century.

Also to be seen throughout the Gairloch/Torridon region are the many areas of ridge-and-furrow strips known as "feannagan". These strips were a clever way of bringing low-lying boggy areas into use and they were excellent for growing potatoes. Large amounts of bracken would be cut in July when the growth was at its most luxuriant. This would then be spread thickly over the ground and parallel ditches would be dug at intervals of about six feet. The soil from the ditches would be thrown up onto the bracken and the resulting "lazy-beds" would be left for around nine months to allow decay to set in. The following spring, holes would be dibbed in each bed to take seed potatoes. Good examples of feannagan can be seen on the Rubha Beag headland (NG 893 963 and 886 973). These can be visited on the Rubha Beag Circuit walk (see Selected Walks). This method of cultivation continued until the mid 19th century.

Scattered throughout the moorland areas are to be found the sites of summer shielings or "airigh". Shielings were small buildings which were used in summer when the people of the townships moved their herds of sheep and cattle on to the peat moors to eat the moss and sedge which grew there. The people lived in the shielings and turned their herds out onto the peat moor, bringing them back twice a day for milking. At night the animals were bedded in small bothies with bracken and moss. When the bothies were cleaned out in spring, they provided excellent manure for growing potatoes. Today, shieling sites can be recognised as little knolls of green grass which are considerably drier than the surrounding peat moor. The tumbled remains of the shieling buildings can often be seen on such knolls. A good example of a shieling site is to be found close to Gairloch, just to the north of Loch Airigh Mhic Criadh - The Loch of the Shieling of the Sons of Criadh (NG 82 76).

Another feature sometimes encountered in the hills is the fail-dyke or "garradh fail". These stone and turf dykes mark the boundaries of former areas of grazing. Some run for miles over the hillsides and following them can give an interesting walk.

A good example occurs close to the deserted village of Innis Bhuidhe (see above). Last but by no means least in this account of recent settlement remains are the old drover's paths and hill tracks which criss-cross the area. One such path is the old track from Midtown to Camustrolvaig (NG 812 859 to 762 917).

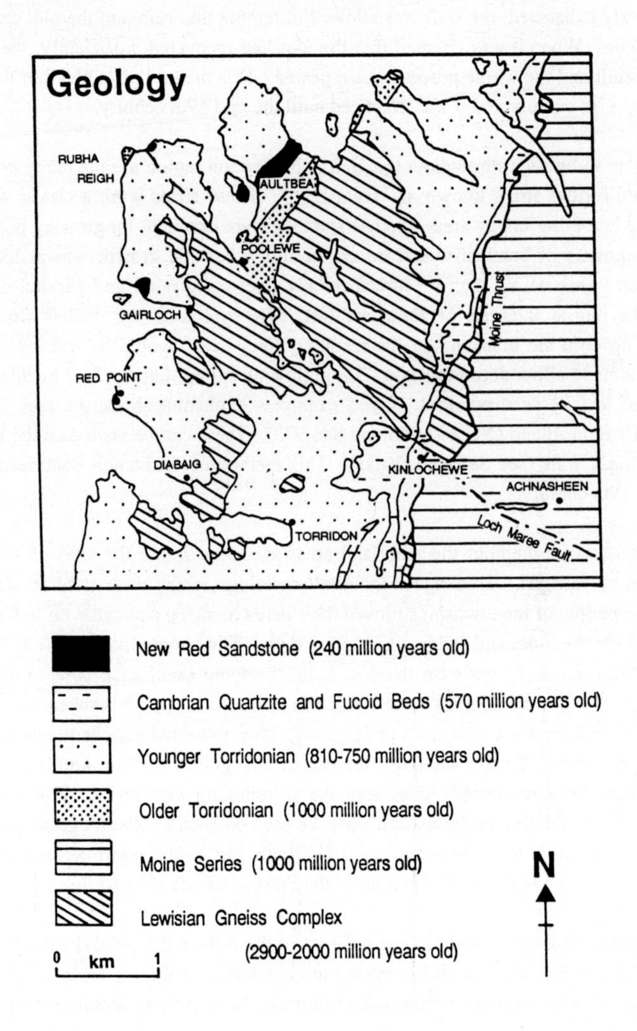

CLAN HISTORY

The beginnings of the clan period in Scotland can be traced back to the time of the Picts. Before the Viking hold over the west of Scotland was broken at the Battle of Largs in 1263, the old Pictish mormaers or king's deputies had been given the title of Earl. It is recorded that the first Earl of Ross was created in 1157 by David I, King of Scots. This title was held by Heth and later by his son Malcolm. In 1220, King Alexander II conferred the Earldom of Ross on Farquhar Macintaggart (Mac an t-Sagairt - "Son of the Priest"). Macintaggart appears to have been the representative of the secularised monastic settlement at Applecross. He was effectively chief of the Applecross church lands which stretched from Kintail to Loch Broom and he and his descendants were largely responsible for bringing together the eastern and western parts of present day Ross-shire.

In the early 15th century, the Earldom of Ross became the subject of a fierce dispute between Robert Duke of Albany and Donald Lord of the Isles. Earl Alexander had married Robert's daughter and had died young in May 1402 leaving only a small daughter, Euphemia, as heir. Robert believed that his grand-daughter should resign the Earldom in favour of his own son, John. This was contested by Donald, Lord of the Isles, who was married to a sister of Earl Alexander. This dispute was to lead to the Battle of Harlaw in 1411 and it was not until 1436 that Donald's son, Alexander, was finally recognised as the Earl of Ross.

For the next forty years, the Earldom of Ross was held jointly with the Lordship of the Isles and this arrangement was ultimately to bring about the forfeiture of the Earldom to the Crown. The Lords of the Isles had rebelled against the Scottish kings on several occasions. In 1462, Lord John, acting as an independent power, made a secret treaty with the Yorkist King Edward IV of England. The Scottish crown officially supported the Lancastrian Henry VI and when John's treaty was discovered, the Earldom of Ross was annexed by the Crown as punishment in 1476.

The MacBeaths

In the years leading up to the forfeiture of the Earldom of Ross, the lands of Gairloch were in a state of turmoil. The district had been taken over by a group of MacBeaths who had arrived in the area sometime during the 13th century from Assynt. The chiefs of the clan had three strongholds in the area: the castle on Eilean Grudidh in Loch Maree, the crannog in Loch Tollaidh and the Dun or Castle of Gairloch.

The MacLeods

Gairloch next came into the possession of the Siol Torquil, a branch of Clan MacLeod, early in the 15th century. The MacLeods were principally an island clan with lands in Lewis, Harris, Skye and Raasay and it is believed that their original claim to Gairloch was derived from kinship with Donald, Lord of the Isles and Earl of Ross. In 1430, King James I granted the lands of Gairloch to "Nele Nelesoun" as a reward for capturing his rebellious brother, Thomas. Neil was a son of Neil MacLeod and this act served to reinforce the MacLeod claim to Gairloch. Thereafter, the MacLeods captured the three MacBeath strongholds and drove most of that clan out of the area. The MacLeods constructed another stronghold on the headland between Port Henderson and Gairloch. This site was known as Uamh nam Freiceadain. It is in the time of the Macleods that the Tigh Dige or Moat House which stood close to the present Flowerdale House is first referred to.

The tragic events which occurred in Loch Thollaidh in 1480 were to lead ultimately to the end of MacLeod power in Gairloch. Allan, the chief of the MacLeods in Gairloch, had three sons by his first wife, a daughter of Alexander Mackenzie, 6th Laird of Kintail. Allan took as his second wife a daughter of MacLeod of Lewis. The MacLeods so hated the Mackenzies that two of the brothers of the second wife came across to Loch Thollaidh and murdered Allan and two of his sons. In this way the brothers hoped that the Lewis MacLeods would gain the lands of Gairloch through their sister. Their sister was horrified at this deed and took the blood-stained shirts of her step-sons to the boys' grandfather, Alexander of Kintail, as proof of the terrible act. Alexander sent his own son, Hector Roy Mackenzie, to see King James IV in Edinburgh where he also produced the shirts as proof of the murders. The King gave Hector a commission of fire and sword to destroy the MacLeods and in 1494 he was officially granted the lands of Gairloch by charter of the Crown. This effectively marked the end of the MacLeods of Gairloch, although they did manage to hold onto a third of their lands for another century.

The Mackenzies of Torridon

A charter of 1584 shows that the lands of Torridon were in the possession of the MacDonalds of Glengarry. Mackenzie power and influence in the area began to increase rapidly at the end of the 16th century and by 1602 the clan had taken over Torridon. The MacDonalds of Glengarry also had possession of half the Dundonnell lands in Lochbroom, while the other half belonged to the Mackenzies of Kintail. This resulted in a deadly feud which raged throughout the 16th century and which came to an end in 1603 when Glengarry surrendered to Kintail all his lands in Ross. This meant that the Mackenzie lands now extended from Kintail to Little Loch Broom and the importance of the clan was subsequently recognised by the Crown when the title of Earl of Seaforth was granted in 1623.

Shortly after this time, the first Mackenzie Lairds of Torridon appear in the records. The Lairds were descended from the ancient families of Coul and Applecross. The Torridon Mackenzies further strengthened their position in the area by intermarriage with the surrounding Mackenzie families of Dundonnell, Gairloch and Applecross. The 3rd Laird, John, was a supporter of Prince Charles and fought at the Battle of Culloden in 1746. That he took one hundred men with him suggests that the economy of the area must have been reasonably strong in those days to support such a large number of families. Although he was sentenced to death for his part in the uprising, John was later pardoned through the intervention of MacDonald of Sleat.

The last in direct line to hold the lands of Torridon was John, the 6th Laird. He was in effect an absentee landlord, having married and taken up residence in London. John sold all of the Torridon lands and died in 1852 without an heir. It was probably during the time of this last Laird that the glens of Torridon were cleared to make way for sheep. Families who had farmed the land for many generations were cruelly evicted and forced to eke out a meagre existence on the shores of Loch Torridon. The little township of Fasag was founded at this time by the evicted families.

The Mackenzies of Gairloch

Hector Roy of the ancient house of the Mackenzies of Kintail took the title of 1st Laird of Gairloch in 1494. He was called Roy or Ruadh because of his red hair and it is said that he was a tall powerful man and a fearless hero - a typical Highland chieftain. It was during Hector Roy's time that the lordship of Kintail was inherited by his nephew, John of Killin. Hector declared John to be illegitimate and took possession of the Kintail lands for himself. He was backed in this enterprise by the whole of the clan with whom he was a great favourite. However, John's grandfather, Lord Lovat, was able to gain the support of Sir William Munro of Fowlis who was the lieutenant of James Stewart, second son of King James III. With a force of seven hundred men, Sir William set out to punish Hector Roy for taking possession of the Kintail lands. This powerful army did not believe that Hector Roy could pose any real threat and this carelessness was to lead to their downfall. Hector attacked suddenly at dusk with only one hundred and forty men and succeeded in completely routing Sir William's army. For this act and for other disturbances of the public peace, a Royal Warrant was issued in 1499 for the death of Hector Roy. The Laird was eventually pardoned, thanks to the intervention of MacCailean, Earl of Argyll and the Kintail lands were returned to John of Killin. Hector was allowed to retain his Gairloch estates which thereafter passed undiminished to his heirs.

The 8th Laird of Gairloch, Sir Kenneth Mackenzie, was granted the title of Baronet of Nova Scotia by Queen Anne on 2 February 1703. This would seem to suggest that the Laird actively encouraged the people of Gairloch to emigrate to Canada as this title was usually conferred upon proprietors who assisted in peopling

Nova Scotia. Sir Kenneth represented Ross-shire in the Scottish Parliament and was strongly opposed to the Union with England.

The later Gairloch Lairds prided themselves on the fair treatment of their tenantry. The Mackenzie family helped the local fishing industry by purchasing wood for boat building and by guaranteeing sale money for the catches. In the 19th century, Gairloch Parish seems largely to have escaped the cruel clearances which occurred elsewhere in Scotland. Indeed between 1801 and 1831 the population of the Parish rose from 1,437 to 4,445 and reached a peak of 5,186 in 1851. On the surface, such a rise would seem to indicate that Gairloch Parish was in a fairly prosperous state at this time, but further investigation reveals that a severe strain was put on existing resources. Despite this strain however, it is clear that the estate trustees gave no thought to making more land available to the tenantry. Indeed they managed to squeeze more rent out of the people by subdividing existing holdings and offering increasingly smaller plots of land. Evidence given by the North Erradale crofters to the Napier Commission reveals that the trustees took away their common grazing and then made separate charges for grazing and arable lots. A similar tale was told by the crofters of South Erradale.

Lady Mary Mackenzie, wife of the 12th Laird, was certainly more enlightened than most in her dealings with the people of Gairloch. It was Mary who hit upon the idea of building the many "Destitution Roads" in the area to help relieve the poverty and suffering caused by the potato famine of 1846-48. She taught herself Gaelic and instructed her sons to learn the language from their Gaelic-speaking nursemaid. Instead of sending her children to public school and university in England as was usual among the landed gentry, she chose to have them educated at home with tutors. They grew to understand the local people in a way that would have been impossible for a non-Gaelic speaker and they were thus better able to run their estates successfully. It is clear however, that she was a rather overbearing lady - her son Osgood, founder of Inverewe Garden, described her as "a very domineering woman". When work was being carried out on the Destitution Roads, meal rations were often withheld from those deemed not to have worked hard enough. It has even been claimed that workers unwilling to give up their Catholic faith were denied rations. Lady Mackenzie and her son Osgood were certainly capable of acts which today would be regarded as downright cruel. They evicted an old woman from her house and set fire to it because she could not pay the rent. The poor woman fled with part of the roof and used this to make a small tent against the walls of Poolewe Cemetery. The Mackenzies followed her there and forced her to move on again. It is said that the old woman cursed them, saying "...there will never be a male heir at Inverewe while a Mary reigns." Lady Mackenzie's name was Mary and Osgood's daughter was called Mairi, the Gaelic version. No male heir lived to maturity.

Today, although somewhat diminished by sales, much of Gairloch Parish still remains in Mackenzie ownership. Flowerdale House at Charleston is currently the west coast residence of the 17th Laird, John Mackenzie.

PLANT LIFE

When the ice finally left Scotland around 10,000 years ago, the denuded landscape was gradually recolonised by plants and trees. Juniper was the first tree species to gain a foothold and by around 9,500 years ago an open woodland of birch and hazel had developed. By 8,250 years ago, a thick pinewood had become established and this great forest, known as the Great Wood of Caledon, spread to cover most of Highland Scotland.

Looking at the Gairloch/Torridon region today, it is hard to believe that most of the glens and lower mountain slopes were once thickly wooded. The area has suffered, as elsewhere, from exploitation by man, both in prehistoric and historic times. Timber was cut for construction, household fuel and tannin production and regrowth was prevented by sheep grazing. Much of the native forest around Loch Maree was felled to make charcoal to fuel the 17th century ironworks at Letterewe (see Kinlochewe to Gairloch). This destruction continued until fairly recent times: sections of forest at Beinn Eighe were felled during the Second World War to make ammunition boxes. Today, an important remnant of the native pinewood can be seen at Coille na Glas Leitire within the Beinn Eighe National Nature Reserve. Further remnants of native forest occur on the islands at the northern end of the loch. The oak woodland on the sunny south-west facing shore of Loch Maree is also worthy of mention: this is the most northerly example of an extensive natural oak woodland in Britain.

Apart from pockets of native pine forest, the poor acidic Torridonian soils support clumps of birches and rowans. These are usually to be found clinging to the sides of burns. On the lower areas of deforested ground, heath, bog and moorland vegetation predominates. Here are to be found ling and bell-heather, purple moor grass, cross-leaved heath, bearberry, lousewort and mountain everlasting. In damp areas you may find carniverous plants such as butterworts, bladderworts and sundews. Bog cotton, asphodel, ferns, bog juniper and various types of mosses and liverworts also occur in wetland areas. In summer, look out for the pretty heath spotted orchid. Higher up, on the broadest mountain slopes, are to be found water avens, alpine lady's mantle, marsh marigold, angelica, bog whortleberry, mountain sedge, dwarf cornel, alpine club moss and starry and mossy saxifrage.

The great Torridonian peaks such as Liathach, Beinn Alligin, An Teallach and Slioch are clear of peat from around 1,750 feet upwards. Wet conditions give way to tiered cliffs of sandstone and this sudden change allows another type of flora to flourish. Here are to be found a variety of plants which can withstand sudden droughts and changes in humidity. There is an abundance of rose-root, alpine saw-wort, thrift, alpine scurvy grass and mountain sorrel. In areas where small rivulets of water come into contact with lime-bearing rocks, a sweeter habitat is created and beautiful natural alpine rock gardens are to be found. These contain plants such as northern rock cress, Arctic mouse-ear, alpine hair grass and alpine hawkweed. In 1950, Norwegian mugwort was discovered on one of the Torridonian hills by Sir Christopher Cox. On mainland Europe, this rare plant occurs only in a few locations in Norway and in the Ural Mountains of the former U.S.S.R.

If you are interested in alpines, the Beinn Eighe Mountain Trail is a worthwhile excursion. Here, various alpines can be seen at relatively low altitudes. The higher reaches of Beinn Eighe contain fine examples of prostrate shrub and moss heaths. Here too, lime rich rocks give rise to montane grass heaths which are rich in species such as alpine lady's mantle, thyme, least willow, mosses and liverworts.

Unusual plants and exotic trees such as Japanese cedar, monkey puzzle and cypress can be seen in the vicinity of the old mansion houses of the area where the owners could afford to plant for pleasure instead of profit. Gardens which fall into this category include those at Dundonnell House, Gruinard House and Inveran. These gardens are occasionally open to visitors under Scotland's Garden Scheme.

No survey of the plant life of the region is complete without a reference to the wonderful garden at Inverewe created by Sir Osgood Mackenzie. Here, a variety of sub-tropical plants flourish at the same latitude as Siberia. A trip to this fascinating collection is a must for any visitor to the Gairloch/Torridon region (see Poolewe and Inverewe Garden for full details).

BIRD AND ANIMAL LIFE

Birds

The Gairloch/Torridon region has much to interest the bird watcher. A wide variety of sea-birds frequent the many miles of secluded coastline including herring gulls, black backed gulls, shags, fulmars, gannets, black guillemots and kittiwakes. The most common shore waders are dunlins and oyster catchers. The area is also visited by migrating groups of skuas, little auks and shearwaters. Eider ducks are also frequently seen. At Gruinard Bay you may find the red-breasted merganser wintering along the coast. This attractive sea duck travels up the Dundonnell River to breed. The elegant long-tailed duck is also a winter visitor here, as is the rare great northern diver. The beach at Redpoint Fishing Station, the sea cliffs between Melvaig and Rubha Reidh and the Rubha Beag headland north of Mellon Udrigle are all excellent spots for watching sea-birds.

The remnant of native pine forest at Coille na Glas Leitire on the shore of Loch Maree is a haven for woodland birds such as cross-bills, siskins, willow warblers and coal tits while on Loch Maree itself may be found the rare black-throated diver, mute swans, red-breasted mergansers, goosanders and greylag geese. Wood warblers occur in areas of birch forest and gorse and alders provide an ideal habitat for redwings. Greenshanks, snipe, curlew and red-throated divers are to be seen on wet moorland, lochs and estuaries.

Birds of prey such as peregrine falcons, buzzards, and merlins are occasionally seen on moorland areas while the rare golden eagle frequents high crags. On the higher hills, ptarmigan and red grouse are commonly seen. Other mountain and moorland birds include ravens, snow buntings, dotterels and ring ouzels.

Animals

The woodland areas in the Gairloch/Torridon region are home to red deer, roe deer, foxes, red squirrels and small rodents such as common shrews, bank voles and field mice. In the woodland fringes, you may be fortunate enough to spot the wildcat, although this rare animal hunts mainly at night.

The remnant of native pine forest at Coille na Glas Leitire contains a healthy population of the elusive pine marten. This attractive animal was once considered a pest and was persecuted to the point of extinction. At the end of the 19th century, the woodland around Loch Maree became the last stronghold of the pine marten in Scotland. Thanks to sensible conservation measures, population numbers began to increase in the 1970's and this little animal has now gradually recolonised much of the Highlands.

The rabbit is as common today in the Gairloch/Torridon region as it is elsewhere in Scotland. It is however a fairly recent introduction to the area, being released at Letterewe around 1850.

Herds of wild goats roam the hillsides around Dundonnell and Diabaig and can also be found on Slioch. These unusual long-haired goats are descended from once-domesticated stock which used to be kept for the milk which the nannies produced. It is said that they were also kept for their ability to graze out narrow ledges thus making them unappealing to sheep and preventing them from straying into dangerous areas. During winter, the herds descend from the hills for shelter and during this time you may spot them by the side of the road. The billie goats have remarkable curly horns.

Above the tree line, the red deer is the only mammal commonly seen. During summer the deer graze on the rough moorland pasture and in winter they descend to the woodland areas for shelter. The beautiful blue hare is seen only very rarely on the higher hills.

Those who are patient enough to study the coastal waters of the region for any length of time may well be rewarded with a sighting of dolphins or porpoises. Minke and killer whales are more unusual visitors. Common and grey seals are frequently seen in sheltered coastal areas such as Gruinard Bay and Camustrolvaig. The otter, mainly a nocturnal hunter, is also to be found close to sea lochs and rivers.

GLOSSARY OF GAELIC AND NORSE PLACE NAMES

O.N. = Old Norse. All other names are from the Gaelic. If anglicised, the correct Gaelic form is shown in brackets.

Abhainn a'Gharbh Choire - River of the Rough Corrie
Abhainn Coire Mhic Nobuil - the River of the Corrie of the Son of Nobul
Achnasheen (Achadh na Sine) - Field of the Storm
Achnashellach (Achadh nan Seileach) - the Field of the Willows
Achtercairn (Achadh a Charn) - Field of the Cairn
Aird - Height
Allt a'Bhealaich - the Stream of the Pass
Allt a Choire Dhuibh Mhoir - the Burn of the Great Black Corrie
Am Feur-Loch - the Loch of the Sedge
Am-ploc - the Lump
An Teallach - the Forge
Anancaun (Ath nan Ceann) - Ford of the Heads
Applecross (Apor Crossain from Pictish Aber Crosan) - the Confluence of the Crossan
Aultbea (Allt Beithe) - the Burn of the Birches
Aultroy (Allt Ruadh) - Red Stream
Badachro (Bad a Chrotha) - Thicket of the Cattlefold
Badcaul - Hazel Clump
Badluarach - Clump of Rushes
Baosbheinn - the Mad Mountain
Bealach na Gaoithe - the Pass of the Wind
Beinn a'Chearcaill - the Mountain of the Girdle
Beinn Airidh Charr - the Mountain of the Rough Shieling
Beinn Alligin (Ailleag) - Jewel Mountain
Beinn an Eoin - the Mountain of the Bird
Beinn Bhan - the White Mountain
Beinn Damph (Beinn nan Damh) - the Mountain of the Stags
Beinn Dearg - the Red Mountain
Beinn Eighe - File Mountain
Beinn Ghobhlach - the Horned Mountain
Beinn Lair - Mountain of the Mare
Braemore (Braigh Mor) - the Big Summit or Hill
Bualnaluib - the Fold of the Bend
Camas Allt Eoin Thomais - the Bay of the Burn of Eoin Thomais
Camas Mor - Big Bay
Camustrolvaig (O.N./Gaelic hybrid) - Goblin or Troll Bay
Carn Dearg - the Red Cairn
Coille na Glas Leitire - Wood of the Grey Slope
Coire an Laoigh - the Corrie of the Calf
Coire Dubh Mor - the Big Black Corrie
Coire Mhic Fhearchair - the Corrie of the Son of Farquhar
Coire Mhic Nobuil - the Corrie of the Son of Nobul
Coire na Caime - the Crooked Corrie
Corrieshalloch (Coire Shalach) - the Ugly or Dirty Corrie

Craig (Creag) - Crag or Rock
Creag-Mheall Beag - Little Hill of the Rock
Creag Mhor Thollaidh - the Big Rock of the Place of Holes
Diabaig (O.N. diup-vik) - Deep Bay
Druim Breac - Trout Ridge
Drumchork (Druim a Choirc) - Ridge of Corn
Dundonnell (Dun Dohmnull) - the Fort of Donald
Eilean Dubh na Sroine - the Black Island of the Promontory
Eilean Ruaraidh Mor - the Big Island of Rory
Eilean Subhainn - the Everlasting Island
Erradale (O.N.) - Gravel Beach Valley
Fionn Beinn - White Mountain
Firemore (Faidhir Mor) - Great Market
Gairloch (Gearr Loch) - the Short Loch
Garbh Eilean - the Rough Island
Glas Mheall Mor - Big Grey Hill
Gleann na Muice - Glen of Pigs
Gruinard (O.N. grunna fjord) - Shallow Fiord
Inveralligin (Inbhir) - the Mouth of the Alligin
Inverewe (Inbhir-iu) - the Mouth of the Ewe
Inverasdale (O.N./Gaelic hybrid) - Aspen Valley
Kinlochewe (Ceann-loch-iu) - the Head of Loch Ewe
Laide (Leathad) - the Slope
Leacnasaide (Leac nan Saighead) - the Flat Rock of the Arrow
Letterewe (Leitir-iu) - the Slope of the Ewe
Liathach - the Grey One
Little Loch Broom (Loch a'Bhraoin) - the Little Loch of the Showers
Loch a'Chroisg - the Loch of the Cross
Loch a'Mhadaidh Mor - the Big Loch of the Wolf
Loch a'Mhullaich - the Loch of the Summit
Loch an Doire Ghairbh - Loch of the Rough Grove
Loch an Eilean - the Loch of the Island
Loch an Fada - the Long Loch
Lochan an Iasgair - Loch of the Fisherman
Lochan Dubh - Little Black Loch
Lochan nam Breac - the Small Loch of the Trout
Loch Bad na h-Achlaise - Loch of the Grove of the Hollow
Loch Bad na Sgalaig - the Loch of the Servant's Grove
Loch Clair (Clar) - Loch of the Flat Place
Loch Damh (Loch nan Damh) - the Loch of the Stags
Loch Diabaigas Airde - Upper Loch Diabaig
Loch Gleann na Muice - the Loch of the Glen of Pigs
Loch Grobaig - the Loch of the Broken Tooth
Loch Maree (Maelrubha) - Loch of the Red-haired Tonsured One
Loch na Beiste - the Loch of the Beast
Loch na h-Oidhche - the Loch of Night
Loch na Sealga - the Loch of the Hunts
Loch nan Cabar - the Loch of the Antlers
Loch nan Dailthean - Loch of the Meadows
Loch Tollaidh - the Loch of the Place of Holes
Londubh - Black Bog
Lonmore - Big Bog
Meall a'Ghiubhais - the Hump of the Fir Tree

Meall an t-Sithe - the Hill of the Fairies
Meall Garbh - Rough Hill
Meall Lochan a'Chleirich - the Hill of the Loch of the Priest
Meall Mheinnidh (Meall Meadhonach) - Middle Hill
Meallan na Ghamhna - Stirk Hill
Mellon Charles (Meallan Thearlaich) - the Little Hill of Charles
Mellon Udrigle (O.N./Gaelic hybrid) - the Little Hill of the Outer Ravine
Melvaig (O.N. mel-vik) - Bent Grass Bay
Mial (O.N. mjo-vollr) - Narrow Field
Mullach Coire Mhic Fhearchair - the Summit of the Corrie of the Son of Farquhar
Naast (O.N. faste) - Castle or Fort
Ob a'Braighe - Summit Bay
Opinan (Obanan) - Little Bays
Ormiscaig (O.N. Ormiskiki) - Orm's Strip
Poolewe (Poll-iu) - the Pool of the Ewe
Rhu Noa (Rudha 'n Fhomhair) - the Point of the Giant
River Grudie (Gruididh) - Gravelly River
Ruadh Stac Mhor - the Big Red Cliff
Rubha Ban - White Point
Rubha Beag - Little Point
Rubha Mor - Big Point
Rubha Reidh - the Smooth Point
Sail Liath - Grey Heel
Sail Mhor - Big Heel
Seana Mheallan - the Old Knoll
Sgeir Dughall - Dugald's Rock
Sgurr Ban - White Peak
Sgurr Dubh - Black Peak
Sgurr Mhor - Big Peak
Shieldaig (O.N. sil-vik) - Herring Bay
Sitheanan Dubha - the Black Hillocks of the Fairies
Slattadale (O.N.) - Even Valley
Slioch (Sleagh) - Spearhead
Spidean a'Choire Leith - the Pinnacle of the Grey Corrie
Strath na Sealga - the Valley of the Hunts
Stuc a Choire Dhuibh Bhig - the Point of the Little Black Corrie
Talladale (O.N.) - Ledge Valley
Tom na Gruagaich - the Knoll of the Fairy Woman
Torridon (Toirbheartan) - a Place of Transference

BIBLIOGRAPHY

Ang, T. & Pollard, M. 1984 "Walking the Scottish Highlands: General Wade's Military Roads". Andre Deutsch.

Brander, M. 1980 "The Making of the Highlands". Constable, London.

British Geological Survey 1936 "The Northern Highlands of Scotland". 4th Edition 1989. H.M.S.O.

Crawford, I. 1986 "Held In Trust: The National Trust For Scotland". Collins, Glasgow.

Darling, F.F. & Boyd, J.M. 1964 "The Highlands & Islands". Collins, London.

Dixon, J.H. 1886 "Gairloch and Guide to Loch Maree". 4th Reprint 1984.

Gairloch Heritage Museum "The Local 17th Century Iron Works". Pamphlet.

Mackenzie, O.H. 1921 "A Hundred Years in the Highlands". Reprinted 1988. National Trust For Scotland.

Macrow, B.G. 1953 "Torridon Highlands". Second Edition 1969. Robert Hale & Company, London.

Murray, W.H. 1985 "The Companion Guide to the West Highlands of Scotland." Collins.

Napier Commission 1884 "The Report of the Royal Commission on Crofting". H.M.S.O.

National Trust For Scotland "Torridon: A Guide to the Hills".

Nature Conservancy Council 1977 "Beinn Eighe National Nature Reserve".

Nature Conservancy Council 1989 "Beinn Eighe National Nature Reserve: Woodland Trail".

Nicolson, J.R. 1975 "Beyond the Great Glen". David & Charles.

Omand, D. (Ed.) 1984 "The Ross and Cromarty Book". The Northern Times Ltd, Golspie.

Pennant, T. 1772 "A Tour In Scotland and Voyage to the Hebrides".

Pitt, B. (Cons. Ed.) 1986 "The Military History of World War II". Guild Publishing, London.

Queen Victoria 1884 "More Leaves From The Journal of A Life in the Highlands".

Ratcliffe, D. 1977 "Highland Flora". Highlands and Islands Development Board.

Ritchie, G. & A. 1985 "Scotland: Archaeology and Early History". Thames and Hudson Ltd, London.

Scottish Natural Heritage 1992 "Beinn Eighe National Nature Reserve: Mountain Trail".

Scottish Review 1888 "Unpublished Letters of James Hogg". Vol. 12, July 1888.

INDEX

INDEX